Local Infrastructure Investment in Rural America

Local Infrastructure Investment in Rural America

edited by Thomas G. Johnson,
Brady J. Deaton, and Eduardo Segarra

Westview Press / Boulder and London

HC
110
.P83
L63
1988

A Westview Special Study

Copyright © 1988 by Westview Press, Inc., except for Chapters 1, 4, 18, 23, and 24, which are works of the U.S. government

Published in 1988 in the United States of America by Westview Press, Inc.; Frederick A. Praeger, Publisher; 5500 Central Avenue, Boulder, Colorado 80301

Library of Congress Cataloging-in-Publication Data
Local infrastructure investment in rural America.
  1. Public investments—United States.
2. Infrastructure (Economics)—United States.
3. United States—Rural conditions. 4. Local
government—United States. I. Johnson, Thomas G.
II. Deaton, Brady J. III. Segarra, Eduardo.
HC110. P83L63 1988   332.6′7252   87-21606
ISBN 0-8133-7460-X

6   5   4   3   2   1

Contents

PART I: THEORETICAL FOUNDATIONS OF
INFRASTRUCTURE INVESTMENT

PART II: MODELS AND APPROACHES FOR COMMUNITY INFRASTRUCTURE ANALYSIS

PART III. INFRASTRUCTURE INVESTMENT DECISION-MAKING: CASE STUDIES

PART V: IMPLICATIONS FOR THE FUTURE OF INFRASTRUCTURE INVESTMENT

Tables and Figures

Tables

Figures

About the Authors

Theodore R. Alter is an Associate Professor of Agricultural Economics/Extension Community Economics Specialist at the Pennsylvania State University. Some of his specialties include public sector economics, public finance, institutional economics, community and regional economics, and land economics and policy. He was awarded with the American Agricultural Economics Association Distinguished Extension Program Award in 1985, and is affiliated with AAEA and Community Development Society of America, among other professional affiliations. His academic background includes a B.A. in Economics from the University of Rochester, and both a M.S. and Ph.D. in Resource Development from Michigan State University.

James G. Beierlein is an Associate Professor of Agricultural Economics at the Pennsylvania State University. His area of expertise is agribusiness management and marketing, with interest in the efficiency of marketing systems, firm level decisionmaking, and marketing. He has recently finished a project in the dairy industry, and is currently involved with a project in the poultry industry. Dr. Beierlein earned a Ph.D. from Purdue University.

Beverly A. Cigler is an Associate Professor in the Department of Political Science and Public Administration, North Carolina State University and a Faculty Research Associate at the Center for Urban and Regional Studies, North Carolina State University, Chapel Hill. She teaches urban/environmental policy, politics, and management. She has published several dozen chapters, journal articles, essays, and technical reports, as well as a co-authored book, on such topics as small city capacity-building, growth management, emergency management, information dissemination, infrastructure policy, and fiscal stress. Dr. Cigler currently serves on three editorial boards, is past president of the Research Triangle Chapter of the

American Society for Public Administration (ASPA), president-elect of ASPA's Section on Public Administration Education, and a national council member of three organizations. She also has a grant from the Economic Research Service, USDA, to develop and co-ordinate a National Small Government Research Network.

Brady J. Deaton is a Professor of Agricultural Economics and Associate Director of International Development at Virginia Polytechnic Institute and State University. Dr. Deaton earned his B.S. and M.A. degrees at the University of Kentucky and his Ph.D. at the University of Wisconsin. Before joining the VPI&SU faculty he was an assistant and later Associate Professor at the University of Tennessee. Dr. Deaton is on the Board of Trustees of the Rural Virginia Development Foundation, a member of the Southern Growth Policies Board's Committee on the Future of the South, and a member of the American Agricultural Economics Association, Special Committee on Issues and Priorities in Agricultural Economics. Dr. Deaton is author of numerous articles on rural and economic development.

Gerald A. Doeksen is Regents Professor and an Extension Economist in the Department of Agricultural Economics at Oklahoma State University. In his current position he conducts research and provides extension programs concerning community service problems. A recipient of the 1986 Elmo Boumann Distinguished Professorship Award, the 1986 Extension Achievement Award, and of numerous other awards, Dr. Doeksen also serves on Board of Directors and as Secretary-Treasurer, MidAmerican Rural EMS Council, and in the Community Development Society. He received his Ph.D. from Oklahoma State University in Agricultural Economics. Formerly, Dr. Doeksen was with the Economic Research Service, USDA.

William R. Gillis is an Assistant Professor of Agricultural Economics and Extension Economic Development Specialist with the Pennsylvania State University. His areas of interest and expertise include rural employment policy, regional economics, downtown revitalization and public finance. Dr. Gillis' current Extension and Research activities focus on local economic development planning and policy. He is a native of the state of Washington. He has a B.S. and Master's Degree in Agricultural Economics from Washington State University and a Ph.D. degree in the same field from the University of Wisconsin with a specialty in community economic development and rural labor markets. Since joining the faculty at Penn State in 1983, Gillis has worked with numerous Pennsylvania communities in planning a local development strategy and has authored a number of articles on rural economic development issues.

John M. Halstead is a Ph.D. candidate in the Department of Agricultural Economics at Virginia Polytechnic Institute and State University. His research has focused on natural resource and rural development issues. He is co-author of *Socioeconomic Impact Management: Design and Implementation (Westview Press), Social Impact Assessment and Management*, and various other journal articles and book chapters. Recent publications include articles on fiscal impact modeling and policy issues in managing ground water contamination from agricultural chemicals. Current research at Virginia Polytechnic Institute and State University focuses on ground water contamination from agricultural nitrates. Formerly research associate in the Department of Agricultural Economics at North Dakota State University, Mr. Halstead received his M.S. from the University of Massachusetts and B.A. from the University of Notre Dame.

Thomas R. Harris is an Associate Professor in the Department of Agricultural Economics at the University of Nevada, Reno. Dr. Harris received his Ph.D. from Oklahoma State University and his M.S. degree from Texas Tech University in agricultural economics and a B.B.A. degree from the University of Texas at Arlington in economics and finance. Dr. Harris' current areas of research are in rural small business development, impact modeling, and rural government financing and budgeting. Dr. Harris has published in *American Journal of Agricultural Economics, Southern Journal of Agricultural Economics, Journal of Environmental Systems, Journal of Computer Applications, Water Resources Bulletin*, and *Journal of Applied Agricultural Research*.

Mark S. Henry is a Professor of Agricultural Economics at Clemson University. He earned his B.A. in Economics from Baker University in Kansas, and his Ph.D. in Economics from Kansas State University. Some of his current projects are the organization and operation of South Carolina water utility systems, an analysis of cost sharing strategies for beach replenishment on Hilton Head Island, South Carolina, and coastal resource management and policy. More general research areas include regional economics, development theory and policy, fiscal impact analysis, modeling regional economic structure, and state and local finance. In 1986 he was a Visiting Scholar at the Research Department of the Federal Reserve Bank of Kansas City, and in 1984 a Visiting Scholar in the Aggregate Analysis Section, ERS, of the U.S. Dept. of Agriculture. He has several publications in various professional journals.

Daryl Hobbs is a Professor of Rural Sociology and a Director of the University of Missouri's Office of Social and Economic Data Analysis. Most of his teaching, research, and extension work focuses on social change and economic development in rural communities. He organized and heads the Office of Social and Economic Data Analysis which was created to supply rural communities and organizations with economic, demographic and other kinds of data to facilitate their planning and analysis. Dr. Hobbs is author of more than 100 articles, chapters, and papers on related topics. Included among his publications is *Rural Society in the USA: Issues for the 1980's* (Westview Press, 1982) co-authored with Don Dillman. He is a past president of the Rural Sociological Society, has served as a visiting professor at Colorado State, Alaska, Iowa State and Wisconsin, and has been a consultant on rural development projects in five foreign countries. A native of rural Iowa, he received his B.S. degree in Agricultural Economics, and M.S. and Ph.D. degrees in Rural Sociology from Iowa State University.

Beth Walter Honadle is the National Program Leader for Economic Development with the Extension Service at the U.S. Department of Agriculture in Washington, D.C. She provides overall leadership and guidance to the Cooperative Extension System programs. Her areas of responsibility include area development, business and industrial development, downtown revitalization, small business management, impact assessment and the exploration of natural resources policy alternatives, among others. She is also an Adjunct Professor of Public Administration at the American University, Washington, D.C. Prior to joining the Extension Service in 1985, Dr. Honadle served as Leader of the Organization and Delivery of Local Services Project, Economic Development Division, Economic Research Service, USDA. She also served as founding Executive Editor of Rural Development Perspectives. She has published two books, several articles, and she is active in a number of professional organizations. Dr. Honadle holds a Ph.D. in Public Administration from Syracuse University and masters degrees in both Public Administration and Economics.

Thomas G. Johnson is an Associate Professor of Agricultural Economics and Extension Specialist-Community Resource Development at Virginia Polytechnic Institute and State University. He earned his B.S. and M.S. degrees from the University of Saskatchewan and his Ph.D. from Oregon State University. Dr. Johnson teaches graduate and undergraduate courses in rural development, resource economics and microeconomic theory. He is involved in several programs in which local decision makers are trained in the use of impact assessment and policy evaluation tools. Dr. Johnson is on the Advisory Committee of American Runs on Local Roads, the Editorial Board of the Southern Journal of Agricultural Economies, and the Executive Council of the Southern Regional Science Association.

Lonnie Lee Jones is a Professor of agricultural economics at Texas A&M University and a co-owner of Southwest Resources Analysts, a consulting firm specializing in research and educational services in resource economics and impact analyses. Dr. Jones was a recipient of a grant from the AAEA to participate in the Fourteenth International Conference of Agricultural Economists at Minsk, Russia, in August 1970, and was selected as the Researcher of the Year--Department of Agricultural Economics, 1976-77. He is also affiliated with several Agricultural Economics Associations. His more active research involves studying the economic impacts of industrialization in rural communities, and economics of institutional arrangements for viable rural communities in Texas. His teaching includes courses in quantitative methods and input-output analysis. He has published extensively on these and related areas. He received a Ph.D. from the Ohio State University.

Marvin Konyha joined the Florida Cooperative Extension Service in 1970. He then came to the Extension Service, USDA, in 1973 as Program Leader, Manpower Development and Community Facilities on the Community and Rural Development staff. He served three years as Program Coordinator, Community and Rural Development, on the Joint Planning and Evaluation Staff of the USDA, Science and Education Administration, and completed the USDA Senior Executive Service Candidate Development Program, September, 1982. Raised on a dairy farm near Memphis, Michigan, Dr. Konyha received his B.A. in 1960 from Kalamazoo College (Michigan) and his M.S. and Ph.D. from Michigan State University in Agricultural Economics in 1967 and 1970 respectively. Dr. Konyha served as an assistant professor at the University of Florida, an instructor and graduate assistant at Michigan State University and a high school english and economics teacher in Michigan before coming to USDA. Dr. Konyha has authored numerous publications on human resource, community, and rural development.

Warren Kriesel received a B.Sc from the University of Wisconsin, River Falls in 1977 and his MSc degree in Agricultural Economics from Virginia Polytechnic Institute and State University. After completing the MSc degree, he was employed as a Research Assistant by the University of Kentucky. He is currently a Ph.D. candidate at Ohio State University. He has served as a Peace Corps volunteer in Malaysia. His research interests include the process and determinants of economic development, regional planning, and resource economics policy.

F. Larry Leistritz is Professor of Agricultural Economics at North Dakota State University at Fargo. He has completed extensive research regarding the economic and fiscal impacts of energy resource development in the western United States. From 1975 to 1978, he served as Associate Director of the North Dakota Regional Environmental Assessment Program, a state-funded research and policy analysis project for analyzing the impacts of energy development. In that capacity he was responsible for managing the development of the REAP Economic-Demographic

Models, RED-1 and RED-2. He is senior author of *Socioeconomic Impact of Resource Development: Methods for Assessment (Westview Press), Social Impact Assessment and Management: A Bibliography* (Garland Publishing), and *Interdependencies of Agriculture and Rural Communities: an Annotated Bibliography* (Garland Publishing), and coauthor of four other books. In 1978-79 he was a Visiting Professor of Agricultural Economics at Texas A&M University, where he advised in the development of the Texas Assessment Modeling System (TAMS). He received his Ph.D. in agricultural economics from the University of Nebraska--Lincoln in 1970.

George McDowell is a Professor of Agricultural Economics at Virginia Polytechnic Institute and State University and an on assignment in Zambia. At the time of the preparation of this chapter he was an Associate Professor of Agricultural and Resource Economics and an Extension Economist at the University of Massachusetts. Dr. McDowell's special focus is on problems of local government finance and financial management, the role that local governments hold in rural development, and the political economy of extension and research in Land Grant Universities. Prior to joining the faculty at the University of Massachusetts, Dr. McDowell was an Associate Director of the United States Peace Corps first in Kenya and then in Malaysia. He received his M.S. in Agronomy from Cornell University and his Ph.D. in Agricultural Economics from Michigan State University.

Steve H. Murdock is the Head and Professor in the Department of Rural Sociology and Sociology at Texas A&M University. He received a M.A. and a Ph.D. in Sociology from the University of Kentucky, Lexington, and a B.A. in Sociology from North Dakota State University, Fargo. Dr. Murdock's areas of interest include demography, human ecology, socioeconomic impact analysis, and applied sociology, to name a few. He is an author of four books on the demographic and social impacts of natural resource development, of over fifty technical articles and book chapters on demographic and social factors in resource development in Texas and the nation, and of over hundred research monographs, reports, and professional papers on related topics.

Glenn Nelson is Professor of agricultural and applied economics at the University of Minnesota. He specializes in research and teaching on the economics of the public sector, with special emphasis on rural and agricultural problems. His publications include "Elements of a Paradigm for Rural Development" and "A Critique of Executive Branch Decision Making Processes" in the *American Journal of Agricultural Economics*. He is co-editor of *Rural American in Passage: Statistics for Policy* published by the National Academy of Sciences. Nelson has extensive governmental as well as academic experience. He has served as State

Economist for Minnesota, Senior Staff Economist with the President's Council of Economic Advisors, and economist with the Cost of Living Council and the Office of Economic Opportunity. Honors include a resident fellowship at the National Center for Food and Agricultural Policy located in Resources for the Future and listing in *Who's Who in the Midwest.*

Daniel M. Otto is an Associate Professor of Economics and an Extension Economist at the Iowa State University. His areas of specialty include Community and Rural Development, Impact Analysis, and Economic Feasibility Analysis of Public Services and Facilities. He has written numerous articles in related areas, and is currently actively involved, at both the community and state level, with various community development workshops and analyses. He is currently developing various data bases, economic forecasts, and input-output models for the State of Iowa. Dr. Otto received a B.A. in Economics and a M.S. in Agricultural Economics from the University of Minnesota, and a Ph.D. in Agricultural Economics from Virginia Tech.

Glen C. Pulver is Professor of Agricultural Economics at the University of Wisconsin-Madison. He holds M.S. and Ph.D. degrees from that same University. He first joined the faculty of the Department of Agricultural Economics at the University of Wisconsin in 1955. His field of specialty is Community Economic Development. In this role he works closely with governmental bodies, economic development committees, organizations, agencies, and educators throughout Wisconsin. His research is focused on community economic development policy and capital acquisition for new and developing businesses. Dr. Pulver also has previous experience as a visiting professor in southern Brazil and Indonesia, as dean of the University of Wisconsin-Extension, and as associate director of the Cooperative Extension Service at Purdue University. He has extensive work experience both in rural and urban settings. He is a past president of the Community Development Society of America and the recipient of its Distinguished Service Award in 1986.

J. Norman Reid is currently chief of the Rural Business and Government Branch, ERS, USDA. He directs a program of research on rural economic and governmental trends and their public policy implications. He has written on rural public infrastructure, rural economic and social trends, entrepreneurship, rural development policy, federal aid to rural areas, and substate regionalism. Dr. Reid received his B.A. in political science from Muskingum College in Ohio in 1967, his A.M. in political science from the University of Missouri, Columbia, in 1969, and his Ph.D. in political science from the University of Illinois, Urbana, in 1975. Before assuming his current position he headed the State and Local Government Section of ERS.

Eduardo Segarra is an Assistant Professor of Agricultural Economics at Texas Tech University. Dr. Segarra earned his M.S. at the University of Missouri and his Ph.D. at Virginia Polytechnic Institute and State University. His research interest include resource economics and conservation, and the use of mathematical programming models.

Ron E. Shaffer is a Professor of Agricultural Economics and Community Development Economist at the University of Wisconsin-Madison. Dr. Shaffer's extension responsibilities include working with community groups to build economic development strategies and understand local and nonlocal forces affecting community economic development. Part of this effort includes the development (with Dr. Glen Pulver) of a micro computer system for community economic analysis. His research is on the local economic impacts of economic development, sources of employment change, identifying types of economic development most likely to employ specific workers, the influence commercial bank policies play in local economic development, and sources and uses of capital for new small businesses. He serves as an advisor to the State of Wisconsin on economic development policies and chaired a national task force preparing a report for Extension USDA on economic development impacts and rural data needs. He developed a methodology to evaluate the community impact of economics development that has been used in Florida, Indiana, Kansas, Michigan, Minnesota, Ohio, Oklahoma, South Dakota, Texas, Virginia and Wisconsin. He has taught impact evaluation at the American Economic Development Council's Basic Industrial Development Seminar. He works with the Organization for Economic and Cooperative Development (DECD) in Paris, France on local economic development strategies. During 1980-81, he was a visiting professor to the Institute of Industrial Economics, Bergen, Norway. In 1985, Ron and Glen Pulver were recognized with the Outstanding Extension Program Award by the American Agricultural Economics Association.

Thomas F. Stinson is a Professor in the Department of Agricultural and Applied Economics at the University of Minnesota. Specializing in rural economic development issues, his current research includes a study of the restructuring of the rural economy, a study of the effect that two decades of changes in the federal system have had on local government finances in non-metropolitan communities, and an assessment of rural infrastructure needs based on a national survey of rural communities sponsored by USDA's Farmers Home Administration. Most recently, he completed a major report, *Governing the Heartlands: Can Rural Communities Survive the Farm Crisis*, for the U.S. Senate's Subcommittee on Intergovernmental Relations. Dr. Stinson received a Ph.D. in Economics from the University of Minnesota. Before joining the faculty at the University of Minnesota,

Dr. Stinson was employed by the U.S. Department of Agriculture's Economic Research Service for more than 20 years.

Patrick J. Sullivan is chief of the Finance and Tax Branch, in the U.S. Department of Agriculture's Economic Research Service. Previously, he worked in the State and Local Government Section and supervised the Financial Markets Section of ERS. Before joining the USDA in 1977, he completed undergraduate and graduate work in economics at Syracuse University and taught economics at the State University of New York College at Oswego. He has written extensively about rural development, public finance, local infrastructure, and financial economics issues. He is a member of the editorial board of the *State and Local Government Review*. In his current position, he directs and conducts research on the impacts of Federal tax policies, credit programs, and financial deregulation on the agricultural sector and rural economies.

Bruce A. Weber is a Professor and Extension Economist in the Department of Agricultural and Resource Economics at Oregon State University. His educational background includes a B.A. in Political Science from Seattle University, and a M.S. and a Ph.D. in Agricultural Economics from the University of Wisconsin, Madison. He is responsible for the extension program in state and local government finance and economic development, and for teaching a graduate applied course and also research in the economics of rural development. During 1984, he was a Visiting Professor of Agricultural Economics at Virginia Polytechnic Institute and State University. Dr. Weber is the author of Coping With Rapid Growth in Rural Communities (Westview Press, 1982) with Robert E. Howell, and of the forthcoming paper "Economics of Rural Areas" with Brady J. Deaton in Agricultural and Rural Areas Approaching the 21st Century: Challenges for Agricultural Economists, eds. R.J. Hildreth, K.L. Lipton, K.C. Clayton, and C.C. O'Connor. (Iowa State Univ. Press), and the author of numerous articles and papers in related areas.

J. M. (Jack) Whitmer specializes in education and training for local government officials, intergovernmental relations, computer applications for local government, and financing of public services. He is a Secretary/Treasurer of the Alpha Mu Chapter of Epsilon Sigma Phi, a National Honorary Extension Fraternity, and a member of various committees. In addition to his position as an Associate Professor at Iowa State University since 1980, he has been a Visiting Professor at the University of Arizona-Extension Service Winter School since 1986. Dr. Whitmer received his B.A. in Political Science from the University of Wisconsin, his M.A. in Political Science from Iowa State University, and his Ph.D. in Adult and Extension Education also from Iowa State University.

Mike D. Woods is an Associate Professor of Agricultural economics and an Extension Economist at Oklahoma State University. He has state wide responsibility for developing educational programs in small business management and economic development. His research interests include impact analysis for rural communities and economic development. He holds a Ph.D. in Agricultural Economics from Oklahoma State University, a M.S. in Agricultural Economics from the University of Arkansas, and a B.S. in Economics and Finance from Arkansas Tech University.

Russell Clark Youmans is a Professor of Agricultural Economics at Oregon State University. He is also the Director of the Western Rural Development Center, and a Program Leader of the Community Development section of Oregon Extension Service. Dr. Youmans received awards, in 1978 and 1980, for Outstanding Extension Programs in Agricultural Economics by the Western Agricultural Economics Association, and in 1982 for Distinguished Extension Program by the American Agricultural Economics Association. His recent publications include "Sustaining American Farm-Ranch Family Income: The Land Grant Institutions Can Help" (September 1985), and "Economic Multipliers: Can a rural community use them?" with Eugene Lewis et. al. (1979). He holds a B.S. in General Agriculture from University of Illinois, and a M.S. and a Ph.D. in Agricultural Economics from Purdue University.

Acknowledgements

This book is the product of many people's efforts. The National Symposium upon which this book is based was the brain child of Dr. Marv Konyha of USDA Extension Service. In retrospect Marv's concerns over the issue of local infrastructure investment were well founded since the issue is even more critical now than then.

The general format of the symposium and, to a somewhat lesser extent, the book were determined by a planning committee comprised of Brady Deaton, Tom Johnson, Lonnie Jones, Mike Woods, Gerald Doeksen, Dan Otto, and Marv Konyha.

The chapters' authors and other participants at the symposium deserve credit for the depth and bredth of the material in this book. It was a very exciting task to compile this enormous amount of information and thoughtful material into a single volume.

The task of physically combining the many chapters into a single volume was only possible with the assistance of several student assistants and secretaries. Thanks are due to Sari Lammivaara, Trevor Hamilton and Jill Albert for their hours of labor. The authors are especially indebted to Linda Kipps who, with immeasurable patience, made the countless corrections and changes in style necessary to arrive at the volume before you.

Finally, the authors wish to express their appreciation for the financial support received from the Extension Service of the United States Department of Agriculture.

Thomas G. Johnson, Brady J. Deaton,
and Eduardo Segarra

1
Introduction

Brady J. Deaton and Marvin E. Konyha

The purpose of this book is to provide an assessment of professional knowledge regarding economic decision tools for local governments. Specifically, the book includes both macro and micro economic analyses of rural infrastructure. Both theoretical and applied analyses are incorporated in order to provide academic researchers, extension personnel, and local government practitioners with a knowledge base for evaluating selected public sector investment decision tools.

The book evolved from an extension project undertaken by Virginia Polytechnic Institute and State University and the Extension Service, United States Department of Agriculture. A National Symposium was organized as a major objective of the project in 1985, at which time most of the chapters contained in this book were presented and scrutinized by professional peers.

A few additional papers were selected for inclusion after gaps in information were identified and the availability of new materials pertinent to the objectives of the book was recognized. A brief description of the rural infrastructure problem, the basic assumptions guiding the development of this book and the project from which it grew, and the set of events leading up to the publication of this book will be presented in this chapter as an Introduction to the book.

SITUATION

Communities and rural areas are feared to be seriously underinvesting in public infrastructure. Concern about dilapidated roads and deteriorating bridges is rampant. Human lives have been lost and the fiscal health of local governments in the U.S. seriously threatened in recent and deteriorating bridges is rampant. Human lives have been lost and the fiscal health of local governments in the U.S. seriously threatened in recent years. Even more alarming is the pervasive expectation that matters are getting worse.

Because of tight budgets and inflation, the maintenance of a growing number of public facilities has been deferred and replacement or rehabilitation of obsolescent public works have been postponed. In many communities, public services are considered deficient because of the inadequate investment in infrastructure such as roads, bridges, fire stations, health clinics, water and sewer systems and solid waste disposal systems. At the same time, cutbacks in Federal funding programs are forcing States and local units of government to find alternative funding sources for community infrastructure investments. Also, the inadequacy of community facilities and services places a severe constraint on the economic development opportunities of many communities.

Several programs have been developed by the Cooperative Extension Service and its research base in Land Grant Universities to help local communities address economic development, community infrastructure, and alternative technology issues. A powerful economic development aid is available in several states through computerized community impact assessment programs. Computerized budgeting decision aids for a limited number of community services and facilities are also available in a few states.

Given the current fiscal situation, communities need to prioritize their community facility or service projects according to which has the greatest economic and social payoff to the community. There is a need to assess the community decision aids being used in the Extension system and to integrate them into a comprehensive community impact analysis tool as a basis for assessing both costs and benefits of all community investment alternatives. Where such information is not available, there is a need to coordinate and evaluate the development of appropriate educational materials and the delivery of Extension staff development programs regionally and nationally. At the same time, the infrastructure issue must be understood in the context of national and international changes in the economy and the emerging role that these changes demand for state and local governments.

OBJECTIVES

Given the assumptions implicit in this situation statement, the Extension Service, USDA entered into a cooperative agreement with the Virginia Cooperative Extension Service (CES) "to assess the cost and benefits of the community investment alternative decision aids used in the

Extension system and to integrate them into a comprehensive community impact analysis tool."*

The initial objective of this project was "to provide CES system-wide leadership for integrating several Community Resource Development, (CRD) computer-assisted, community impact assessment and infrastructure decision aids into one comprehensive community assessment and decision aid." A second objective was "to expedite the organization, development, and implementation of a "networking" model for development and dissemination of community infrastructure technology, program delivery innovations, computer assisted teaching, and other resources."

PRELIMINARY EVENTS

An ad hoc group of members of the American Agricultural Economic Association (AAEA) Community Economics Network (CENET) met during the AAEA annual meeting August 6-8, 1984, at Cornell University to explore networking potentials. The group agreed to participate in a "community infrastructure network" and to assist with assessing the current state-of-the-art and the future potential for decision-making models to help local officials plan and implement infrastructure investments.

Several members of this ad hoc group also agreed to serve on a planning committee to develop a national workshop/symposium as the first step in the process of assessing existing infrastructure decision-making models and integrating them into a comprehensive community impact analysis tool. Members of the planning committee were Gerald Doeksen, Oklahoma State; Dan Otto, Iowa State; Mike Woods and Lonnie Jones, Texas A&M; Brady Deaton and Tom Johnson, VPI & SU (project leaders); and Marv Konyha, ES-USDA (project coordinator).

The planning committee organized this symposium with several general dimensions in mind. First, it was expected that we would recognize both the demand for and the supply of infrastructure from a broad-based economic and political perspective. Secondly, it was recognized that the theoretical bases of community infrastructure decision-making models, both economic and political, should be explored in order to put the economists' supply and demand models into more realistic perspective. Next it was thought necessary to present a brief overview of models and approaches that have been used by Extension specialists and other providers of decision-making aids. Lastly, the question of "where do we go from here?," should be thoroughly examined.

---

*Cooperative Agreement 84-EXCA-2-0711, Extension Service, USDA, August 1984.

The answer should be sought both in terms of synthesizing existing models into some general model or approach and in terms of institutional changes deemed necessary to meet the growing needs for infrastructure decision aids at state and local levels.

Above all, it was agreed that the symposium should be an opportunity to examine ourselves as researchers and as change agents. Are existing models and decisions aids for infrastructure decision-making adequate? Is there a need to synthesize existing approaches into a common model or common delivery mechanism useable in all states or regions? Is the development of such a common model feasible or even possible? In other words, are the objectives of this project attainable? The symposium planners didn't know the answer to these questions. The workshop, itself, and the presentations included in this book mark only an important beginning in developing answers to these questions.

We do not expect that this book will provide the last word on these issues. And we expect it to generate more questions than answers. However, the participants in this process were challenged by the prospect of helping chart future program directions for Cooperative Extension's CRD work vis-a-vis local government, community infrastructure, and economic development by taking a hard, objective look at where we are and where we might be, or ought to be, headed in our local infrastructure investment decision models.

This book is offered to the reader as a challenge. Practitioners need more complete theoretical foundations and more accurate decision tools as they face new social and economic demands, an evolving and sometimes uncertain form of "New Federalism," and an increasingly restless local public. Research and extension professionals must respond to these needs in a scholarly and committed fashion, drawing on the best research-based knowledge that can be generated. The future dimensions of Cooperative Extension will be significantly influenced by its success in assisting local governments in meeting this challenge. Likewise, academic professionals will find that the intellectual challenges inherent in the important issues addressed in this book are both imposing and gratifying. We hope that these contents will serve to bring the researcher and the practitioner together into a more enlightened debate about rural infrastructure problems.

PART I: Theoretical Foundations of Infrastructure Investment

2
Economic Theories of Infrastructure Decision-Making[1]

Thomas G. Johnson

It is difficult to lay the foundations of infrastructure investment decision-making processes without dealing simultaneously with supply and demand. At its simplest level, this decision-making process is one of equating supply and demand for infrastructure. While many of the issues involved in this process are fundamentally political in nature, economists have important contributions to make to the understanding of the local government infrastructure investment decision-making process. The economists' contributions stem from 1) their dichotomous view of theory (normative and positive), 2) their chief contributions to rationality (the concepts of marginality, opportunity cost, and incentive systems), and 3) their growing preoccupation with an institutional view of economic phenomena and processes.

As Paul Barkley has pointed out, the normative theory of public goods deals with the issues of efficiency, equity and population distribution. The addition of population distribution to the usual list is made necessary by the indivisible characteristic of public goods and the possibility of economies of size in their provision. The positive theory of public goods deals with the use of limited or nonexistent economic information (preferences, relative prices, cost functions, measures of access, and future population) to make expenditure and investment decisions.

Marginality indicates, for example, that efficient provision of infrastructure will occur where marginal cost of the facility equals the

---

[1] This chapter has benefited immeasurably from reviews by Drs. Eldon Smith, and George McDowell.

Marginality indicates, for example, that efficient provision of infrastructure will occur where marginal cost of the facility equals the marginal benefits to the constituents and that population should rise if the marginal person contributes more in tax revenues than he or she costs in marginal variable costs and congestion costs. The concept of opportunity costs is essential when facilities and services are being provided in the absence of firms willing to bear costs and risks in order to generate economic rent. Incentive is the concept which economists use to relate normative and positive theories of private good production (the invisible hand) and the element which is so obviously altered when the good in question is public in nature.

Finally, the economist offers an institutional view of the decision-making process. Insititutional views generally suggest that the political constitution, the system of property rights, tradition and the social structure determine the system of incentives facing the local government decision-maker. Furthermore, it suggests that while these institutions do change, they change slowly, and this stability allows the decision-making process to become more efficient and effective in providing the types, sizes, qualities and locations of infrastructure which people demand.

This chapter first considers the current normative theory of public service provision. Much of this theory does not pertain exclusively to infrastructure but includes the broader concept of public services and public goods in general. Next various positive theories of public service provision are reviewed and their implications discussed. Finally, the two are synthesized in an economic context.

THE NORMATIVE THEORY OF PUBLIC SERVICE PROVISION

Normative theories deal with what should be--that is, how public infrastructure investment decisions ideally would be made. In the standard neoclassical theory, the invisible hand leads the perfectly competitive market to produce the optimum level of product and to distribute it optimally at the optimum price. Under these circumstances the normative theory is also positive in the sense that if it were correct then it would also occur in the real world. There are several reasons why we should not expect the market or any other institution to automatically lead to socially optimum levels for all goods and services. These include:

1. For many goods and facilities, residents cannot be excluded (or can only be excluded at very high costs) from receiving benefits from the facility. Furthermore, there are no reasons to try to exclude an individual because he/she causes little or no extra costs.

2. The necessary investments are large relative to the population to be served, and competition among private firms is unlikely.

3. The operation of the facility is subject to diminishing costs, and a private firm would lose money if it equated marginal costs with price.

In those cases where one or more of these characteristics occur, provision of the service or infrastructure by the local government is warranted. In the following section a theory of local public goods is presented and discussed.

PUBLIC GOODS

Assume a locality with n individuals (families) each demanding some level of public good, G. Then the total cost relationship for this aggregate good can be expressed as:

$$TC = h(G)$$

and the average cost as

$$C = C(G).$$

If G were a perfectly exclusive good, the total production would equal the sum of the quantities consumed by all constituents that is:

$$G = \sum_n G_i.$$

where

G_i = the level of public good consumed by the ith individual.

If, instead, it is an indivisible, or jointly consumed good as assumed here, each constituent consumes the entire production level, that is:

$$G = G_i = G_j.$$

If the government balances its budget, and collects revenues from constituents through taxation, the sum of taxes will equal the total cost of producing G, that is:

$$\sum_n T_i = CG; \tag{2.1}$$

and each constituent will pay,

$$T_i = CGt_i \tag{2.2}$$

where:

T_i = the taxes paid by the ith individual;

t_i = the ith individual's share of taxes ($\sum_n t_i = 1$).

Assume individuals have utility functions such as:

$$U_i = u_i(X_i, G_i), \tag{2.3}$$

and incomes,

$$Y_i = PX_i + T_i \tag{2.4}$$

where,

U_i = utility of the ith individual,

X_i = private goods consumed by the ith individual,

Y_i = income of the ith individual, and

P = the price of X.

Combining equations (2.2) and (2.4) gives

$$Y_i = PX_i + CGt_i . \tag{2.5}$$

Maximizing the ith individual's utility (2.3) with respect to X, and G, subject to the budget constraint (2.5) yields the first order conditions:

$$u_x - \lambda P = 0;$$

$$u_G - \lambda t(C + G*\partial C/\partial G) = 0;$$

and

$$Y - PX - CGt = 0 .$$

where the subscript i has been dropped for simplicity.

These conditions lead to the optimizing condition:

$$MRS_{GX} = t(C + G*\partial C/\partial G)/P; \tag{2.6}$$

and the demand function,

$$G = D(C,t,P,Y) . \tag{2.7}$$

The Samuelson Condition indicates that given the non-rivalness of public goods, the social optimum occurs where the sum of individual marginal rates of substitution at each level of output, equals the marginal rate of transformation of G for X, that is:

$$\sum_n MRS_{GX} = MRT_{GX}.$$

The Lindahl Solution (or benefit pricing model) demonstrates that the demand function (2.7) may be inverted and solved for t to calculate the tax share which will make the optimum output of G, optimum to each constituent. This solution is:

$$t = D^{-1}(C,P,Y,G).$$

The Samuelson Condition and Lindahl Solution are illustrated graphically in Figure 2.1.

If the good X is a numeraire good measured in dollars, then the ith individual's MRS is his or her marginal benefit, the sum of MRS's is the social marginal benefit, and the MRT is the marginal cost of producing G. Given the total cost curve (2.1),

$$MC_G = C + G(\partial C/\partial G). \tag{2.8}$$

If $\partial C/\partial G = 0$, then average cost and marginal cost are equal and each constituent's opportunity cost of consuming G, Ct, is at the same time optimal, and the level required to allocate resources and generate sufficient revenues to exactly cover the total cost of the public good, that is:

$$\sum_n Ct_i = C\sum_n t_i = C.$$

This is, of course, similar to the case of the competitive market under similar circumstances. Private firms, if faced with constant unit costs, would also just cover costs at equilibrium. However, if the $MC \neq AC$, as is most likely, then the private and public cases diverge. If production is subject to increasing returns to size, average cost will decline and marginal cost will be lower than average cost. A private firm faced with declining average costs would not be able to cover its total cost by pricing its product at its marginal cost. The local government, by charging each individual a share of average cost, will exactly cover costs and, at the same time, send the constituents the optimizing "price" signal, MC. To see this, notice that the change in tax liability associated with a change in G is exactly equal to MC of G, that is if one takes the partial derivative of equation (2.2) with respect to G, one gets the expression:

$$\partial T_i/\partial G = C + G*\partial C/\partial G.$$

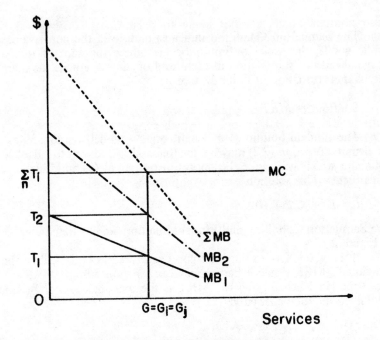

Figure 2.1: Samuelson Condition & Lindahl Solution

This is precisely the MC of the public good in equations (2.6) and (2.8).

Similarly, if average cost is increasing and marginal cost is greater than average cost, the private market will generate profits. Government, on the otherhand, can send the same "price" signal while balancing the budget.

Since the optimum level of G is determined by the sum of constituents' MB, or demand curves in this model, the addition of new constituents raises the level of G and lowers the tax share, t, sufficiently to induce the current residents to demand it. This suggests a continuous process of growth, even when the locality faces increasing costs. However, pure nonrival goods are not likely to occur in the real world. The following section introduces the concept of congestion.

CONGESTION

Assume, not a pure public good (one in which consumption is entirely joint), but rather, one in which congestion costs appear at some level of production. This case is particularly appropriate to a discussion of infrastructure provision since facilities are frequently subject to the following conditions: 1) it is difficult or costly to enforce exclusion, 2) costs are frequently large relative to the population, and 3) they are frequently subject to decreasing costs.

In this case, the marginal benefits of the public good are, at some point, a function of the number of constituents. The utility function becomes:

$$U = u(X,G,n); \text{ where } \partial u_i/\partial n < 0.$$

This declining marginal utility effectively creates an optimum community size (or facility size) in terms of public service provision. This optimum occurs when the marginal benefits of additional constituents (due to reductions in the cost of services) exactly equal the marginal costs (due to congestion). At this optimum size the tax share, t, will just equal the marginal congestion cost. Again, this good will be provided publicly if exclusion is not possible at low cost, if the size of the facility is large relative to the population, or if the service is subject to decreasing costs. Congestion in public goods is discussed further in the next chapter.

OTHER ISSUES

The above model can be altered to allow for such real world considerations as variability in the rate of use. Variability is particularly important in decisions related to infrastructure since roads, bridges, water, sewer, and other facilities are characterized by large variations in useage. The rate of use has important influence on the optimum size of a facility.

Another issue is that of location of facilities. For many types of infrastructure, one's proximity to the source of the service is important since the private costs and the level of the benefits are affected by the ease, time and expense involved in using the service. The normative dimensions of this question are largely unexplored except through such approaches as benefit-cost analysis. The equity dimension of this issue is of particular importance as well.

BENEFIT-COST ANALYSIS

Given the conceptual basis provided above, the normative role of the decision-making body is to compare the benefits and costs of the various alternatives facing it. If completed correctly this process will lead to the optimum type, size, and location of the facility. In the perfectly functioning private market case, the market itself plays this role. In the absence of a market, the public sector must explicitly determine the optimum strategy. Benefit-cost analysis is a formalization of this process. It formally incorporates and introduces the economic concepts of marginality and opportunity cost into the decision-making process.

While benefit-cost is not, itself, a theory, its usefulness is predicated on its relationship to the normative theory above. As in the case of many analytic tools, the theoretical basis of benefit-cost is often ignored by practitioners. But an understanding of the theoretical basis is essential if we are to correctly apply it to emerging issues.

As a normative economic tool for measurement of "...'public benefits' or 'general welfare'..." (Krutilla, 1964), benefit cost analysis must necessarily reflect some social welfare function and thus be based on certain value judgments (Nath, 1957). A minimal set of value judgments which must be accepted in order to use benefit-cost analysis would include:

1. Individuals are the best judge of their own well-being;

2. Social welfare depends on individual well-being;

3. Non-monetized issues may be ignored;

4. Each person is of equal importance;

5. Individual utility is approximately proportional to the consumption of goods and services (and is therefore cardinal and additive); and

6. The marginal utility of money is constant and equal for all individuals.

The first five assumptions are coincident with utilitarian economics. The sixth must be made in order to sum the expenditures of individuals with different incomes. It can be demonstrated that together these assumptions lead to a social welfare function which is equivalent to an expanded concept of National Income in which certain shadow prices replace distorted and otherwise non-monetized values (Johnson, 1977).

Among the many implications of the normative theory above for benefit-cost analysis, are the following:

1. Benefits are determined by the constituents' "demand function" for public services. These demand functions, while not revealed by market transactions, must be estimated in order to calculate benefits.

2. The appropriate measure of cost is the marginal cost of the service or facility. This rather obvious implication is sometimes ignored in favor of average cost. It is particularly important that marginal cost be employed when such issues as congestion and size of a facility are being considered.

3. When marginal benefits and costs are not constant, a surplus is generated which, because of the non-profit nature of governments, is entirely consumer surplus. In these cases, reliable estimates of supply and demand elasticities are essential data.

Benefit-cost analysis does not, itself, provide all the answers to the infrastructure investment question. Because it values social benefits and costs, its treatment must be very comprehensive. It must, therefore, be used in conjunction with fiscal and economic impact models, and employ a large number of data.

A critical issue in the success of the benefit-cost analysis is whether valid measures of constituent demand (marginal valuation) are available. This issue leads conveniently to a discussion of positive models of public service provision.

POSITIVE MODELS OF PUBLIC SERVICE PROVISION

Normative models of private production and consumption largely double for positive models because of the system of incentives in the private market. In the case of public services, no comparable correspondence exists between normative and positive models. A critical problem with normative models of public service provision is that without a well developed market mechanism for measuring the preferences of individuals, it is difficult to know precisely what these preferences are. If it is assumed that the consumer is rational and the best judge of his/her own well-being, then some knowledge of this system of preferences is essential if we are to apply normative theory to real world cases.

On the other hand, the same system of preferences is the criterion by which public decision-makers must make public service and infrastructure decisions. Thus, it is important to consider how constituents make their preferences known. Various positive models of constituent behavior have been suggested. These will be reviewed briefly in the next few pages.

A common view in many positive models of public service decision-making is that the consumer makes his/her preferences known directly. Other models attempt to determine the conditions under which group decision-making will result in optimum levels of public services. In most, however, it is assumed that the decision-maker simply carries out the will of the people, i.e. the "majority" which is taken to be the utility maximizing solution for the group.

THE TIEBOUT HYPOTHESIS

One of the more commonly analyzed models of individual behavior is the Tiebout Hypothesis. This theory suggests that individuals "vote with their feet" -- that is, they move from one jurisdiction to another in order to receive the type of public services (and public goods in general) that most closely match their preferences. The theory assumes:

1. perfect mobility of consumers,

2. perfect information,

3. a large number of communities offering a wide choice of public services and tax rates,

4. no labor supply or production effects related to choice of residence,

5. no spillover effects between communities, and

6. each community has an optimal size.

This model can be expanded to take into consideration production-side effects and can be extended to explain some of the location behavior of industry. One important implication of this theory is that communities will compete for residents (both households and firms) until they achieve their optimal size.[2] This hypothesis is supported by the evidence that communities are competing very vigorously for migrating and expanding firms.

The Tiebout Hypothesis is frequently criticized because of its assumptions of zero relocation cost (perfect mobility). While this is perhaps not too serious for relocations over very short distances (within cities or counties) it is likely to become very serious as distance increases. Furthermore, over short periods of time, the mobility of individuals is very low.

It is perhaps best to view the Tiebout phenomenon as a long run tendency of individuals. If the preferences of individual constituents are viewed as a continuum (as certain voting models to be considered later do), then at any point in time the number of constituents with any

---

2 Since in-migrants to one community are out-migrants of another, the overall optimality of any equilibrium depends on the number of communities relative to the number of residents.

preference would be from a frequency distribution (in some cases assumed to be normal). The Tiebout Hypothesis suggests that over time, if preferences are fairly stable, the frequency distribution will become narrower without any changes in the policy of local governments. This process is illustrated in Figure 2.2. Of course, conditions are always changing, as are preferences, and the equilibrium predicted by Tiebout is not likely to be realized--even in very small communities. The theory does lead, however, to some interesting hypotheses about the relationship between homogeneity of service demand and the stability of populations. Among other things, it suggests that as a community matures, it will become more homogeneous, and that rapidly growing communities will be less homogeneous.

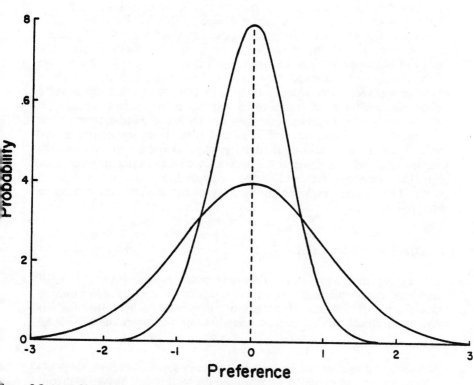

Figure 2.2: Voter Distribution Before and After Migration

VOTING MODELS

Various voting models have been offered as explanations for the behavior of decision-makers. Given the hypothesized frequency distribution of preferences above, these models try to determine the likely level and mix of services that communities will provide. These models--the optimal constitution model, the median voter model, and the Buchanan and Tullock model--each take a different tact but have in common their assumption that individuals directly influence the decisions being made.

Another group of models takes the alternative view that decisions are made by elected or appointed officials. The Downs Model of political parties, for example, is based on a concept of representative government. The model suggests that political parties will adopt platforms which will maximize their probability of election and re-election. This rather self-serving motivation is an important difference from the other models since it admits that decision-makers may not always translate the preferences of voter exactly.[3] Even here, however, the model maintains that preferences are considered. A similar model by Breton views this process as an economic system producing policies in return for political support.

An even more extreme model has been suggested by Niskanen. The theory of bureaus contends that elected officials have complete knowledge of the constituents' demand curve for public services but know nothing of the cost curves for producing them. The bureaucrats that produce the public services have an incentive to maximize the budget under their supervision since this will enhance their esteem, power, and income. Since they must equate total expenditures and total revenues, they tend to choose a means of producing the service which is as expensive as possible without reducing the demand. This is achieved by extracting revenues along the demand curve until the real marginal costs equal the demand curve. This is very similar to the strategy of the perfectly discriminating monopolist.

MUDDLING THROUGH

Yet another theory of the decision-making process is offered by the "disjointed incrementalism", or "muddling through" view of policy making (Lindbloom, 1979). This school describes other theories as rational-analytical models because they assume unambiguous knowledge

---

[3] This model is less relevant in our federal primary system, where platforms are more discrete and candidate oriented. At the local level, however, platforms are most frequently based on party deliberation.

of all alternatives and their consequences, and consistent preference orderings. In contrast to the rational-analytic models above, disjointed incrementalism suggests that preferences evolve as individuals learn the consequences of alternatives. Furthermore, it is hypothesized that policy-makers do not come to a consensus but, rather, strive for compromise. Each actor is guided by his or her own ideals as well as some broader common value or social consensus. "Common values are the store of preference information generated by the feedback from previous choice making" (Shabman, 1983). Common values reflect some imperfect image of individual preferences for alternative policies, while the process of compromise reflects the appropriateness of the policies. Such a theory predicts that policy change will occur incrementally, rather than abruptly, and that with suitable lags and allowances, it brings about changes which reflect the electorate's will. The process of change will, in turn, result in an evolution of preferences. A particularly important implication of this theory is that decisions are not based on the result of analysis but on the basis of different ideologies (or perceptions of ideology).

CONCLUSIONS

The above, noncritical review of infrastructure investment theories, leaves us with a menagery of sometimes complementary, sometimes contradictory, views of local government decision-making. What can we learn from these theories? Regardless of the particular mechanisms involved, the models analyzed above have one thing in common which allows us to proceed analytically. That commonality is that decisions are made with the goal of reflecting some view of the electorate's system of preferences (or what it would be if they had perfect knowledge of their consequences).

Another conceptual mechanism, which is complementary (or at least not contradictory) to each of the theories discussed, is induced migration in response to local public goods. The Tiebout Hypothesis, while unproven itself, implicitly incorporates the highly plausible concept of induced migration. Other theories, especially the median voter model, are enhanced by introducing the possibility of changing preferences through migration of households and firms.

The concepts of supply and demand themselves, while attractive to economists and highly complementary, are unproven in public good provision where markets, prices, and units of production do not exist. If one accepts the validity of utility functions, then the concept of marginal benefits follows logically. But unless some concept of supply response can be logically defended, then the framework is lacking. A danger in relying on a framework such as this (if it is not in fact adequate) is that it may fail to direct attention to other, more pertinent aspects of the problem.

The voting models contain a number of contradictions and most are, at best, applicable under limited circumstances only. In general, these models are not very satisfying because they overlook so many important issues. Most troublesome is the observation that they have very little predictive power. The "muddling through" view, while appealing because of its universality and evolutionary nature, has even less predictive power.

An important difference between public and private goods which is entirely overlooked by the theories above, is the social, intergenerational and distributional implications of joint consumption. Whereas consumption of private goods allows a heterogeneity among any community, consumption of public goods enforces homogeneity. Thus, to a considerable extent, the values of the community (however determined) are forced upon the individuals. Levels of law enforcement, education quality, and infrastructure are consumed more or less equally by all who choose to live in the community.

How might the theory of infrastructure investment and provision evolve? Theoretical advances are necessary in two areas. First, better theories are needed to understand the process by which resident preferences are translated into local government decisions. Second, better theories are needed to understand the demand or preferences themselves.

One theoretical framework which may serve as a point of departure is household production theory. In the proposed framework, the local government would be a producer and a surrogate consumer of public services. Just as the household production theory internalizes the processes of production and consumption, with 1) implicit prices of the produced services based on prices of factors, 2) implicit technologies, and 3) income and other constraints, the local government could be viewed as producing public services at levels which equate the marginal social value with the marginal cost of production. In this model, migration would homogenize the constituents over time, and lead to competition for growth until an optimum sized community is achieved.

In the meantime more empirical validation and rejection of the various theories must take place. Where possible, those concepts which are not rejected during empirical testing should be synthesized and incorporated into more general theoretical frameworks.

APPENDIX 2: GRAPHICAL PRESENTATION OF A TWO-PERSON, TWO-GOOD (ONE PUBLIC AND ONE PRIVATE) WORLD

Daniel M. Otto

This analysis proceeds as in chapter 2 for an economy consisting of two individuals (A and B), two goods (a private good X and a public good G). The private good is allocated between A and B in such a way that supply equals demand:

$$X_A + X_B = X.$$

In the case of a pure public good, the joint consumption and non-exclusion properties implies that the consumption of the good by one individual does not prevent its consumption by another so that we have:

$$G_A = G_B = G.$$

If it is assumed that the production efficiency conditions for providing X and G are satisfied, the combination of X and G which can be produced by resources and technology in the economy can be represented by the production possibility curve PP in Figure 2A1. Individuals A and B benefit from the consumption of goods X and G as represented by the indifference maps for each of them. Figure 2A1 depicts A's indifference maps drawn from the origin O_A while the lower diagram depicts B's indifference curves drawn from O_B.

The Pareto optimality conditions can be found by taking an arbitrary utility level for A and finding the allocation of resources that maximizes the utility level of B. If we choose I'_A to be the arbitrary utility level for A, we need to find the combination of G and X_B available to B that is consistent with the level of G and X_A which allowed individual A to achieve utility level I'_A. Choosing any point along the production possibility frontier, such as C, defines the level of X and G produced in the economy. The output of G produced here ($O_A E$) can be consumed by both A and B since it is a public good. However, the production of X is (EC) and must be divided between individuals A and B. In order for A to achieve utility level I'_A, he must consume ED leaving CD for consumption by individual B. The difference between the production possibility frontier PP and the indifference curve (CD at the optimal level for A) represents the consumption opportunities available to B. The locus of these points is represented by TT in Figure 2A1. The maximum level of utility that B can attain is that of the indifference curve J'_B where TT is tangent to J'_B. This entails an output of the public good given by $O_A G_0 = O_B G_0$ and an output of the private good $O_A X_O$ of which $O_A X_A$ is consumed by A and $ZX_A (= O_B X_B)$ is consumed by B.

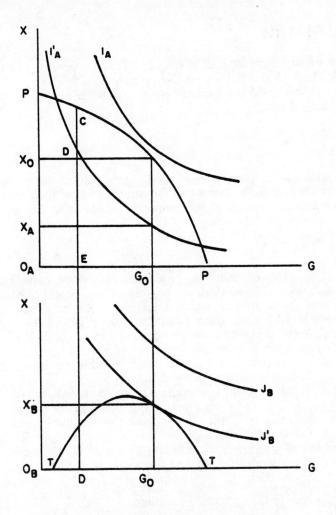

Figure 2A1: Derivation of Efficiency Conditions

At these points of tangency a series of marginal equality conditions can be used to characterize the Pareto optimal allocation of resources. The slope of B's indifference curve, which is B's marginal rate of substitution of X for $G(MRS^B_{GX})$. Since TT was derived by vertically subtracting I'_A (which is the slope of MRS^A_{GX}) from PP (which is the slope of MRT_{GX}), the slope of TT is the difference between PP and I'_A which can be written as $MRT_{GX} - MRS^A_{GX}$ therefore at the point of tangency between TT and J'_B, the optimal allocation of resources can be represented as:

$$MRS^B_{GX} = MRT_{GX} - MRS^A_{GX};$$

or

$$\sum_{i=A,B} MRS^i_{GX} = MRT_{GX}.$$

This last equation is referred to as the Samuelson condition which implies that at the optimum, the marginal cost of supplying the last unit of G in terms of foregone $X(MRT_{GX})$ just equals the marginal benefits that all users of G obtain in terms of $X(\sum MRS^i_{GX})$ the condition will also hold for more general cases where there are many consumers.

In an economy where money is used, these efficiency conditions can be expressed as marginal benefits in monetary terms and as marginal costs, also in monetary terms. The marginal rate of transformation is the ratio of the marginal costs of producing G for the marginal cost of producing X:

$$MRT_{GX} = MC_G/MC_X.$$

Similarly, the marginal rate of substitution for an individual is the ratio of the marginal utilities of the two goods, which in turn is the ratio of the marginal benefits of G for X in monetary terms:

$$MRS^A_{GX} = \mathrm{MU}^A_G/\mathrm{MU}^A_X = MB^A_G/PX.$$

In an economy in which competitive producers follow marginal cost pricing ($P_X = MC_X$) the efficiency conditions for the production of public goods imply that the sum of the marginal benefits to all individuals from G must equal the marginal cost of producing it:

$$\sum_{i=1}^n MB^i_G = MC_G.$$

This discussion of efficiency conditions for public goods assumes that it is possible to assign prices to the benefits and costs. However, this becomes a difficult task when attempting to deal with all possible primary and secondary benefits.

These efficiency conditions in terms of marginal costs and benefits can also be expressed using the constructs of demand and supply curves. The supply curve in Figure 2A2 shows the marginal costs of producing G for various points along the production possibility curve. The curves D^A and D^B represent "demand" curves for individuals in the sense that they show the marginal benefit placed on G by the individuals (MB^i), or the price they would be willing to pay for each output of G if they had to pay a price. Defining this relationship abstracts from a number of problems associated with eliciting demand functions for public goods. These "demand" curves for G must be added vertically, rather than horizontally, to obtain an "aggregate" demand curve because the joint consumption property means that one person's consumption of G does not preclude others from consuming.

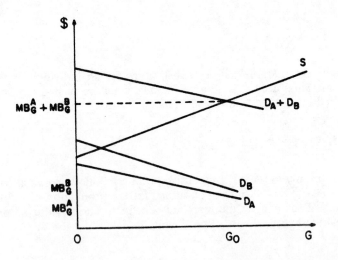

Figure 2A2: Individual and Aggregate Demand Curves for Public Goods

The optimal output of G occurs at the point at which the aggregate demand curve ($D^A + D^B$) intersects the supply curve. The total social costs is the area under the supply curve while the total benefit is the area under the "aggregate demand" curve. By producing G jointly between individuals A and B, the net social benefits are greater than the level which would have been provided if A or B's individual optimal level had been chosen. The allocation of this net benefit among various individuals in society depends upon the nature of the pricing strategy for the good or taxing scheme for financing the public good which are issues beyond the scope of this discussion.

3
Issues in the Supply of Public Infrastructure

Daniel M. Otto

Infrastructure of an area refers to the basic public investment in transportation systems, water and energy supplies and distribution systems, education, housing and expenditures on the social and cultural environment. These investments in social and physical overhead make possible the provision of basic services to the commodity producing sectors as well as to the social services and other human resource development institutions. In other words, infrastructure provides important services to existing population as well as the capacity for retaining local industries, facilitating expansions and attracting new jobs to the community. The importance of infrastructure to the performance and growth potential of communities has raised interest in the quality of rural infrastructure.

Population growth in rural areas and increased interest in economic development may put additional pressure on improving the quality and availability of public services to these areas. Attempting to meet these demands for new services will create a need for continued information and assistance by researchers and extension workers on various public service provision considerations such as estimating benefits and costs for various service and facility plans, evaluating financing alternatives and identifying appropriate scale and mix of services for different communities. This chapter focuses on economic dimensions of infrastructure supply with implications for future economic viability of communities. It begins with an examination of some of the underlying theoretical issues, followed by a discussion of efforts to empirically examine public service supply questions, and finally a discussion of the implications of these issues for rural areas of the U.S.

THEORETICAL FRAMEWORK

Although this chapter focuses primarily on supply issues related to the provision of public goods and services, it is necessary to include some demand related elements as the theoretical framework is developed. Beginning with a normative view of public goods provision provides a standard for evaluating how efficiently factors of production used in the production of public goods are being utilized. This framework is useful for discussing technical considerations such as service quality, appropriate scale of provision, and the divisibility of inputs and services.

Supply of both public and private goods are determined by their respective production functions. From an economy-wide perspective, there is no difference between an economy producing X and G and one producing two private goods. The same production efficiency conditions must exist in a mixed economy as in a purely private goods economy. Because of this, the marginal rate of technical substitution (MRTS) between any two factors of production (K, L) must be the same in the production of both X and G. This condition can be written as:

$$MRTS_{LK} = MP_{LX}/MP_{KX} = MP_{LG}/MP_{KG}.$$

In a competitive market, it is assumed that the price mechanism will ensure satisfaction of the production efficiency conditions, provided all firms or individuals are price takers for factors of production and all firms pay the same factor prices. If these production efficiency conditions are met, then the combinations of X and G which can be produced by the economy given its supplies of factors of production and technology in a production possibility curve such as in Figure 3.1, can be determined.

From the last chapter, pareto efficient production occurs where the marginal cost of supplying the last unit of G in terms of foregone private good X, (MRT_{GX}) just equals the sum of the marginal benefits that all users of the increment of G simultaneously obtain where benefits are in terms of the marginal rate of substitution of the private good for the public good (MRS_{GX}):

$$\sum_n MRS_{GX} = MRT_{GX}.$$

These same general conditions hold in an economy with many persons, many public and private goods and for each of the public goods in terms of any arbitrary private good.

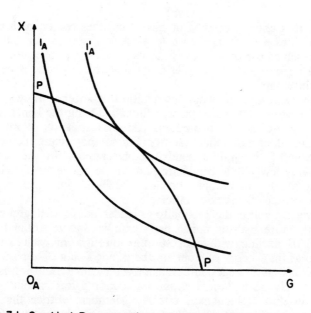

Figure 3.1: Graphical Representation of Production Efficiency Conditions

PRICING OF PUBLIC GOODS

The Lindahl Solution (discussed in the last chapter) suggests a scheme of charging individuals according to the benefits they receive, for allocating public goods in a manner similar to a market mechanism. However, because of free rider problems, there is no incentive for individuals to voluntarily pay their benefit price (which could be different for each individual) to consume G. Even if exclusion were possible, it should not be done on efficiency grounds since no one's utility is reduced by an additional individual consuming G. Also prices do not play the same role in allocating public goods as they do with private goods since by definition everyone could consume the same quantity of G once it has been provided. The only function of a pricing scheme would be to determine how the costs of financing the public goods are to be shared among the users.

While there is no reason to prefer benefit pricing to any other pricing scheme on efficiency grounds, there may be equity arguments depending upon the value judgment that is made about the distribution of benefits. The initial ownership of resources and the financing scheme will determine which of the Pareto-optimal allocations (if any) is achieved. Different starting points in terms of resource endowments would result in different optima so that choices need to be based on other criteria such as equity. In certain cases society may wish to achieve a non-pareto allocation of resources such as use of progressive taxes to finance public projects in less developed regions. Again, further discussions of this issue is beyond the scope of this chapter.

In this simple framework the addition of another individual would add another source of tax revenue without reducing the benefits enjoyed by previous users. This outcome assumes that the third person's consumption does not reduce A's or B's so that economies of size in consumption of the public goods are generated. In the real world, however, very few public goods are pure in the above sense. As we saw in the last chapter additional users will usually begin, at some point, to reduce the benefits for previous users.

If we generalize the theory to consider goods that are subject to congestion, more realistic conclusions can be drawn. One theoretical approach for dealing with congestion is through an exclusion process referred to as the "theory of clubs" in the public finance literature. A club good is defined as a congested public good for which exclusion is possible and which may be replicated within an economy for different groups of persons, or clubs (Buchanan, 1965). Members within the club are assumed to have identical utility functions so that they group into communities according to their similar preferences for public goods and services. According to the theory of clubs, the optimal number of users for G is reached when the per person tax price benefit, (the tax savings benefit to existing producers from adding one more user) is just equal to the marginal congestion costs imposed on all users.

Under these "club conditions" where exclusion is possible at zero cost and if the costs of providing the good are constant, the competitive market mechanism can be relied upon to provide an economy of many individuals with the correct size of facility and the correct number of members and the correct number of facilities for the entire population. Although it is not a pure form of a club, one aspect of the post World War II (WWII) development of the suburbs in the U.S. was that many families with similar characteristics chose to live in communities that would support the kinds and qualities of public services (such as schools and parks) which closely matched their life stage and preference patterns.

In situations where clubs for a particular public good subject to congestion costs are not likely to form, a similar approach to determining optimal use of facilities can be followed. Although some means of controlling or regulating the facilility would be needed, the optimal use of a facility occurs when the marginal benefit from the additional use equals the marginal congestion costs incurred. The optimal size of a facility would be at a level where the marginal cost of expanding the facility equals the marginal benefits to members in the economy.

EMPIRICAL STUDIES

In order to evaluate the appropriateness of the supply related concepts of public services looked at above, and to relate them to questions of efficient scale of provision, it is useful to draw upon empirical work on the subject. Although production economists have long been concerned with measuring output, relatively few have focused on the public sector. Much of the scarcity of empirical studies on this issue may be due to the difficulties in formulating the supply concept properly and measuring the output and costs of public sector services. Conceptually, outputs of public sector goods and services are the amounts, expressed in physical units, that result from the production process. Difficulties arise because output has quality characteristics as well as quantity characteristics. These difficulties often lead to a reliance on proxies to measure different dimensions for the type of services involved. For services such as garbage collection, water and sewer and other utilities, volume serves as a good measure of output. In other cases such as police, fire and health, the major output is in the form of a deterrence, or the prevention of an outcome such as crime, fire, or disease outbreaks. As a result of these difficulties, efforts to measure output seems to have focused on activity measures, primarily expenditure for services.

In addition to the difficulties of conceptualizing and measuring output, there are problems in dealing with the cost components of these expenditure functions. These difficulties include separating capital costs from operating costs, allocating costs to different financing arrangements for these services, and separating leased properties from owned.

Despite these difficulties, researchers have attempted to estimate factors that influence the provision of public services, usually in a form of an expenditure function which is amendable to estimation (Hirsch, 1968 and 1973). In estimating factors determining expenditure levels, researchers often include demand as well as cost factors. Abstracting to a long-run concept where all inputs are variable, the long-run average unit cost (AUC) of a given service (total cost/output) is affected by the service quality (Q), quantity (A), prices of factor inputs (I), service characteristics affecting input requirements such as population density (S) and the state of technology (T). This can be formally expressed as:

$$AUC = f(Q, A, I, S, T).$$

Expenditure functions based on this conceptual model can provide information on why expenditures levels differ among communities and among services. This line of research can also be used to evaluate cost implications of growth or consolidation of local governments. These governmental consolidations can be inclusions of many different services into a single administrative system (vertical integration) or dispersed delivery units of the same service (school system or fire stations) into one administrative unit. Since relatively few short-run changes can be made in physical infrastructures in order to adjust to changing population or other demand conditions, economists have been more concerned with long-run expenditure functions. The typical shape of the conceptual long-run average cost curves for firms is U-shaped with the per unit cost of output declining as the size or volume of output increases (Figure 3.2). Although the expenditure function for public services by local governments is an analogous concept exhibiting similar properties, there are significant differences. Among the major differences are: (1) that no assumptions of cost minimization and equilibrium among marginal contributions of factors of production can be made for government production as is done for private firms; and (2) the units of measurement are usually number of people served rather than a unit of good or service output. In both the private firm and the government sectors, there is a relationship of declining per unit costs as size or volume of units increase, at least in the initial stages. The point at which the long-run average cost curve begins to increase is a matter of much debate for both private and public goods.

Factors which contribute to economies of size include greater specialization and division of labor and technological improvements such as capital investments and labor saving machines. However, as Hirsch (1968) points out, many of these conditions are missing in local governmental units that are growing or consolidating. Few supplies are purchased in sufficient quantity to obtain major price concessions, legal restrictions on debt and salary levels may affect efficient allocations and citizen access considerations may limit the size of many services.

Based on these expenditure surveys, Hirsch and others conclude that there are no significant economies of size for services such as police, fire, refuse collection, libraries, street maintenance, and primary and secondary education for all but the relatively smallest political jurisdictions. This lack of significant economies of size reflects the fact that these services seldom operate in genuine long-run conditions as few changes can be made to school buildings, police and fire stations, libraries, water treatment plants, etc., in order to achieve efficient operation levels. Communities tend to operate under short-run conditions where extra policemen, teachers or firetrucks are added until it reaches a size where an additional station or building is needed. These are represented by short-run average cost curves SAC_1, SAC_2, SAC_3, in Figure 3.2. Expansion by the addition of extra services have little effect on per capita costs so that long-run average costs are expected to remain relatively flat until such a large geographical area, or population, is served that diseconomies set in from management or coordination problems. These inputs to police, education or fire protection services represent a "lumpy" input problem where communities overinvest in a service if they purchased a whole new unit, such as a firetruck, until they are of a sufficient size. Arrangements to lease or purchase part-time services may help provide an appropriate match.

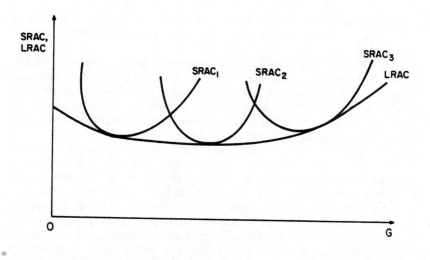

Figure 3.2: Typical Long-Run and Short-Run Average Cost Curves for Private
or Public Goods

There is evidence that economies of size do not appear to exist for
water supply, sewage disposal and electric power production. The
Advisory Commission on Intergovernmental Relations (1970) suggested
that efficiencies were most dramatic in cities up to 25,000 in population,
with relatively little gain in efficiency for cities in the 25,000-250,000 range
with diseconomies beyond that size. A review by USDA of potential
economies of size in public services which affect rural communities suggest
that many economies of size are possible for communities of up to 10,000
population (Fox, 1981). These economies of size gains can best be
achieved when services (1) have high fixed costs such as capital facilities,
(2) are centrally located, (3) have efficient, large-scale machinery available.
Thus water and sewage treatment services are more likely to possess
economies of size characteristics than more labor intensive services such
as police and fire services. Since many of these gains from economies of
size are dependent upon population size and density, it is difficult for
communities to influence the population or cost variables in the short-run.
Efforts to lower per capita costs by consolidating the service area typically
have offsetting expenses associated with a more extensive service delivery
area. Another factor limiting potential economies of size savings for
communities is that different services achieve their gains from scale of
operation at different population levels. Unless there are means for

vertically integrating services efficiently, there are likely to be different degrees of efficiency across the different types of services within a community.

While this examination of economies of size in public infrastructure has focused on the technical relations and physical production processes, the question of economies in public services is linked to several other related issues. In addition to technical considerations, economies of size involve the issue of managerial effectiveness. Larger size units of government are likely to have a competitive advantage by being able to afford the technical skills, quality of staff and use of ancillary services and management tools needed for sound administration. However, this potential gain from "managerial efficiencies" may be offset by losses from diseconomies associated with administrating large units of government.

Another related issue is that the most efficient city size, in terms of providing services, may not be the most efficient in terms of financing these services. There is often a wide gap between the demand for services and the ability to pay for them within a region such as economically depressed central cities surrounded by affluent suburbs. Factors such as population densities and inter-jurisdictional relations also may affect the role of effective financing and efficient service provision.

Finally, there is the non-economic factor that the suitable size of local government may have to do more with the desire for political participation than what is an efficient scale for goods and service provision. The benefits of local community identity, active political participation and involvement in decisions that affect them, particularly in regard to the provision of education, health and welfare, and the planning function may be so great as to favor small areas of governmental organization except where economic efficiency advantages of large size are very strong.

These arguments for a smaller scale of governmental organization which allows citizen participation are strengthened further with the suggestion that the appropriate measure for the output of public services is in terms of "consumer-citizen satisfaction." As stated by the public choice perspective, the opportunity for citizens to interact in determining the level and mix of services provided by local government is seen as a fulfillment of the primary goal of a democratic government (McDowell, 1978). By involving citizens in determining production goals for their unit of government, the scale and mix of services will necessarily be specific to that group. Although the goal implied by this perspective of local government activities is to promote citizen involvement in service provision decision, technical and analytical capabilities of various management science related disciplines are still expected to play a role in helping determine service provision options and the potential consequences of different courses of action.

SUMMARY AND CONCLUSIONS

This chapter has attempted to focus on issues related to the supply of public services from a conceptual and empirical basis. As this discussion has indicated, the supply issues quickly become intertwined with demand related issues of the level and mix of services to be provided and the issue of appropriate organization for the financing of these services.

The theoretical discussion presented a normative analysis of conditions guiding the optimal provision of pure public goods. Because of the joint consumption and non-exclusion characteristics of public goods, expanding participation in a particular public service reduces per capita costs without reducing benefits or utility of others in the economy. In a world of less than pure public goods, levels of services would be provided until the marginal cost in terms of crowding or congestion is equal to the marginal benefits of reduced per capita costs.

The discussion in the empirical section of the chapter focused on the difficulties of identifying and obtaining reliable measures of these public service supply concepts. Despite these difficulties, many researchers have formulated models to estimate factors influencing the provision of public services for local government. The most common procedure in these empirical studies have been to use expenditure functions as a proxy for public service output. While most of these studies agree that there are economies over the smaller range of city sizes, there is considerable disagreement as to size of local government at which all significant economies of size are achieved. Services requiring large capital investments such as water and sewage treatment plants are most likely to achieve some degree of economies of size. These attempts to estimate relationships affecting the supply of services have continually confronted problems of properly identifying and measuring public service output and supply determinants.

Most of this chapter has been concerned with technical and efficiency concerns in the provision of public goods and services with the implicit judgment that larger local government size was an important goal in order to achieve significant per unit savings from economies of size effects. However, if consideration is given to achieving citizen satisfaction with the level and mix of public services via their participation, increasing city size can quickly create diseconomies. This last issue suggests that the efficient city size for service provision needs to consider costs from economic, political and social perspectives and that the "optimal" size will be different for different communities.

The current interest in the provision of public goods and services reflects local communities' concern with providing adequate services to residents as well as an interest in using these public services as a means of attempting to attract and retain industry. Much of the block grant activity for infrastructure in Iowa, for example, is linked to the potential for job creation. The assessment of a community's proposal for job creation potential is an added criterion beyond community need. This standard puts pressure on communities in declining areas to organize their economic development efforts or deal with their infrastructure problems from their own resource base. The increased emphasis on the economic development potential of infrastructure investment at the state level suggests further financial strain on smaller rural communities outside the eligible "developing set" as they attempt to deal with infrastructure problems from their own resources. Loss of revenue sharing and tighter budgets can only exacerbate these problems.

Under these conditions there remain ample opportunities for research and extension activities in helping communities and local government determine their service provision options and the potential impacts of different courses of action. Additional options for providing services could be developed. Borrowing from the public choice literature with their emphasis on competitive market-oriented approach, further opportunities for private sector involvement in the production of public goods need to be explored. Current examples of this approach include hospital chains, garbage collection services, some utilities and prisons. Other conceptual tools suggested by the public choice literature are to encourage competitive behavior among bureaucracies and allowing managers to share in more of the savings that are achieved. In the more traditional approach, further refinements in the tools of community analysis such as community fiscal impact models, regional input output models, public service budgeting and feasibility models and local government management assistance programs can help communities move toward efficient and appropriate scale for providing local service.

4
Life Cycle Behavior, Uncertainty, and the Demand for Infrastructure

Thomas F. Stinson

News of collapsing bridges, deteriorating highways, unsafe drinking water, and polluted rivers and streams has focused national attention on the quality of public infrastructure. Nearly everyone agrees that more public sector investment is needed. There is, though substantial disagreement over how much more is necessary. Estimates of needs by the year 2000 range from $1.2 trillion by the Joint Economic Committee (1984a and 1984b), to $3 trillion, by the Associated General Contractors (1983). For wastewater treatment alone, 1982 EPA's estimates are that about $58 billion would be necessary to bring the existing system up to the standards set by the Clean Water Act of 1972. Recent USDA findings indicate that more than $16 billion of that backlog is in rural America.

These needs estimates are highly subjective. They are obtained by defining a minimum adequate standard for a particular service, and then estimating of the cost of bringing all communities into compliance with that standard. The size of the estimated shortfall (or the additional investment necessary) depends largely on one's definition of a minimum adequate service level. Such estimates do not allow for differences in local tastes and incomes. Often they depend greatly on the value of those estimating the backlog.

The alternative approach--relying strictly on consumer judgments about the optimal level of public infrastructure given household incomes, time preferences, preferences for public and private goods, and the relative costs of each good--also has problems. The most serious is that such estimates do not take into account any of the positive externalities produced by public infrastructure.   Consequently, less than optimal amounts will be made available.

The traditional demand-supply framework of economics does offer insights into the infrastructure issue, however, even though it cannot be used to precisely determine the nation's future public sector investment requirements.   This chapter highlights some results which emerge when public sector investment is examined using a model based on consumer demand under uncertainty.   The discussion proceeds as follows.   First, private sector investment under certainty is reviewed.   Demand for public sector investment under certainty is then developed and contrasted with the private sector results.   Uncertainty is then introduced into both the private and public sector frameworks and the differences again noted.   The chapter concludes by discussing likely impacts of key demographic and policy trends on demand for infrastructure.   Throughout, the analysis proceeds from the consumer's point-of-view.

PRIVATE SECTOR INVESTMENT WITH CERTAINTY

Begin by considering a consumer with initial endowments or incomes (y_1, y_2) available for consumption in each of two time periods. The consumer's goal is to maximize the utility of consumption over both time periods, subject to a set of potential investment opportunities and a subjective rate of time preference.

In the absence of a capital market consumers with identical endowments and investment opportunities may make very different decisions on how much to invest due to their differences in time preferences.   Individuals with a strong preference for current consumption will invest less (requiring a higher return on investment) than those with strong preferences for future consumption.

When perfect capital markets are introduced the familiar results emerge.   Perfect capital markets, where borrowers and lenders are charged the same interest rate and there are no transaction costs or restrictions on the amount one can borrow other than ability to repay, allow consumers to maximize utility by following a two-step process.   First, everyone invests until the marginal return on investment equals the market interest rate.   Then, each consumer maximizes utility by borrowing or lending along the capital market line, (the inter-temporal equivalent of the budget constraint) equating his or her subjective rate of time preference for consumption with the market rate.

The separation of investment and consumption into two distinct decisions, formally known as the Fisher Separation Theorem, is one of the foundations of the theory of finance.   In simplest terms it says that if managers choose investments in such a way as to maximize the value of their firm, they will automatically allow investors to maximize their utility of consumption.   Investors gain because they know that if management follows a profit maximizing strategy, each individual management decision need not be monitored to insure outcomes which will maximize investor utility. That is, investors can leave decisions on the firm's operation and investments to management.

Management gains because with separation it need not consider the time preferences of each of the firm's investors when making a decision. No matter what investors' time preferences may be, their utility of consumption will be maximized by generating the most wealth. Investors may then borrow or lend along the capital market line to reach optimal annual consumption levels. The existence of perfect capital markets allows management to simplify the capital budgeting decision rule to that of selecting all independent projects with net present values greater than zero.

An important result obtained directly from the separation theorem is that all stockholders if asked, will vote unanimously either in favor of or against any particular investment of the firm, depending on whether its net present value is greater or less than zero. This finding, termed the unanimity principle, implies that all investors have identical interests in the firm's behavior, independent of their individual time preferences. As long as managers choose all projects whose net present value is greater than zero, investor wealth and utility of consumption will be maximized.

Relaxing the assumption of a two period time frame by allowing multiple time periods changes nothing. The separation theorem still holds, and management still maximizes investor utility by following the net present value rule. Individuals continue to use the capital market to adjust consumption in line with their time preferences. There is, of course, no restriction on the time preferences of consumers, and individuals may oscillate back and forth between being net consumers and net investors as many (or as few) times as they desire over their lifetime.

Ghez and Becker (1975) in their studies of household activity present strong evidence of such life cycle behavior. They hypothesize that time preferences for consumption combine with the time path of market wage rates to produce a pattern of net borrowing, then net saving, followed by dissaving over the household's life cycle. Typically, it is assumed that the shift from net debtor to net saver takes place as individuals enter their peak earning years, while dissaving begins around retirement age.

Life cycle behavior will have no impact on aggregate consumption or investment levels if age cohorts in the population are relatively uniform. But, if one age cohort dominates the population distribution, market interest rates, and the level of investment in the economy could be affected.

Life cycle behavior by the post-war baby boom generation appears to have the potential to affect interest rates and savings levels. At present, while this group is in the net borrowing phase, aggregate investment may be reduced. But, as this cohort reaches its peak earning years, private investment levels should increase substantially correcting the earlier trend toward under investment. The correction will only be temporary though, since as that cohort enters the dissaving phase in retirement, it will again depress savings rates in the economy.

PUBLIC SECTOR INVESTMENT WITH CERTAINTY

Attempts to use the model of private investment reviewed above to analyze demand for public infrastructure run into immediate difficulty. The first problem is defining return on public sector investment. Unlike private sector investments which are freely convertible into any consumption good, investments in public sector capital facilities only increase the amount of a particular service available for consumption, or lower the cost of existing levels of that service to the consumer. Such investments increase consumer's utility in the present and in the future, but that increase is tied to a fixed annual level of consumption of a particular commodity at an established price.

This right to a specific level of government services at a fixed cost expands the consumers' opportunity set, and it can be assigned a value by consumers. But, in the absence of a perfect, Tiebout-like world where net benefits from a community's public services are capitalized into local property values, there is no market for that right and it cannot be sold. As a result, individuals cannot fully adjust their consumption so as to maximize utility of consumption subject to their time preferences. Thus, the separation theorem does not hold for public investment.

Consumers' inability to use the capital market to convert returns from investment in infrastructure into other consumption goods forces use of a different framework to analyze demand for public sector infrastructure. In the absence of a market for claims on government services, demand models, such as those used for private investment, which postulate that investment demand is a function of the vector of future incomes, the market rate of return, and individual's subjective rates of time preference are clearly insufficient.

Public sector investments must be analyzed in a derived demand framework. Because the return on investment comes from the guaranteed level of consumption of a particular service, consumers must see their investment decision as closely linked with their demand for that service. The arguments of the infrastructure demand function then expand to include the arguments of the demand function for the particular government services provided by the infrastructure including relative prices of all other consumer goods, factor prices and tastes, as well as expected incomes and relative time preference.

This formulation emphasizes that the public sector investment decision cannot be viewed simply as one of adjusting the timing of one's total consumption pattern. Instead, it is a more complicated adjustment of the timing of all consumption by purchasing a contract for fixed levels of future consumption at a guaranteed price.

Life cycle behavior may still appear, but it could be less important. One can imagine, for example, consumers at life cycle positions where additional investment will maximize utility, but for whom consumption levels of government services now and in the future are already sufficient. The result will be a decision to invest only in the private sector, and no public investment will occur. Situations in which life cycle behavior would call for investment, but where demand for the particular service decreases with age--schools, for example--also exist, as does the reverse, an increased demand for particular services and facilities--such as hospitals--during the dissaving phase of the life cycle.

A second implication of the lack of a market for public services rights is that all consumers will be unable to maximize their utility of consumption no matter what investment rule public decision-makers follow. Use of the net present value rule will not maximize each individual's utility unless all consumers have identical subjective rates of time preference and demand for public services. Nor can the decision-maker assume that the net present value rule will maximize using utility for the entire community over time.[4]

To insure that a particular infrastructure investment will maximize a community's utility, decision-makers need knowledge of each resident's subjective rate of time preference and their demand for the service in question. It would then be technically possible to calculate the increase in consumer surplus for each alternative, including investment in the private sector, and to choose the alternative for which the aggregate increase was the greatest.

Such calculations would be extremely complex and time consuming. As a result, decision-makers must choose a simpler rule. To reduce the necessary calculations, they focus their attention on the reactions of a limited number of voters. Two models of government decision-making allow this narrowing of information requirements, the median voter model and the dominant party model.[5] For simplicity in exposition, in this chapter it is assumed that public decision-makers base their investment decisions on the net present value of the project to the median voter. Use of a dominant party model would make only minor changes in the analysis, however.

---

[4] This does not, however, mean that the net present value rule should be rejected. Under no circumstances would it be appropriate for the public sector to invest in projects whose net present value using the market rate of return was less than zero. For a more complete discussion of the social discount rate issue see Wilson (1982).

[5] Inman (1979) gives a good review of the median voter and dominant party models.

Decisions made on the basis of the derived demand for public investment of a median voter will be different from those which would be predicted if a pure private sector investment model were used. Unlike the private sector result localities will differ in the amount of investment required in equilibrium. Communities will require the same levels only if their median voters are identical. Differences in tastes, time preferences, incomes, or appropriate production technology will produce different levels of local public facilities.

Such decisions will not necessarily be optimal from society's point of view, however. The problem of externalities (both positive and negative) remains. Public decision-makers who follow the preferences of the median voter are likely to invest less in infrastructure than is socially optimal. To increase local public sector investment to more nearly optimal levels, states and the federal government typically use matching grants to lower the future costs of the service to the consumer, thus increasing the return on the investment seen by the consumer.

PRIVATE SECTOR INVESTMENT UNDER UNCERTAINTY

Uncertainty is introduced into the demand for private sector investments by allowing actual, realized returns to differ from the expected return. The variation comes from two general types of risk, systematic risk, or variation due to changes in the national economy, and non-systematic risk, or variation due to the particular investment chosen, holding the national economy's performance constant.

Non-systematic risk in any portfolio can be eliminated by diversification. When an individual has a large number of investments some will yield less than expected and others more. But, actual and expected returns for portfolios of sufficient size will coincide in the absence of systematic risk. Households will be unwilling to pay to reduce nonsystematic risk because they can do so at no cost simply by broadening their portfolios.

Systematic risk, on the other hand, cannot be eliminated by diversification. Changes in the economy will affect the value of the portfolio no matter how many separate investments it contains. As a result investors will pay more for (or accept a lower rate of return on) assets which reduce the systematic risk of their portfolios. Attempts to determine rules for portfolio selection which minimize systematic risk are what drive the theory of financial policy for private sector investments.

When uncertainty is introduced in the analysis, the individual's choice problem becomes more complex. Consumers no longer simply maximize utility of consumption subject to a vector of incomes, the market interest rate, and their subjective time preferences. Now, they maximize expected utility subject to those same constraints plus their attitudes toward risk.

For the purpose of this chapter three results are particularly important. Assuming perfect and complete capital markets the separation theorem still holds, the net present value decision rule is still valid, and the unanimity principle still holds. Even under uncertainty managers will maximize expected utility of all investors if they choose projects so as to maximize the expected value of their firm. Consumers continue to be able to adjust consumption along the capital market line until it matches with their time preference. And, if one allows the existence of a risk free asset, consumers can choose a degree of risk consistent with their preferences by the allocation of their portfolio between the risk free asset and the market portfolio.

These results, obtained through state preference theory have little empirical content, although they are valid under very general assumptions. To provide a framework within which risk can be discussed in a quantifiable manner, financial theorists have turned to discussing portfolio decisions in terms of mean-variance equilibria. The models developed provide special insights into how to value risky assets. They also provide guidance about the discount rate which should be used when the net present value from a particular investment is to be calculated.

The capital asset pricing model (CAPM) is the best known of these models.[6] Its basic result is that the required expected return from any asset, $E(R_j)$, depends on the correlation between that asset's return (R_j) and the return on market portfolio. Formally, the CAPM is defined as:

$$E(R_j) = R_f + E(R_m - R_f)\beta;$$

where R_m is the return on the market portfolio; and
   β = covar (j,m)/var (m).
In the *CAPM* β measures systematic or non-diversifiable risk between the particular investment under consideration and the market as a whole.

The CAPM provides several key insights. For investments whose volatity is perfectly correlated with the market portfolio ($\beta = 1$) the return required is that of the market portfolio. Investments more volatile than the market ($\beta > 1$) will require expected returns in excess of that of the market, while those with $\beta < 1$ will require returns less than those on the market portfolio. If $\beta = 0$, the risk free return is all that is required, while if $\beta < 0$ (a negative correlation between market returns and returns to the asset) expected returns less than the risk free rate are called for.

Use of the CAPM modifies the capital budgeting decision of the firm slightly. The appropriate discount rate for use in determining the net present values now becomes the required rate from the CAPM, $E(R_j)$,

---

[6] The CAPM was developed almost simultaneously by Sharpe (1964), Mossin (1966), and Lintner (1965). A good overview is provided in Copeland and Weston (1983).

and not the market rate. Consequently, projects or investments with different βs --different degrees of correlation with the national economy--may have different net present values even though their net cash flow streams were identical.

Introduction of uncertainty will not change life cycle investment behavior unless some systematic relationship between age and relative degree of risk aversion is hypothesized. However, if, as seems reasonable to expect, relative risk aversion is hypothesized to increase with age, one would observe an increase in the proportion of an individual's portfolio holdings of the risk free asset and a decline in the market sensitive holdings with the age of the investor. If one age cohort is sufficiently large to influence the market, as it ages one would expect to observe higher returns on the market portfolio, reflecting the decreased amount of funds available for risky investments.

PUBLIC SECTOR INVESTMENT UNDER UNCERTAINTY

When public sector investments with uncertain outcomes are among the choices available to consumers the portfolio planning problem becomes more complicated. An additional type of risk, local or community based risk, is introduced into the problem.

Returns from public investment--the expected value of a service claim at a known price--still are subject to the nonsystematic risks associated with particular projects. These risks, as with those for private sector investments, can be limited by increasing the number of private and public sector investments in one's portfolio.

Systematic risk associated with the economy's performance also exists. The net benefit (consumer surplus) an individual receives from a fixed amount of any public or private sector good at a fixed price will increase or decline with one's income. Changes in net benefits from public sector goods may be substantially less volatile than income changes, however, resulting in a situation where the β in the CAPM is close to zero. If such results hold, investors would require a lower return from public sector investments than that for the market portfolio, if there were no local risk.

Local or community risk is a systematic risk attached only to the public sector investments in each community caused by unanticipated population changes. Large unexpected population changes will decrease the quantity and/or quality of publicly provided services available to each consumer. Decreases in population may reduce revenues available for services producing in turn either a decrease in local service levels or an increase in per capita costs above those expected. In either instance the claim on services is less valuable than expected.

Because local risk is associated only with public sector investments, it is possible to limit its impact by diversification. However, public sector investments are a large part of the total capital structure of the United States economy. Therefore, for many individuals, particularly those of middle and lower incomes, it may not be possible to diversify sufficiently to eliminate local risk.[7] If local risk is significant it will drive the return required by local investors on public sector investments above what would have been necessary for a private investment with the same systematic risk.

It is important to note though, that local risk will be completely diversified away when the public infrastructure investment decision is viewed from a national perspective. Consequently, local risk creates another reason for a divergence between optimal levels of public sector investment when seen from the local and national levels.

Adding uncertainty to the public sector investment decision does not change the need for decision-makers to rely on the preferences of the median voter or some other small subset of local residents. The separation theorem still does not hold in the absence of a market for public service claims, and the unanimity principle also fails. Indeed, since uncertainty would require decision-makers to have information about individual's risk preferences as well as all other information required in the certainty case, there is an even stronger incentive to focus on the median voter or some subset of residents.

Life cycle behavior will be reinforced or modified depending on whether or not risk aversion varies systematically with age. Just as in the private sector analysis, if one cohort's size is sufficient to dominate the age distribution, there can be a life cycle investment pattern in the public sector. Further, since localities do not have identical age distribution of residents, one would expect to see different levels of public infrastructure demand depending on where in the life cycle a community's median voter was.

Finally, introducing uncertainty into the local public investment decision creates additional problems for the decision-maker when substantial community growth is expected. First, there is the uncertainty associated with the expected growth. An expected source of employment may not start up at the time expected, or it may not require the number of employees expected. Migration and location decisions may not be as expected, and either more or fewer new residents may move to the locality. Commuting from other localities, for example, may supply much of any needed increase in the labor force. All of these project related uncertainties affect decisions on timing of infrastructure investment. And, while they are diversifiable for the nation, localities will be unable to diversify such problems away.

---

[7] Kendrick (1976) estimates that about one-fourth of the nation's capital stock is in the form of government capital. This is about the same as business' holdings of capital and about one-half the amount of tangible and intangible capital including human capital, held by individuals.

The second problem for the decision-maker is uncertainty over the characteristics of the median voter. When major population changes occur the local power structure is unlikely to remain the same. For an official concerned about maximizing chances for re-election, such shifts will produce substantial uncertainty over the proper level of public sector investment.

One way local officials can reduce such uncertainty is to postpone decisions, taking additional time to gather information. In situations where issues are particularly volatile, or where the timing and composition of growth is only generally known, purchasing information in addition to that evolving naturally over time may be rational. In all instances, though, strong incentives exist for officials to minimize uncertainty by delaying decisions to invest in infrastructure.

FEDERAL POLICIES AND THE DEMAND FOR INFRASTRUCTURE

Federal tax and expenditure decisions also play an important role in determining the demand for local infrastructure. Federal programs create a set of incentives which, under ideal circumstances, can be managed to produce more nearly optimal levels of local public sector investment. By adjusting out-of-pocket local costs federal programs can expand or contract the scale of proposed projects to take account of any possible externalities which may accompany the project.

Three policy instruments are available: interest rates, direct subsidies, and tax expenditures. All can affect whether particular projects can meet the criterion of having a positive net present value, by either changing the stream of benefits or the discounting factor, or both.

Current federal budget problems and the administration's tax reform proposal have reduced incentives for local infrastructure investment. The current budget deficit, by keeping interest rates on government bonds high, has increased the risk free rate of return available to investors. The result has been that all consumers' portfolios contain a smaller proportion of risky investments that they would with lower government bond rates. At current high real interest rates fewer public and private projects can show net present values greater than zero. Even using the CAPM model, which allows the required rate of return to depend on the covariance of each investment's returns with those of the market portfolio, an increase in the risk free rate yields an increase in the discount rate applying to all investments. As long as existing federal deficit problems go unsolved and government bond rates remain high, or increase, investment in public infrastructure will tend to be depressed.

The administration's proposals for reducing the deficit are likely to exacerbate the situation, even if they succeed in bringing down interest rates. Cuts in, or elimination of, programs providing federal matching grants for infrastructure development will reduce incentives for local investment in two ways. First, as is well known, such cuts will raise the project's cost to the locality, lowering expected rates of return. Other things equal, investment in public sector facilities which benefitted from matching grants will decline.

Elimination of existing matching grants will also decrease public sector investment, other things equal, by increasing the variance of returns from public sector investments. Both systematic risk and local risk will increase in the absence of federal aid because the maximum potential loss in adverse states of nature will increase. The result, an increase in the covariance between returns on public sector investments and those from the market portfolio. This in turn will lead to a higher discount rate for public investment.

Thus, cuts in some domestic programs are likely to have a double barrelled impact on demand for infrastructure. The resulting lower net returns and higher discount rates will lead to a decreased demand for local infrastructure at the community level, even though social benefits from increased public sector investments remain unchanged. Current federal budget problems are major barrier to any long term increase in public sector investment levels.

Provisions in the administration's current tax reform proposal will, if adopted, have a smaller impact. By eliminating existing deductions for state and local taxes, this reform would increase the amount of consumption foregone by communities financing public infrastructure through the tax system. The increase in the after tax cost of infrastructure will cut the number of projects available with a positive net present value. And, just as with cuts in matching aids, the risk of investment also increases, which in turn requires a higher discount rate, limiting even further the number of feasible projects. Existing budget and tax proposals can only widen the gap between estimates of infrastructure needs such as those mentioned above, and actual investment levels in communities across the country.

IMPLICATIONS FROM THE MODEL FOR THE CURRENT POLICY DEBATE

The heuristic model of demand for public infrastructure outlined above provides several key insights for the current infrastructure policy debate. First, it is vital to think of demand for public facilities as a derived demand, dependent upon the demand for the public services produced by those facilities. Because there is no market for future claims on government services the separation theorem which allows households to treat investment and consumption as two separate decisions does not hold.

Introduction of uncertainty into the analysis yields a reason in addition to the usual externality argument for local perceptions of optimal infrastructure investment levels to be less than those required from a national or social perspective. Local, or community based risk is a key element in each community's decision on the amount to be invested in public sector projects. This risk is particular to each community and it cannot be fully diversified away due to the size of public sector investments. As a result, the appropriate discount rate for determining the net present value of a public sector project from a local resident's point of view will be higher than that for a private sector investment with similar systematic (market related) risk. That discount rate will also be higher than that for the same project if viewed from the nation's perspective since at the national level the risk due to major population change in any particular community is spread over many communities.

Probably the most intriguing insight the model provides--and certainly the one about which the least is known--is that household life cycle behavior can have an impact on the demand for public infrastructure. While the impact would be small if the age distribution were relatively uniform, the post-war baby boom cohort is of sufficient size to affect national investment patterns in both the private and public sectors.

There have not been econometric studies which verify that life cycle behavior has influenced the investment rate, nor are there studies showing systematic changes in risk preference with age. But, both are reasonable hypotheses with important implications for the future. Because baby-boomers are now moving toward the investment stages of the life cycle, increased demand for investments in both the public and private sectors is likely. Further, since public sector investment appears to have lower systematic risk than private sector investment, one would expect to see public sector investment increasing as a percentage of total investment over the next two decades. Life cycle behavior appears to be such that it will stimulate an increase in the demand for public infrastructure, adding to the nation's stock of public capital.

But, because infrastructure demand is a derived demand, investors are likely to be selective. All types of facilities will not benefit equally. Instead, we should expect to observe increased investment in infrastructure for services used most by the dominant age cohort or the age cohort containing the median voter, and only a modest change in facilities primarily benefitting others. Investments will vary, of course, depending on the age structure of the community.

Life cycle investment behavior offers some solace to those who see large existing infrastructure needs and fear that those needs will never be met. Currently perceived shortages may not be due to unknowing neglect during the past decade, nor to the outright rejection of the value of investment in the public sector as some have supposed. Instead, what we observe may be the result of conscious, utility maximizing strategy by a dominant age cohort. Observations of deteriorating infrastructure, or disinvestment in the public sector, are fully consistent with individuals early in the life cycle who are following a utility maximizing strategy which calls for an emphasis on current composition until peak earning years are reached. The real test of whether life cycle behavior has influenced infrastructure investment will come during the next decade, as the baby boom cohorts enters the net investor phase.

5
Factors Influencing the Demand for Rural Infrastructure

Daryl Hobbs

Lacking any solid information base on which to make a judgment, it could be asserted that the demand for infrastructure in rural America is greater than can be met from a combination of local, state and federal investments. The National Rural Community Facilities Assessment reveals an absence of basic public services such as sewer and water for a substantial minority of rural communities and significant problems in maintaining roads, bridges and other services already in place (Reid and Sullivan, 1984). Future demand will likely also include new forms of infrastructure as technologies contribute to new methods of delivering rural services.

The overall demand for rural infrastructure investments will materialize as a "politically effective" demand, which surely is some fraction of total demand. Thus, this chapter addresses "which" rural infrastructural demands are most likely to be met, and "what" new demands are likely to surface to take priority over those traditionally included on rural infrastructure shopping lists.

WHAT IS "RURAL" INFRASTRUCTURE?

Experience of the past 30 years or so leads to the observation that the largest public infrastructure investments in rural areas, and those having the greatest impact on rural America, have been undertaken for reasons other than improving the quality of life of rural residents. Reference is mainly made to the Interstate Highway System and related trunk roads, hydroelectric dams and other power generating facilities, military establishments and related support infrastructure, etc. Rural interests have come down on both sides of these investments; yet they were made and their impact on rural localities has been substantial. Despite their obvious impact on diversifying the rural economy and adding jobs, either directly or through subsequent relocation of industry, the rationale for undertaking these investments was clearly something other than rural development.

Perhaps because of the kind of investments noted above, the distinction between "rural" and "urban" America has become increasingly blurred, even leading some to question whether it is useful to continue to employ the term "rural" to refer to anything other than population density (not an irrelevant consideration when it comes to providing services and rural infrastructure) (Friedland, 1982). As if shared lifestyles, sources of income, and connecting transportation and communication technology were not sufficient to produce a rural-urban blend, the movement of sizable numbers of ex-urbanites to selected rural areas in recent years (a movement greatly facilitated by past public infrastructure investments) has made it even more difficult to separate rural from urban interests.

Some rural areas have even become "metropolitan extensions", serving principally as play grounds for urban visitors as well as attracting urban private capital. These resort-like localities have been the object of substantial infrastructure investment by governments at all levels, but it is clear that such investments have been influenced by both rural development intentions and the enhanced political influence accruing from the combination of rural and urban interests.

In contemplating which rural infrastructure investments are most likely to be made in the future, it seems safe to conclude that those which combine urban with rural interests are most likely to move up the priority list. Below, reference will be made to some specific types of infrastructure for which "effective political demand" is most likely to converge.

THE CURRENT STATUS OF RURAL INFRASTRUCTURE

With completion of the National Rural Community Facilities Assessment Study (NRCFAS) (Reid and Sullivan, 1984), some data are now available on the extent and condition of rural community infrastructure. A principal conclusion from that study is that for many rural communities the problem is to establish some components of infrastructure for the first time rather than repairing deteriorating facilities (Reid and Sullivan, 1984).

In general their survey showed that:

• 2/3 of rural "communities" are unincorporated places including such local units of government as townships, special districts and the like. More than 80 percent of incorporated places have fewer than 2,500 residents: only 5 percent have a population above 10,000. But more than half of non-metro residents live outside incorporated places. The size of rural "communities" influences the demand for, and the capacity to provide and support, many infrastructural features.

- more than half of the rural communities are served by one or more public water systems. Nearly all incorporated places have a public water system; 3/5 of unincorporated do not. In about 1/5 of the communities with a public water system the pipeline was largely deteriorated.

- nearly all towns above 2,500 were served by wastewater treatment plants, about 5/8 of incorporated places under 2,500 had such a service, but only about 1/8 of unincorporated places. In about 1/4 of the communities with waste treatment facilities current flows exceeded designed capacity.

- rural America is generally within 30 miles of one or more hospitals. Only 2 percent of the rural population is outside such a service radius. But as discussed later, having access to a hospital does not necessarily translate into adequate health care.

- 58 percent of rural governments have responsibility for construction and maintenance of roads and bridges. About half of all rural communities having bridges longer than 20 feet had one or more bridges restricted to relatively light loads.

While these data provide some indication of the distribution of rural infrastructure, they do not provide as clear an indication of either need, or demand, or the kinds of infrastructure that may contribute most to improving quality of life in rural areas. Therefore, the remainder of this chapter is directed to the infrastructural implications of changes occurring in rural areas, and new technologies that may supplant some of the infrastructural features incorporated in the NRCFAS.

THE "GREENING, GRAYING, BROWNING, ETC." OF RURAL AMERICA

Important to determining the "which" and "what" of rural infrastructure investment is a brief summation of some of the more notable social and economic changes in rural America in recent years. Since the changes have varied substantially from one part of the country to another, and from one type of community to another, they have contributed to differentials in how much "urbanization" has occurred. Some parts of rural America are still very rural.

Sources of Income

Manufacturing employment, transfer payments, government employment, and property income have left agriculture far behind as sources of rural income. The most recent USDA chart book (1984a) includes a colored map showing the principal source of income for rural counties. It is only in the Plains states and the upper Midwest where there is a significant concentration of counties which count agriculture as the leading source of income. Observation of the map shows counties in the eastern half of the country being about equally divided between those where transfer payments is the leading source and those that depend most on manufacturing income. An additional consideration is the increasingly high proportion of rural residents who commute for employment to other counties. An important implication, especially for local infrastructure investment decisions, is the declining proportion of rural residents who are dependent on the locality they live in for their income.

These changes in income sources interact with infrastructure investment decisions: increased manufacturing in rural areas has often been associated with communities providing infrastructure as an inducement; increased transfer payments translates into a higher proportion of retired persons (an implication discussed below); and increased reliance on property income often contributes to a reluctance to support local financing initiatives.

Changes in Agriculture

Little can be added about the severity and magnitude of the commercial farm crisis in the country. It is important, however, to emphasize that the geographic and farm size distribution of the crisis is limited. The most serious problems (and the greatest regional dependence on agriculture) are in the Corn Belt and Plains States. Farmers most seriously affected are those who are large enough to fall into the "commercial" farming categories. Approximately 75 percent of all the "farms" in the country are not commercial, are not seriously affected by debt service and commodity price problems, and are principally dependent on off-farm sources of income.

However, fewer and larger farms in commercial agriculture areas will continue to contribute to discussion of infrastructure needs in those areas. Some attention has been devoted for example to what roads can justifiably be maintained in areas experiencing further rural depopulation.

Where commercial agriculture is dominant there are also indications of present and future problems in funding of local services. Harl (1985) reports survey results indicating that the rate of property tax delinquency in rural Iowa counties averaged 10 percent this spring, and ran as high as 25 percent in some principally agricultural counties. He adds that the dramatic decline in land values, and value of machinery and equipment, will further erode the fiscal capacity of local governments to provide services and make infrastructure investments.

Rural Population Turnaround

As in the case of agriculture little can be added to the volume of attention to the "rural population turnaround" of the past 2 decades except to review its selective nature and to speculate on where, and to what extent, it is likely to continue. In general the shift of net-migration flow from urban to rural is best understood as part of the general process of urbanization; past rural infrastructure enhancements have contributed to it, and its existence adds to a growing demand for further investments.

Like everything else not all parts of rural America have shared in the rural re-population. Regionally, the South and West have gained the most. The urban dependency of much of the migration is reflected in the disproportionately large share occuring in belts around major metropolitan areas. Important also have been various recreation and resort areas. While all ages of people have been included, most notable have been a sizable population of what might be referred to as "early retirees";--people who have gained retirement benefits after 30 or so years of work and have exchanged their urban equity for a place in the country. These contribute importantly to the large number of rural counties counting transfer payments as the leading source of income (Beale, 1982).

This graying of significant parts of rural America is productive of questions pertaining to future infrastructure investments. First is the question of investments and services to meet the needs of an older population. Meeting these needs would seem to be a contributing factor to the substantial increase in non-metro government borrowing for health, housing and transportation from 1977-1982 while borrowing for other purposes remained at about the same level (USDA Chartbook, 1984a). The second question for rural communities which have experienced an in-migration of people who have "brought their income with them" is the extent to which they will remain as they become older, less active and in greater need of specialized health care. Analysis of census data for rural Missouri shows that many counties that have recently had a net in-migration of 55-65 year olds, have at the same time experienced an out-migration of those over 65. Receiving counties appear to be those having a larger regional service center (10,000 or more). One piece of conventional wisdom about the implications of the population turn-around for receiving communities appears to be dispelled by several recent rural sociological studies which have found that recent migrants tend not to differ much from long-term residents in their expectations for local services.

Decline in Community Autonomy

Numerous authors have described the decline in community autonomy associated with the economic diversification of rural America. For example, Gartrell (1983: 151-155) notes that "...industrial technology originates outside the rural community and its diffusion is part of an asymmetric rural-urban relationship that creates uneven development and lowers community autonomy...insofar as market dependency reduces community self-sufficieny and community autonomy, the traditional basis for integration is undermined". An implication for infrastructure investments is the nature of linkages between community and regional, state and national levels of government and the extent to which these linkages contribute to infrastructure decisions and acquisitions. The work of several researchers who found differences between communities in the acquisition of external investments based on the external connections of their leaders is noted below.

A feature of these local external linkages however is that they also lead to increased differentiation within the community. For example, school boards tend to relate to state departments of education, County Commissioners to various regional and state funding agencies and service providers, etc., which has resulted in a reduced degree of coordination at the community level among public decision-making bodies.

As an associated feature of declining rural community autonomy, it can be noted also the extent to which various centrifugal forces (e.g. commuting, regionalization, dependency on outside sources for income) combine to adversely affect community participation. Insofar as infrastructure planning and funding depend on local mobilization of residents and resources, the decline in community participation and affiliation influence the community's ability to act to meet its needs.

THE COMMUNITY AS THE LOCUS FOR INFRASTRUCTURE DECISIONS

While local governments are clearly not responsible for most of the infrastructure rural people depend on, it is at the level of community that concerns are often expressed. There have been numerous studies in recent years of community satisfaction and community initiatives pertaining to provision of services. Below is a brief review of some salient findings.

Community Satisfaction and Availability of Services

Recent studies by Molnar and Smith (1982) and by Sofranko and Fliegel (1984) indicate that residents' overall satisfaction with their community tends to be importantly independent of their satisfaction with the quality and availability of services. The researchers report that quality of social relationships is as, or more, important to overall community satisfaction as the objective availability of services.

Effect of Local Initiative

Studies by Lloyd and Wilkinson (1985), Martin and Wilkinson (1984) and McGranahan (1984) indicate that communities whose leaders are more externally involved and who take development initiatives are more likely to be successful in adding to their economic base and local services. It appears from these studies that differences in initiative between communities is a factor in translating infrastructure needs into a "politically effective demand".

Regionalization

Whether accompanied by regional forms of government or not, there has been extensive regionalization of rural people's use of services. Some of the regionalization (such as school consolidation) occurred as a matter of public policy; much of it occurred in response to a combination of improved roads, declining population in small towns and the subsequent centralization of services in larger rural service centers. This trend has included among its effects a redefinition of the community. If where people go for services is used as the criterion for the community, then the "service" community for most rural residents includes several towns they depend on regularly.

Some forms of rural infrastructure and services have been explicitly designed to serve a region such as area vocational schools, regional libraries, etc. A special case of regionalization is the pattern of utilization of hospitals. It was reported above that nearly all of rural America is within 30 miles of one or more hospitals. It is questionable however what this translates into from the standpoint of meeting rural needs for health care. A hospital may be of little value if there are no specialized physicians to staff it. Missouri data indicate that many rural hospitals are underutilized primarily because there are no local medical specialists. Medical specialists have tended to locate in larger towns and cities. Therefore, rural people requiring hospitalization may more often be hospitalized in larger regional towns than in their local hospital if they require specialized medical attention.

Rural production in the past has leaned heavily toward bulky commodities requiring highways and rail services for transport. When natural resource exploitation and agriculture are considered, there will continue to be a requirement for heavy transportation. It appears, however, that the production of such commodities is well established in certain locations and much of the transportation infrastructure is already in place, although there is major concern for the bridge capacity and repair in many commercial agriculture areas as a result of increasing scale of farm production and corresponding use of larger load equipment. Recall, however, the earlier observation that large scale agricultural production is becoming more geographically constricted and therefore the bridge issue is of greater importance in some parts of the country than others.

But there are moves toward non-bulky production in rural areas at the same time that there is a decline in some rural durable and non-durable goods production. There are many reports for example of the closing of mature product cycle industries, especially in the South, and their subsequent relocation outside the U.S. (Bluestone and Harrison, 1982). But at the same time there are indications of the growth of production (Tweeten, 1984), and research and development facilities (Buck, Hobbs, and Meyer, 1984) of technology based industries in non-metropolitan areas. A characteristic of such industries is that the products are typically of high value, but not bulky, including production of "information".

In 1984, a survey of "high-tech" firms located in 57 non-metroplitan, research-oriented, college and university towns was conducted in Missouri. Included were places such as State College, Pennsylvania; Blacksburg, Virginia; Stillwater, Oklahoma; etc. The primary purpose was to determine the extent to which the research base of the university was a factor in the location decision of the firms. We were able to identify about 1500 firms in the 57 communities that met our criteria of being science and technology based. We found that a majority of the entrepreneurs of these firms were alumni or former faculty members of the university. Yet we found that they placed a much higher value on community quality of life factors and availability of technical personnel than on factors traditionally associated with industrial and firm location. We also found that they placed great value on local availability of a "technology support structure". For example, they ranked such factors as "availability of overnight package service", "sophistication of the telephone system", "air service", and "dependable electrical supply", higher in terms of location considerations than such factors as "industrial parks", "capacity of sewer and water system", "average wage rates", "interstate highway", "rail service". While admittedly research oriented college and university towns are atypical of non-metropolitan America, these findings do suggest that future infrastructure investments, made with an eye toward enhancing a local economic base, will need to pay attention to some kinds of investments that traditionally have not been included among economic development strategies.

It is not, however, for economic development alone that a new form of infrastructure investment may be indicated for rural America. There are those who have been saying for some time that technology has made it cheaper to transport information than to transport people in providing rural services (Kaye, 1982). The traditional problem for rural schools, for example, has been to overcome the friction of space in cost-effective ways. For the past several years, one cluster of schools in Wisconsin and another in Minnesota have been offering courses to students in various locations by use of an interactive Low Power Television network (Hobbs, 1985). Similarly, Oklahoma State University is offering German and Physics to students in more than 150 rural high schools across several states. Several other similar programs (Utah, Texas, and Washington) are in operation. The infrastructure needs of the participating public schools is shifting from buses to dishes and from roads to telephones and microwave relay towers.

NEW AND EXPANDING NEEDS FOR SERVICES

The social, demographic and economic changes that have occurred in rural areas have contributed to the emergence of a demand for new and different kinds of services as well. For example:

Women in the labor force

There has, along with metropolitan areas, been a dramatic increase in the proportion of women entering the labor force over the past two decades. A consequence is that a corresponding demand is generated for services formerly provided in the home. Important among these is the increasing demand for child care. While child care is most often provided by individuals and the private sector, it is not uncommon for there to be a public involvement in providing this increasingly demanded service.

Education

Throughout much of the nation there is a declining enrollment in elementary and secondary schools largely because of the declining birth rate in recent years. Many rural localities experience the added effect of a general population decline. At the same time there is a growing demand for adult and vocational education. Some rural localities may become involved in re-directing use of their educational facilities to include greater attention to adult education.

This is but one potential for changing and expanding the role of a traditional component of the rural infrastructure. There are others pertaining specifically to schools, such as Jonathan Sher's (1976) call for rural schools to become more directly involved in community economic development through the formation of School Based Development Enterprises.

Social Services

As rural communities have become more like metropolitan communities in life style it is also becoming apparent that some forms of social disruption, most often identified with urban areas, are increasing as well. It is well documented that there has been a general increase in rural crime rates and it has recently been demonstrated that farming is, or has become, one of the most stressful occupations. While a strength of rural communities has always been thought to be their ability to cope with both public and private problems it is less clear that that capacity has been fully retained in the face of significant economic changes.

There is a growing trend toward shifting more responsibility to communities and localities for the provision of services, a situation which, for both economic and political reasons, can be expected to increase infrastructural differences between rural communities in the future. It was suggested that the demand for rural infrastructure will likely be expressed as a "politically effective" demand, with the expectation that some kinds of communities will be more successful in representing and meeting their needs than others. As pointed out, research shows that initiative of community leaders contributes to community's ability to attract resources and investments.

Although rural America is generally becoming more urbanized the effects are uneven across different communities. Some rural communities have been substantially converted to metropolitan extensions, with corresponding increases in income, population, and economic and lifestyle diversification. Most other communities remain relatively isolated and largely dependent on agriculture, transfer payments or labor intensive manufacturing for an economic base. Agriculture is under economic stress and some rural manufacturing plants are closing. Such communities are also often the location of persistent pockets of poverty. It is unlikely that these communities will fare as well in adding to their infrastructure stock.

It was also suggested that some of the components of rural community infrastructure are likely to change as new technologies modify the methods of providing services. Because new telecommunications technologies give promise of overcoming some of the traditional costs of space, there is reason to believe that rural communities may lead the way in application of these technologies. The possible applications for education and health care are particularly promising. However, their effective use depends on coordination and/or collaboration with other communities or with organizations who supply the service. Therefore, expectations of meeting future infrastructural needs will depend at least, in part, on effective cooperation among rural communities and support agencies.

6
Limitations of Theoretical Foundations of Infrastructure Investment Decision-Making

George R. McDowell

The previous chapters review an array of theoretical foundations of government decision-making as it relates to infrastructure and publicly provided services. The reviews are helpful because there is a need to know those routes well. However, there are some limitations which must be addressed with respect to the normative theories and benefit/cost analysis in particular. The problem here is, of course, with the ceteris paribus conditions that includes the initial resource endowment - implicitly an acceptance of that endowment or income distribution. That is an analytical problem when much of our public decision-making, including infrastructure investments and public service provision, is directed at redressing income distribution issues. It is analytically inconsistent to use the outcome of a theoretical construct that starts by accepting the distribution we are trying to change as a guide in evaluating the policy being assessed.

If these limits are acknowledged, in terms of the theoretical underpinnings of the benefit/cost analysis and the implicit value judgment that protects the status quo, then it can be used to display as much information about the consequences of a public decision as is possible. We are then, as honest analysts and as more humble economists, rather like the street corner flasher in his rain coat - we show all that we have, even if it is not very much.

In order to make this point more concrete, consider the frequently identified problem of a divergence between market values and social values in the context of benefit/cost analysis. It is frequently presented as though market values do not reflect values of the society. While the market may not perfectly reflect the ethical values of the society, it is certainly true that it reflects a great many of those values and therefore affects the benefit/cost calculus. That is certainly true of the American economy under the Reagan administration, which was also true under previous administrations and will be true under future administrations.

This brings up a bit of a side issue which may be of limited practical value and only useful to improving our intellectual honesty. Implied in discussions with respect to infrastructure investment decisions are questions about the appropriate role for government to play - "more" government or "less" government. While there may be some differences in the management and treatment of garbage collectors if they are employees of government or of private firms, it is difficult to argue that government has no role when it decides to leave garbage collection to private firms. It is even less defensible to argue that government provision of garbage collection by either franchising a single firm or by use of a contract is "less" government or "privatization" as compared to direct provision of the service by government.

Government is always present! It anoints one set of rules or another. It is clever to be able to call your use of government, "less government", and my use of government, "more government", but they are both the use and presence of government. When we say "Government of, by and for the people", we mean government of, by and for the people who can use it.

In Chapter 2, we got some insight out of the various economic theories - the public good theory, the Tiebout voting with the feet, the median voter, the Buchanan and Tullock constitutional calculus, and the Downs notions - when looking at infrastructural investment decisions. For example, in the rush to "capacity build" in local government, I have wondered, as a result of Downs insights, if the employment of professionals where there were none before was not itself an upward influence on local budgets. If each of the theories identified in Chapter 2 gives insight, then each is partly right, but only partly because of the insight we get from each of the other constructs. Therefore, I feel that we have a long way to go in getting our theories straight.

The Lindbloom "still muddling" thoughts from Chapter 2 strike a particularly sympathetic note. The specific reference is to the role of "individual" and "collective ideology" in local decision-making. In a new book in progress by Samuel Bowles and Hebert Gintis (1984), they suggest that one of the major errors of neoclassical economics is that it limits its perceptions of individual behavior to a self interested calculus - "maximizing utility" or acting to "reveal" already held preferences. They argue that much of voting and other political behavior is not explainable by this logic. In its stead they suggest the "principle of constitution through practices" - the notion that people act, not merely to fulfill predetermined ends, but to "constitute themselves". They vote, picket, sign petitions, or hold office because it asserts who they are. They are for a world without nuclear arms, or they are for a town that provides redress for victims of dogs that are not on a leash. They vote because it is right, regardless of the calculus of its significance to the electoral outcome, much less to their personal advantage. Perhaps that is what explains the ability to overcome petroleum and cement lobbies and to decide to build the Washington, D.C. METRO. Bowles and Gintis suggest that this implies that preferences are as much formed by the act of choosing as they are revealed by choice. Thus, we have yet another insight that strikes a responsive chord; but that is, implicitly and explicitly, a critique of the other theories or constructs.

Some of the actions being taken by the local governments with respect to local services and infrastructure were discussed and described in the preceeding chapters as a kind of phenomenology without developing particular explanatory threads. Those efforts are very helpful in reminding us that real decisions are made with or without information to guide them and with or without theories of how they are made. There are imperatives to action that will not wait for scholarly deliberations. However, the complexity of the problems and the urgency for action make clear that there is much for scholars to contribute if we can get on with it. The four preceeding chapters are useful in appraising us of where we are on the question of theories of local government decision-making and that there are miles to go.

PART II: Models and Approaches for Community Infrastructure Analysis

7
Budgeting: The Foundation of Community Service Research and Extension Programs

Gerald A. Doeksen

Leaders in many local government units are under pressure to provide more and better community services with stable or even reduced budgets. Reduced local revenues in recent years have resulted from a slowdown in the economy and a reduction in federal and state funds. The economic picture is improving in many areas of the country, but federal and state sources of revenue are often remaining constant or decreasing. Along with the revenue problems, constituents are demanding more and improved services. These quality increases cost money. For example, in the 1970s, many rural residents were satisfied with basic ambulance service; now residents are asking for paramedic type services.

The local leaders must seek ways to provide the maximum quality of service within their limited budget. In Oklahoma for example, the Cooperative Extension Service has a program which provides information of alternative community service delivery systems. The overall purpose of the program is to provide information which will assist local government leaders as they make decisions. By providing them with information as to all alternatives, they can use their limited funds to their maximum efficiency.

The purpose of this chapter is to illustrate how budgeting is the base of a community service program and how it leads to other problems. More specifically, the chapter will:

1. Demonstrate the research behind the community service budgeting process;

2. Illustrate how research is used in Oklahoma's extension program; and

3. Discuss budgeting strengths and weaknesses.

COMMUNITY SERVICE BUDGET RESEARCH

Local government leaders have requested budgets for most community services. A budget is defined as a plan for the future in which all items of costs and returns are estimated. A complete budget makes it possible to estimate net income or loss expected for alternative plans. The main purpose of budgeting is to compare profitability of different kinds of organizations (Castle, et al. 1972, p. 93). In discussing the budget in regards to decision-making, Hirsch states:

> Consistent with the economic approach to public decision-making is program budgeting, a planning and management process which applies notions of economic efficiency to public decision-making. It involves choice among alternatives in order to achieve the most cost-effective use resources; involving achievement of the greatest effectiveness for given costs and given effectiveness at minimum costs. (Hirsch, 1973, p. 310)

Budgets can be prepared by survey methods or engineering methods. The method chosen to develop the budget is not important. What is important is that budget information is developed from the latest data, reflecting current prices and technology.

The various budget studies resulting from the projects take on essentially similar forms. Each budget study is completed such that costs and revenues can be estimated for alternative delivery systems. For example, if community leaders are evaluating how to provide emergency medical services, the budget will summarize: (1) alternative revenue sources and amounts (e.g., charge per call, ad valorem tax, sales tax, utility charge per household); and (2) costs of alternative emergency medical service delivery systems (e.g., fire station based, hospital based, private subsidized, volunteer). The local leaders will then be able to compare costs and receipts and make a decision as to which type of systems they desire and can afford.

Budget studies have been completed for emergency medical service (Doeksen, et al. 1981c), fire services (Nelson and Doeksen, 1982), clinics (Gebre-Selassie, 1983), water delivery systems (Goodwin, et al. 1979), solid waste disposal (Goodwin and Nelson, 1981), transportation systems for the elderly (Webb, et al. 1980), wastewater collection and treatment (Nelson and Fessehaye, 1981) and mobile home park developments (Nelson and Johnson, 1982). The most recent emergency medical service study (Doeksen, et al. 1981c) is used to illustrate the research involved in a budget study.

BUDGET ANALYSIS

Detailed data were collected from about one-third of the ambulance operators in Oklahoma. This included information on ambulance runs, so that the number of calls could be predicted. Also, information was obtained as to operating expenses of the system. Dealers of capital equipment provided data on cost of capital items such as buildings, vehicles and communications equipment.

Estimating the Annual Number of Calls

Two methods are suggested to estimate the number of ambulance calls per year. One method is to collect information on the previous year's operations concerning the ambulance calls made. Useful data include time, date, location of patient, charges and collections. The data can be sorted to provide a clear picture of the need for the service.[8] If the population of the area is stable, the number of calls made during the past year provides a good approximation of the number of calls to expect during the coming year. If the population is growing, the number of calls made during the past year should be adjusted upward by local use coefficients as discussed below and presented in Table 7.1.

Table 7.1. Ambulance Medical Calls by Age and Population in the Study Area for Counties, 1980

AGE	UTILIZATION RATE/1000 IN AGE GROUP
< 19	8.57
20 - 29	17.07
30 - 39	13.66
40 - 49	16.82
50 - 59	28.04
60 - 64	46.42
65 - 69	59.91
70 - 79	137.32
> 80	255.10
TOTAL	36.45

Source: Doeksen, Gerald A., Leonard G. Anderson, Jr. and Vanessa Lenard. "A Community Development Guide to Emergency Medical Services: A System Approach to Planning, Funding and Administration." Ag. Exp. Stat. Bull., Stillwater, Oklahoma, 1981.

---

[8] Some state offices have computer sorting programs, which can sort data quickly and efficiently. For example, in Oklahoma, the Agricultural Cooperative Extension Service has an ambulance call sorting program.

If records from the previous year are not available, a model has been developed that can be used as an alternative method for predicting annual calls. This model divides calls into three categories which include:

1. Highway accident calls (all calls in response to accidents occurring on the highways involving automobiles or other vehicles);

2. Transfer calls (the movement of patients between hospitals); and

3. Other medical calls (those not otherwise listed, including heart attacks, strokes and home or industrial accidents).

The number of highway accidents requiring ambulance service depends on such variables as population, highway miles and highway conditions. For this study, highway injury statistics were provided by the Oklahoma Department of Highways and ambulance operator records. The average number of highway injuries over the past several years provides the means for predicting the number of such calls in subsequent years.

Hospital-to-hospital transfer calls depend on the size and services provided by the local hospitals, the local medical staff, and other personal and medical factors. For the study area, data were collected from ambulance operators to estimate the number of patient transfers. It is impossible to use a rule of thumb to predict transfer calls in a given area, but an estimate can be based on records supplied by ambulance operators and local hospitals.

Other medical calls can be projected on the basis of age distribution of the population.[9] Ambulance utilization rates (the number of ambulance calls per 1,000 population per year) for other medical calls were derived from the ambulance call data and data on population by age groups (Table 7.1). For example, there were 8.57 calls per 1,000 population among those 19 years old or younger and 255.10 calls per year per 1,000 population among those 80 years old and older. These utilization rates can be used with area population data to predict the number of ambulance calls, or they can be applied to other areas by following a similar procedure.

The research developed a procedure for estimating the number of miles the vehicle(s) will travel annually from the estimate of call volume. In addition, a procedure was derived to estimate yearly revenue. The typical rate charged in the Emergency Medical Services (EMS) System in the survey was a base rate per call of $65, plus one dollar per mile one way.

---

[9] Population projections were made from a demographic model which utilized birth rates, death rates and migration data. Most state governments have a department responsible for population projections between census years.

The percentage of patients who paid their bills ranged from very low to very high, the typical collection rate being 60 to 70 percent. The operators who made special efforts to collect their fees by sending out monthly statements reported the higher payment percentages.

Capital Expenditures

Depreciable items typically in an EMS system are vehicles, communication equipment and buildings. Three specific types of vehicles are recommended for ambulance service by the U.S. Department of Transportation. These include a Type 1 ambulance (conventional cab-chassis with modular ambulance body), Type 2 ambulance (standard hightop van, forward control, integral cab-body), and Type 3 ambulance (specialty van, forward control, integral cab-body). In 1983, the approximate costs were Type 1 - $37,753; Type 2 - $26,040; and Type 3 - $37,648.

The life of the vehicle or chassis depends primarily on how much it is used and the quality of maintenance it receives. In general, dealers and operators preferred to use the unit as a backup vehicle or trade it in after it had been driven 75,000 miles or used seven years.

Communication costs were obtained by interviewing dealers of communication equipment. Two options are available to local decision-makers in installing a communication system. These include using an existing communication system or constructing a new one. If the community has a fire or police department with an existing system, it is possible to use it at a cost much lower than establishing a new one. If the system is very high frequency (VHF), a two-way radio for the vehicle would cost approximately $2,771, including installation.

If the community does not have an appropriate communication system, costs of constructing a new one can be estimated. A choice must be made between a very high frequency (VHF) and an ultra high frequency (UHF) system. Both VHF and UHF systems are specified in Table 7.2. In both systems, one frequency would be available for paging personnel within a 10 mile radius. An advantage of the UHF system is that it can accomodate up to 4 frequencies. The base station, remote console, and mobile radio have an average life of ten years, while the life expectancy of the tower is 20 years.

An existing facility or a new one may be used to house the ambulance(s). In 1983 for example, a 2,250 sq. ft. building containing two bays, a meeting room, a bathroom, a kitchen, etc., had a cost of $94,118 and an expected life of 30 years.

Operating Costs

These costs include vehicle, medical and building costs. Vehicle costs include such things as gasoline, tires, oil, oil filters, lubrication, tune-ups and miscellaneous repairs. The 1980 costs of these items are based on records of ambulance operators in Oklahoma, and have been increased to reflect 1983 costs.[10] These costs are presented in Table 7.3. The cost of vehicle insurance was also based on operators' records and has been increased to reflect 1983 costs. The cost of vehicle insurance is $1,221 per ambulance per year.

Table 7.2. Estimated Communications Equipment Costs (1983)

EQUIPMENT	VHF SYSTEM	UHF SYSTEM
Base Station & Remote Console	$5,893	$7,320
Mobile Radio & Installation	2,771	3,305
100 ft. Tower	1,490	1,490
Antenna	356	460
Tower Installation	915	915
Pagers	416	416
First Responder Kits	934	934
First Responder Radio (20 watt)	2,745	2,745
First Responder Radio (5 watt)	1,569	1,569

Plus Transmission lines $3.67/ft.

Source: Doeksen, Gerald A., Leonard G. Anderson, Jr. and Vanessa' Lenard. "A Community Development Guide to Emergency Medical Services: A System Approach to Planning, Funding and Administration." Ag. Exp. Stat. Bull., Stillwater, Oklahoma, 1981.

Table 7.3. Estimated Vehicle Operating Expenses, 1983

ITEM	COSTS & USAGE
Gasoline	Type 2 (Hightop Van) 8 miles/gal $1.25/gal
	Type 1 or 3 (Modular) 6 miles/gal $1.25/gal
	Transfer Vehicle (Van or Suburban) 11 miles/gal $1.25/gal
Tires	Replaced every 20,000 miles $89/tire
Oil, Oil Filter & Lubrication	Changed every 3,000 miles $17.00
License	$5.00/year/vehicle
Tune-ups	Every 10,000 miles $111
Miscellaneous Repairs	$355 every 10,000 miles
Insurance	$1,221/year
Communication System	$133/year for service contract

Source: Doeksen, Gerald A., Leonård G. Anderson, Jr. and Vanessa Lenard. "A Community Development Guide to Emergency Medical Services: A System Approach to Planning, Funding and Administration." Ag. Exp. Stat. Bull., Stillwater, Oklahoma, 1981.

Operating expenses for communications equipment can be assumed to equal the costs of service contracts for the separate components. A service contract for an ambulance mobile unit costs about $133 per year

---

[10] Inflated from 1980 prices to 1983 prices by the Consumer Price Index.

(UHF or VHF equipment). The base station and remote console service contract will cost approximately $500 per year. Expenses for medical supplies were estimated from 1980 records of ambulance providers and have been increased to reflect 1983 costs (Table 7.4). The cost of medical equipment maintenance is the largest item, increasing with other medical supply costs and the frequency of ambulance calls. Some operators used disposable paper "linens", while others contracted with a linen supply company.

Table 7.4. Estimated Medical Supply Expenses, 1983

ITEM	COST
Linens	$2.93/call
Medical Equipment Maintenance*	$3.87/call
Sterile Bandages, & Related Items	$3.46/call

*Include splinting kits, dead-on-arrival (DOA) kits, oxygen, etc.

Source: Doeksen, Gerald A., Leonard G. Anderson, Jr. and Vanessa Lenard. "A Community Development Guide to Emergency Medical Services: A System Approach to Planning, Funding and Administration." Ag. Exp. Stat. Bull., Stillwater, Oklahoma, 1981.

Decision-makers in rural areas planning within a limited budget need to understand their options in staffing the emergency medical service in order to choose the most economical solution. Since payroll is a major budget item, labor requirements under several alternative arrangements must be considered. These alternatives include a fully staffed service, a hospital-based service, and several types of volunteer services. Annual building operating costs were also estimated, varying by locality, type of building, and tied to the general price level changes. Estimated costs for insurance, utilities, etc., are presented in Table 7.5. Miscellaneous costs such as office supplies and Emergency Medical Team (EMT) training expenses occur in the operation of an ambulance service and should be included in the budget.

Table 7.5. Estimated Building Operating Expenses, 1983*

ITEM	COST
Insurance	$2.66/$1000/year
Water, Sewer & Trash	$168/year
Electricity* $1.42/sq. ft./year for office & living area	
Maintenance	$222/year

*If local cost data are available, they should be used in estimating operating costs, replacing data in this table

*Electricity is used for heating and air conditioning in this study. The local utility company can provide the most accurate estimate of yearly electrical costs.

ILLUSTRATION OF RESEARCH USE

For illustrative purposes, reference will be made to a recently completed EMS study for Noble County (Lenard, et al. 1983). Noble County has a population of around 11,600 residents and is in north central Oklahoma. Perry is the county seat and is located 60 miles north of Oklahoma City. The city decision-makers called the Cooperative Extension Service for information as to alternative EMS systems available, because they were losing money on the present system and could not continue under the current situation. The previously mentioned research tools were applied to determine alternative systems. The tools were applied in reverse order because information on location of vehicles and the number of crews is needed prior to preparation of the budgets for alternative systems. Call estimation and budgeting will be discussed in this section while ambulance locations will be discussed in the next section.

Analysis of Runs

In order to estimate the number of runs occurring annually in Noble County, the population by age group had to be obtained. This was done by consulting the 1980 census data for Noble County. Very little population change has occurred since 1980. If a population shift had occurred, the numbers would need to be updated to 1984. The research coefficients were applied to the census data. Given this, an estimate of annual other medical call numbers was developed (Table 7.6). It was estimated that 428 other medical calls occur annually in Noble County. From hospital records, it was determined that 93 hospital transfers could be expected. From other records, it was found that an average of 45 injury highway accidents occurred annually in the county. This information provided an estimate of 566 annual ambulance calls in Noble County.

Budgets of Alternative Systems

From the location analysis, the local decision-makers inferred an interest in a vehicle located at Perry and possibly at Red Rock. The first two budgets presented examined one location at Perry. The third looked at two locations. The three alternative systems were prepared based on the budget research. It was expected that the local decision-makers would modify the budget which came closest to their desires. A discussion of each alternative follows.

Alternative 1 (Fire Department Based System). The capital items needed for this system included two standard hightop vans, three vehicle radios, 4 pagers, three first responder kits, and three 5-watt first responder radios. Hightop vans were $26,040 each; so, the total cost of the vans was $52,080. This alternative assumed that 2 VHF vehicle radios which cost $2,771 each, and 4 pagers which cost $416 each were included. The price

Table 7.6. Estimated Annual Calls Occurring in Noble County, Oklahoma

AGE GROUP	POPULATION	AGE COEFFICIENTS	ANNUAL CALLS
< 20	3580	8.57	31
20 - 29	1739	17.07	30
30 - 39	1389	13.66	19
40 - 49	1267	16.82	21
50 - 59	1139	28.04	32
60 - 64	517	46.42	24
65 - 69	575	59.91	34
70 - 79	904	137.32	124
80+	443	255.10	113
Total Other Medical Calls			428
Hospital Transfers			93
Highway Accidents			45
TOTAL ANNUAL CALLS			566

of a VHF base communication system was $5,893. The EMS service will be housed in existing parts of the fire station at no additional cost.

First responder teams often have provided life saving emergency aid to persons in remote rural areas until a vehicle arrived from a nearby service to transport the patient. These persons are trained to a minimum of an approved first responder capability, but may be trained to a higher level. The minimum training period is about 41 hours and provided at no costs by instructors certified by the State Health Department. These persons were provided with first responder kits. This alternative assumed that three kits at a cost of $934 each, and three 5 watt radios which cost $1,569 each were needed. These kits were placed with key people in the Noble County area (possible locations included Billings, Red Rock and Morrison). The teams were dispatched by EMTs when on duty or by the hospital or police when the EMS crew was out on emergency calls. The radios were used to communicate with law enforcement personnel, fire personnel, the ambulance enroute to the emergency, and other medical personnel. Thus, the total capital needed to initiate this alternative was $66,795 (Table 7.7).

Once the system was operational, a yearly budget to cover on-going expenses was needed. Annual budgets are presented in Table 7.8. From an earlier survey of EMS operators (Doeksen, et al. 1981a), the EMS operators indicated they depreciated their vehicles at 75,000 miles or seven years. It was estimated that the EMS system would travel 20,000 miles or 10,000 miles per vehicle. The vehicles were replaced every 75,000 miles. Yearly vehicle depreciation was $7,440 (Table 7.8). VHF radios for the vehicles had a cost of $5,542 and had a 10 year life. Thus, yearly

Table 7.7. Total Capital Costs of Proposed Alternatives for Noble County Emergency Medical Service[a]

CAPITAL ITEMS	ALTERNATIVE 1	ALTERNATIVE 2	ALTERNATIVE 3
Vehicles	$52,080	$52,080	$78,120
Vehicle Communication	5,542	5,542	8,313
Base Communication	5,893	5,893	5,893
Pagers	1,664	1,664	2,496
First Responder Radio (5 watt)	4,707	4,707	3,138
First Responder Kits	2,802	2,802	1,868
TOTAL	$66,795	$72,688	$99,828

[a]Building costs are not included as this cost is included in building loan costs.

Table 7.8. Alternative Costs for Noble County Emergency Medical Services, January-December, 1984

COSTS	ALTERNATIVE 1	ALTERNATIVE 2	ALTERNATIVE 3
Capital Costs:			
Vehicles	$7,440	$7,440	$11,160
Vehicle Communication	554	554	831
Base Communication	---	589	589
Pagers	555	555	832
Building	---	11,684	11,684
First Responder Kit	560	560	374
First Responder Radio	471	471	314
TOTAL CAPITAL COSTS	$9,580	$21,853	$25,784
Operating Costs:			
Vehicle			
Gasoline	$3,125	$3,125	$3,125
Maintenance	1,411	1,411	1,411
Insurance	2,442	2,422	3,663
Communications	266	266	399
Base Communication	---	500	500
Building	---	2,410	2,410
Medical Expenses	5,807	5,807	5,807
Labor			
EMT Supervisor	2,760	15,180	15,180
EMTs	76,176	101,568	114,264
Volunteers	---	---	750
Training & Misc.	1,000	1,000	1,000
TOTAL OPERATING COSTS	$92,987	$133,709	$148,509
TOTAL COSTS	$102,567	$155,562	$174,293
Cost Per Run	$181	$275	$308

depreciation was $554. A VHF base communication was currently in place at the fire department. It was available for EMS use. The 4 pagers had a cost of $1,664 and had a three year life; so, annual depreciation was $555.

The 3 first responder kits were priced at $2,802 and had a five year life. The annual depreciation charge was $560. The three 5 watt radios had a total cost of $4,707 and a 10 year life. Annual depreciation was $471. Total annual yearly capital costs were $9,580.

Operating costs for 1983 were estimated based on the number of runs and the miles traveled. A hightop van gets 8 miles per gallon, and if gasoline costs $1.25 per gallon in 1984, then yearly gasoline costs were estimated at $3,125. Vehicle maintenance was a function of mileage and was estimated at $1,411. Insurance was calculated based on the number of vehicles. Insuring the vehicle at relacement value, the yearly insurance premium was $1,221 per vehicle. This does not include malpractice insurance. If decision-makers desired malpractice insurance, it would have to be added to the budget. Vehicle radio repair was estimated on the basis of a service contract and was $133 per radio. Medical supply costs were a function of the number of calls and were estimated at $5,807.

Labor was the largest iem in the budget. This alternative assumed that a captain-supervisor and 6 EMTs were paid through EMS. The captain-supervisor was paid $200 per month bonus pay. The EMTs were paid $920 per month and worked as firemen when a fire alarm rang. A fifteen percent overhead charge was added to cover employee costs, such as vacations, social security, and workmens' compensation for all salaried employees. Training and miscellaneous expenses of $1,000 were included in the budget. Thus, the total operating cost was $92,987. Total yearly costs for this alternative were $102,567 or $181 per run.

Alternative 2 (Independent System). Under this alternative, EMS would need to assume the base communication system charge. The capital cost of the base communication system was $5,893. This alternative used two hightop vans. Two hightop vans were $52,080. A building would be included at a cost of $41.83 a square foot for a 2250 square foot building. The building would be purchased on a 30 year, 12 percent FmHA loan. Loan payments will influence annual capital costs but not the capital needed to begin the system. The total capital needed to initiate this alternative was $72,688 (Table 7.7).

Yearly vehicle depreciation was $7,440 (Table 7.8). A VHF base communication system has a cost of $5,893 and a ten year life; so, the yearly depreciation charge was $589. Building annual capital costs were $11,684 on a 12 percent, 30 year loan. Total annual capital costs were $21,853.

Gasoline costs were reduced to $3,125. The base communication operating cost was estimated on the basis of a service contract and is $500. Labor costs were also changed. This alternative uses one EMT supervisor and eight EMTs. EMTs will dispatch themselves, except when on call.

The sheriff's office will then pick up dispatching until the EMTs $920 per month. Total operating costs were $133,709. Thus, the total cost of this alternative was $155, 562 or $275 per run.

Alternative 3 (Two location, Independent System). This alternative was very similar to the second, except for the addition of a location at Red Rock. This alternative assumed that a vehicle and a full-time EMT are placed at Red Rock. Volunteers would aid the EMT and be paid $25 per call. Volunteer labor expenses were $750. The total operating costs were $148,509. Thus, the total cost of this alternative was $174,293 or $308 per run.

One important component of the decision-making process was where would the money come from to support the EMS system. Several alternatives are presented in Table 7.9. First, the amount of revenue which would be obtained from EMS calls was depicted. For example, if a base rate of $140 was charged, and a $2.00 per mile one way charge for out of town calls was enacted, then $92,640 would have been charged. However, not all persons pay their bills. At a 60 percent collection rate, $55,584 would have been collected.

Table 7.9.   Estimated 1983 Revenue from the Noble County Emergency Medical Service

	BASE RATE			
	$80	$100	$120	$140
Chgs/run x 566 calls	$45,280	$56,600	$67,920	$79,240
$2/mile one way	13,400	13,400	13,400	13,400
TOTAL CHARGES	$58,680	$70,000	$81,320	$92,640
Collection at 40%	$23,472	$28,000	$32,528	$37,056
Collection at 50%	$29,340	$35,000	$40,660	$46,320
Collection at 60%	$35,208	$42,000	$48,792	$55,584
Collection at 70%	$41,076	$49,000	$56,924	$64,848
522 EMS COUNTY DISTRICT REVENUE				
1 Mill*	$104,510			
2 Mills	$156,765			
3 Mills	$209,020			
One cent sales tax (Perry)		$368,942		

*Estimated from 1982 evaluations.

Another method to generate revenue would have been for the residents in Noble County to create a 522 EMS County District. In 1976, Oklahoma passed a constitutional amendment (Article 10, Section 9C of the Constitution of the State of Oklahoma) which permitted the establishment of an EMS district (called "522 Districts"). This amendment created a procedure by which any political entity (county, city, school district) could bring the issue to a vote of the people. Three mills for the Noble County district would have generated $209,020 in revenue.

In addition, a portion of a unit of sales tax or a whole unit may have been designated for EMS use. Funds generated by a whole unit of sales tax (typically, one cent) were usually sufficient to support most community EMS functions.

Also, communities in some instances have started applying an assessment fee for ambulance services along with their other community service fees such as water, sewer, sanitation, and electrical services. These charges averaged between $1.50 and $3.00 per month. In full county or multi-county EMS systems, subscriptions equal in price to the assessments made in the municipalities were offered for sale to rural residents. When services were supplied without further fees to residents in these EMS systems, service rates approximated the actual costs per run. Thus, persons not within the geographical boundaries of the system or not subsidizing the EMS system as well as third party payers would have paid their fair share of system costs.

The data in Table 7.9 is intended to allow decision-makers the information necessary to calculate various alternatives. For example, if an:

1. EMS county district was created which generated $104,510
   one mill

2. Residents of Murray County were charged $140/call
   $2/mile one way and had a 60% collection rate $55,584

   Then total revenue collected would be: $160,094

Total revenue collected would support the second alternative, while the one mill alone would support the first.

Another alternative would be to support the system with two mills and third party collections, with no charge to Noble County residents for EMS services. For example, if an:

1. EMS county district was created which generated $156,765
   2 mills

2. EMS system collected from third party payers $12,045

   Then total revenue collected would be: $168,810

This alternative funding arrangement could support either alternative 1 or 2. Under the current interpretation by medicare, this alternative is possible and is used by other EMS systems. In addition, policies must be established as to the number of free calls allowed so that people will not abuse the system. The above alternatives were used to illustrate how decision-makers can use the data in Table 7.9.

OTHER CONSIDERATIONS

Decision-makers often ask the following questions when determining emergency equipment location sites: (1) where should ambulance facilities be located to provide the best emergency service to the citizens; and (2) where should fire stations or substations be located to provide the best protection. To answer these questions a transportation procedure model could be used. For illustration purposes, a theoretical programming model is presented in Appendix 7A which addresses these questions.

In addition to the location of units, information on the number of personnel to staff at alternative time periods during the day can be obtained by using Queueing theory. In 1983, Gebre developed a Queueing model which addressed this question. Time periods during the day can be ranked according to the profitability of multiple calls via probability methodology. With some information, staff schedules can be arranged for maximum coverage during periods with high probability of multiple calls. Another request often made by decision-makers is one for assistance in selecting routes. These occur for solid waste and school bus systems. An outline of a theoretical routing model is presented in Appendix 7B for illustration purposes.

STRENGTHS AND WEAKNESSES OF BUDGETING AS A DECISION TOOL

The strengths and weaknesses of using budgeting as an approach to infrastructure decision-making are intertwined. The main strength is that local decision-makers are clamoring for budgets of alternative community service delivery systems. For example, Oklahoma State University (OSU) Extension completed over 60 community service budget or related studies during the first three months of 1985. Related to the requests is the tremendous clientele base and support that Extension is receiving.

Another important strength, or maybe a weakness, is the importance of a strong research base. As prices and technology change, the budgets need to be updated and revised. Based on various experiences, OSU budgets need to be updated and revised about every two to three years. Each revision contains more data and alternatives. For example, the first EMS study was completed in 1975 and was for basic emergency medical services. In 1978, the budgets were updated and included first responders as part of a rural system. The latest revision was in 1982 and included budgets for advanced life support systems as well as basic life support systems. Also, budgeting lends itself to computerization and the quick delivery of studies.

In a majority of cases, when OSU Extension is requested to conduct a study, the community leaders have a crisis. For example, a recent request from the Tillman county commissioners was for a budget study of alternative solid waste landfill operations. The State Health Department is in the process of closing their current landfill and they have 90 days to find a solution. Since many of the requests have similar time frames, it is imperative that OSU Extension responds quickly. The goal of OSU Extension is to complete all studies within 4 weeks of the request. In some emergency cases, the need is great enough that studies have to be completed within two weeks.

Many of the computerized models currently in use in Oklahoma can be directly accessed from rural communities by way of portable computer terminals. Such terminals are sometimes taken to meetings where reports of community studies are being made. Then, if consideration of additional alternatives is desired by community leaders, appropriate computer analysis can be completed in the field.

SUMMARY

In a period when rural development is being evaluated by college administrators, state and national legislators and other policy-makers, it is imperative that constituents be provided with the products for which they have real needs. The degree of support which can be generated by such "real need" oriented programs is evidenced by the large number of requests of these studies and by their easy applicability.

The need for this type of educational information will not cease. A recent ECOP report stated "Assistance in financial planning and budgeting is a serious need likely to remain over a long period."

With over 53,993 rural local governments (e.g. cities, townships, counties, schools and special districts), the audience is extremely large. In addition, there are over 318,000 elected officials (e.g. mayors, councilors, and supervisors). Of these, forty percent leave office after one term. Each time that work is done with a community, its leaders gain from the information and educational materials presented to them. They become more aware of the implications of alternatives and can more effectively use the community's limited resources to serve the residents. With the large number of local entities and paid and elected officials, as well as the turnover, there is a tremendous need to provide information and educational materials and thus serve the rural residents of our respective state and nation.

APPENDIX 7A: GENERALIZED LOCATION OPTIMIZATION SELECTION SYSTEM

The computerized transportation procedure algorithm designated as GLOSS (Generalized Location Optimization Selection System) was used to assign the demand areas (townships) to an origin in such a way as to minimize the transportation mileage. The transportation procedure model is used to optimize a linear objective function with respect to a specific type of restraint (Heady and Candler, 1958). In a generalized form, the model can be stated as follows:

M = number of possible locations of ambulance service facilities

n = number of locations of ambulance facility users

a_i = ambulance service capacity at the ith ambulance service facility

b_j = amount of ambulance services demanded by the jth location of ambulance service users

X_{ij} = amount of ambulance services to be supplied by the facility at location "i" to ambulance service users at location "j"

C_{ij} = "cost" of supplying one unit of ambulance service from ambulance facility location "i" to each user location "j" (One-way miles were used as a proxy for "cost") and

$C_{ij}X_{ij}$ = cost of applying X_{ij} units of ambulance services from ambulance facility location "i" to any user at location "j".

The transportation problem can be stated in the following general mathematical relationships.

Minimize an objective function of the form,

$$(1) \quad z = \sum_{i=1}^{m} \sum_{j=1}^{n} C_{ij}X_{ij}$$

subject to the constraints

$$(2) \quad _{j=1} \text{ to } n \; X_{ij} = a_i \text{ where } i = 1, 2,.....m$$

$$(3) \quad _{i=1} \text{ to } m \; X_{ij} = b_j \text{ where } j = 1, 2,.....n$$

$$(4) \quad X_{ij} > 0$$

$$(5) \quad a_i \text{ from } i = 1 \text{ to } m = b_j \text{ from } j = 1 \text{ to } n$$

The following assumptions must be satisfied before the transportation procedure can be used to solve either transportation problems or other kinds of problems.

1. Services being provided by each of the various facility location origins are homogenous. In other words, availability of services at each origin will equally satisfy the demands in any service user location (Equation 2).

2. Service capacities at various origins and demands at various locations of service users are known, and total demand must equal total capacity (Equation 5). When discrepancies occur between service capacity and user demand, a dummy service capacity or user demand vector is used to produce equality. This dummy vector is used to signify unused capacities or unsatisfied demands.

3. Costs of providing services by any one origin to other locations of service users known, and are independent of the amount of services provided. That is, there is a constant per unit cost of service provided between locations.

4. There is an objective function to be optimized (Equation 1).

5. The activities cannot be executed at negative levels (Equation 4).

Two objectives are often identified for use in location analyses given multiple origins (Schmidt, et al, 1978).

1. To minimize the maximum response time to reach an emergency; and

2. To minimize average response time to reach an emergency.

These objectives are based on the idea that service users, decision-makers and policy-makers partially identify quality of emergency service with response time (i.e. the lower the response time, the higher the quality of service). The current emphasis in emergency medical service is to get the trained emergency medical personnel to the patient and to stabilize the condition of the patient. These two objectives were designed to reflect these ideas and to also allow some quantifiable measure of quality.

To adapt the general transportation procedure for use in this problem, certain modifications are made. When Objective 1 is used, each location of ambulance facility user is given a value of 1 (i.e. $b_j = 1$, where $j = 1,\ldots n$). This means that an ambulance has to make only one trip to each user location. The facility location(s) which has the smallest solution value (see Equation 1) represents the optimum solution and the location(s) which minimize the maximum response time. When Objective 2 is considered, each location of ambulance facility user is given a value equal to the frequency of calls for ambulance service. This means that an ambulance travels to each user location as many times as necessary to handle the number of calls for each user location. The facility location(s) with the smallest solution value(s) (see Equation 1) represents the optimum solution(s) and location(s) which minimize the average response time. Given that ambulances are to be placed in X < m locations and given each objective, a complete enumeration of all possible combinations of "m" locations taken "x" at a time yields the optimum solution. The algorithm designated GLOSS provides the necessary data to derive maximum and average distances for each combination.

APPENDIX 7B: THE ROUTING MODEL

A set of customers, each with a known location and a known requirement for some good or service, is to be supplied from a single origin by pickup or delivery vehicles of known capacity. The problem is to design the vehicle routes such that total cost of pickup or delivery is minimized. This objective is subject to the following constraints:

1. The requirements of all customers must be met;

2. Vehicle capabilities (e.g. weight or volume, capabilities) are not violated;

3. The total time or distance for each vehicle to complete its route may not exceed some predetermined value; and

4. There is an earliest and latest time interval when a customer can accept delivery that may not be violated.

Determining a route for a solid waste truck fits the general description of a vehicle scheduling problem. Any community service area contains a set of customers or points of known geographical location. Each household would have one base located nearby (i.e. single origin). Each of the constraints (2), (3), and (4) may or may not apply to a specific community service. However, a typical constraint would be that only a certain volume can fit into a truck (e.g. 16 cubic yards).

The ROUTE algorithm (Hallberg and Kriebel, 1972) was designed to develop vehicle routing schedules. The computer routine is an operationally and computationally efficient procedure that is generalizable to many different types of vehicle scheduling problems.

The algorithm incorporates a procedure for vehicle scheduling suggested by Clark and Wright, 1964. Initially, it is assumed that there are sufficient vehicles available so that a single customer is served on each route (i.e. the number of routes equals the number of customers). This initial solution to the scheduling problem can be characterized as the worst of all possible solutions, unless it is the only solution. The decision rule is then used in an attempt to find a better solution, if one exists. This rule pairs two customers on one route so that the cost saved would be the greatest from all choices available. This cost saving is determined from one of the following relationships:

$$S_{ij} = C_{oi} + C_{jo} - C_{ij} \text{ (symmetrical cost matrix)}$$

OR

$$S_{ij} = C_{io} + C_{oj} - C_{ij} \text{ (asymmetrical cost matrix)}$$

where:

S_{ij} = savings coefficient associated with linking customers "i" and "j" on the same route;

C_{oi} = the least cost (in distance, time or dollars) from the distribution center, (o) to customer "i", (where i = 1, 2, ... n; n = number of customers);

C_{ij} = the least cost (in distance, time or dollars) involved in traveling from customer "i" to customer "j" (where ij = 1, 2, ... n; and i = j).

For the initial state of the system (i.e. when one customer is on each route), the cost involved in serving customer "i" is $C_{oi} + C_{io}$ (asymmetrical cost matrix) or $2C_{io}$ (symmetrical cost matrix). Thus, by linking customers "i" and "j" on the same route, the amount saved is represented by Equation 2.

The algorithm calculates savings coefficients (S_{ij}) for each pair of customers for which cost data are provided. These savings coefficients are ordered from highest to lowest. The procedure begins combining pairs of customers onto the same route based upon the linking which would result in the largest savings, assuming no restrictions are violated. The routine continues linking two or more customers onto a single route until a final solution is reached at the end of n(n-1)/2 states although not all stages result in a linking of customers.

When several customers are already linked by one or more existing routes, another decision rule is used to determine which routes to combine. The basic rule of selecting links based upon the largest saving coefficient still applies with the additional condition that breaking up an existing route is prohibited at any stage of the procedure. Thus, a link is selected by choosing that link with the largest saving coefficient among the possible links that exist at the current stage in the procedure.

The procedure used by ROUTE generates a heuristic solution (i.e. an optimal solution is not guaranteed). Finding the optimal solution to even a small problem of this nature is very expensive with known optimizing algorithms. This is due to the large number of possible solutions that must be considered.

8
Economic-Demographic Projection Models: An Overview of Recent Developments for Infrastructure Analysis

Lonnie L. Jones, Steve Murdock, and F. Larry Leistritz

Economic - demographic projection models have received extensive attention over the last two decades as a means of analyzing economic, demographic, public service provision, and fiscal impacts of industrial developments, and as a means of forecasting basic economic and demographic change in rural as well as urban areas. Three factors have been responsible for much of the emphasis on model building. These are new federal and state legislation requiring socioeconomic impact analyses, notably the National Environmental Policy Act (NEPA) of 1969; the development of large mineral and energy projects in the Western states; and the population turnaround in many rural areas during the 1970s. An ability to respond to modeling needs created by these and other factors was made possible by the concurrent advance in the capacities of electronic computers.

In this chapter, a partial overview of economic - demographic models as they have evolved in recent years, as well as a description of current and future directions in the area of infrastructure analysis are provided.

BACKGROUND OF MODEL DEVELOPMENT

Economic and demographic impact models have been developed and refined over a considerable period of time. Economists and others have long recognized the myriad of interdependencies that exist among the various factors involved in impact analysis. However, earlier work concentrated on developing more complete and detailed models for single dimensions (e.g., regional input-output or economic base analyses and population projection models). The integration of more than one dimension into a single impact assessment model had to await the arrival of analytical machinery capable of solving the complex set of equations that characterize such models. Nevertheless, by the end of the sixties, some attention had been given to both the integration of economic and demographic factors and to the application of integrated models for projecting change in rural areas.

One regional economic-demographic model, developed during the late 1960s, had a substantial influence on subsequent socioeconomic modeling efforts. The Susquehanna River Basin Model differed from most earlier models in that it specifically linked the economic and demographic sectors. It also included nonmetropolitan areas in the analysis, whereas previous models had generally focused only on a single large city (Hamilton et al. 1969). The model made extensive use of feedback loops to link its various components, a structure which was influenced at least in part by the earlier work of Forrester (1969).

The research group at Battelle Columbus Laboratories who developed the Susquehanna Model subsequently constructed similar models for the City of San Diego (San Diego Comprehensive Planning Organization 1972) and for the State of Arizona (Battelle Columbus Laboratories 1973). The Susquehanna Model also influenced the structure of a regional forecasting model developed by the Tennessee Valley Authority (Bohm and Lord, 1972). These models, in turn, influenced subsequent model development efforts (Figure 8.1). Notable among these were the series of economic-demographic models developed by the states of Arizona and Utah (Bigler, Reeve, and Weaver, 1972) and the MULTIREGION model developed at Oak Ridge National Laboratory (Olsen et al. 1977).

These models all provided for linkages of the economic and demographic sectors through a submodel which simulated the operation of the labor market and provided for in- or out-migration from the study area in response to changes in labor market conditions (i.e., if the demand for labor increased more rapidly than the "natural increase" in labor supply, in-migration would occur). The models differ somewhat in the degree of sectoral disaggregation within the economic module, however. For example, while the Susquehanna Model includes only three employment categories, the ATOM-3 Model had 88 employment sectors. The models also differ in the degree of spatial detail of their outputs; some provided employment and population projections at the county level (e.g., ATOM, UPED, CPE), and others provided projections only at the multicounty regional level (e.g., Susquehanna, MULTIREGION). Finally, these models differ significantly in the time increments associated

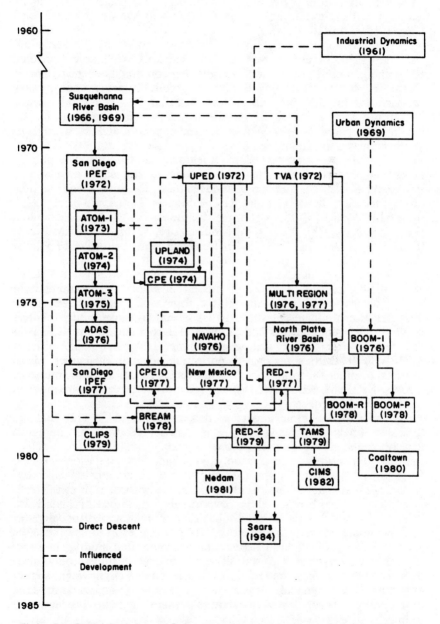

Figure 8.1: Partial Genealogy of Socioeconomic Impact Assessment Models, 1960-1985

with their projections. While a few models provide projections annually (e.g., ATOM-3), several produce estimates only at five-year intervals (e.g., UPED, MULTIREGION).

Socioeconomic projection models developed during the late 1960s and early 1970s were employed primarily as tools for state and regional economic planning. As interest in evaluating community-specific impacts of major projects grew, however, these models were found to have substantial limitations as impact assessment tools. The two principal limitations were a failure to include a number of significant impact dimensions, particularly public service requirements and fiscal impacts, and insufficient spatial and temporal disaggregation of outputs. Thus, in the mid-1970s attention turned to developing models that incorporated additional impact dimensions and provided outputs at county and subcounty levels. A number of models were developed to meet these needs, including the RED-1 and RED-2 models (Hertsgaard et al. 1978), the TAMS Model (Murdock et al., 1979), the BREAM Model (Mountain West Research 1978), the BOOM Model (Ford, 1976), the SEAM Model (Stenehjem, 1978), the West Model (Denver Research Institute 1979), and the SIMPACT Model (Huston, 1979).

These "second-generation" models differ from the earlier economic-demographic projection models primarily in the number of impact categories included and in the degree of spatial and temporal disaggregation of their outputs. Thus, several of these models address public service requirements and public sector cost and revenue effects as well as economic and demographic impacts (e.g., RED, WEST, SIMPACT, TAMS); some provide projections for individual cities, school districts, or other subcounty areas as well as for counties and regions (e.g., TAMS, BREAM, RED, WEST); and most provide yearly projections of key impact indicators.

The socioeconomic impact models discussed so far are the types typically used for analyses of large-scale resource or industrial developments and to simulate regional or state economies. They include multiple dimensions (e.g., economic, demographic, public service, and fiscal impacts) and usually provide impacts for an area including several counties, municipalities, and/or other local jurisdictions. Another "breed" of models that has been developed over roughly the same time period also exists and is widely used in rural infrastructure analysis. Although most of these models are now computerized, their origin seems to have been the "pen and pad" case studies of community-specific rural industry location. Unlike the large-scale and spatially comprehensive simulation models discussed above, these models take a marginal analysis approach to analyzing the marginal impact of a resource and/or economic development, usually in a single development and single community setting.

Considerable direction and focus was provided to this line of modeling by a study of Oklahoma rural communities in 1972 by Shaffer.

The structure of this model influenced the development of community-specific models throughout the 1970s in states including Texas, Florida, Kentucky, South Carolina, Nevada, and Ohio. Most of these models are referred to as industrial impact models and concentrate on a detailed analysis of only one or two impact dimensions, such as economic, population, or fiscal impacts on the various public sectors of a local community. Typically, these models make maximum use of local data and, consequently, do not require the maintenance of large data bases. They also tend to be less complex in terms of methodology and are frequently used for purposes of extension education rather than for making long-range projections in a socioeconomic impact assessment. As such, they have been proven to be useful tools for assisting local decision makers in thinking through the economic and fiscal impacts of a development for their community.

For their intended purpose, community-specific models have a distinct advantage over the large multidimensional, regional models because they are simpler in structure and are much easier to apply in a one industry-one community setting. In most rural growth situations, the community-specific model structure is likely to be a satisfactory tool of analysis that can handle most of the impact questions that arise in a very timely manner. However, in those instances where geographic spillover of economic or demographic impact is significant, community-specific models have been found to have serious limitations.

MODEL EVALUATION

The specific socioeconomic information needs of local decision makers may be expected to vary widely. Consequently, criteria for evaluating models will vary, and no single set of criteria will serve all purposes. Nevertheless, several general considerations must enter into the process of model selection in almost all circumstances. Three important criteria are

1.   information requirements,

2.   methodology and validation, and

3.   use characteristics.

Each of these factors is discussed briefly below.

Information Requirements

Clearly, the starting point in selecting a modeling system is the information needs of the user--what information is needed, for where, and for what periods of time. Environmental impact assessments and community planning are requiring an increasingly larger volume of socioeconomic data. These data usually include, at a minimum, information on the economic, demographic, public service, and fiscal changes likely to occur under both baseline and impact conditions, and for both construction and operational phases during impact periods (Council on Environmental Quality, 1978).

The economic data usually include information on changes in income, employment, and business activity, and changes by type of industry. Information on demographic changes usually includes data on population increases and, increasingly, information for particular age, ethnic, and other groups, and for small geographic units, such as municipalities, as well as total impact areas. Public service data tend to concentrate on the number of new service facilities and personnel required to serve new, in-migrating populations, on the costs of such increased services, and on the public revenues likely to be generated by new populations. Fiscal changes include an analysis of the revenue and expenditure positions of all jurisdictions affected by the impact. These are likely to be the most politically sensitive of all projections and, unfortunately, are usually the most difficult to estimate. Because the costs of acquisition of single data sets (fiscal, economic, etc.) are likely to require investments that may exceed those for an entire modeling effort, the inclusiveness or lack of inclusiveness of a model may be particularly significant. Those models that provide larger proportions of the necessary data items are clearly of greater utility.

Equally important is the need to ascertain both the levels of geographic output provided by the model and its ability to provide outputs for alternative time periods. Many of the available models provide output only at the total impact area level or for counties, but not for individual cities or other government districts. As a result, such models, though useful for those involved in regional planning and decision making, are likely to be of little use to the decision maker charged with allocating resources or assessing impacts for school districts or other local units of government.

At the same time, it is essential to ensure that results are provided for the necessary time periods. That is, impact periods, particularly construction periods, often show rapid changes from year to year, and these changes often require careful planning and resource allocation. However, if such models provide results for only five-year periods rather than for yearly periods, year-to-year changes will not be detected.

Finally, it is essential that the model provide separate outputs for baseline, construction impact, and operation impact periods. Since impact assessment involves comparing impact-induced changes to a projection of baseline changes over time, data for both baseline and impact conditions are essential. Also, since construction and operational phases are separate in impact assessments, and have distinct types of impacts, the production of separate results for each impact phase is usually needed. Hence, both the temporal and geographical specificity of model outputs should be analyzed.

Methodological Considerations

Although the methodologies employed in various models involve numerous technical distinctions that are not appropriate to our discussion here, several aspects of model methodology should enter into evaluations of alternative models.

First, some methodologies are simply likely to be more adequate than others. Although under any set of circumstances, several alternative methodologies may be of equal utility, general assumptions can be made about such methodologies. For instance, even a brief examination of information on demographic projection techniques will suggest that techniques using age cohorts are generally superior to those with less detail (Shryock and Seigel, 1973). A short consultation with appropriate experts will generally provide similar information in regard to other model dimensions.

Second, it is essential to evaluate the extent of submodule integration in such models. Most of the existing models involve a major premise that economic and demographic aspects of developments require careful integration. Some, however, make no attempt at effective integration of key components, but rather simply apply separate methodologies (i.e., for economic and demographic projections) to a common set of project characteristics.

Finally, the assumptions underlying the methodologies employed in such models must be evaluated carefully in terms of such dynamic modeling capabilities as

1. the ability to incorporate changes in the structure of model relationships over time,

2. the inclusion of the key structural dimensions of the phenomena of interest, and

3. the incorporation of feedback loops for updating baseline figures.

In general, models that allow the use of multiple rates for various factors during different phases of the projection period (such as changes in labor force participation rates or fertility rates), that utilize factors that most closely differentiate between key dimensions (such as industries or age cohorts), and that incorporate procedures that feed back changes, such as alterations of population age structures or changes in the economic structures, are superior to those lacking such features.

It is, of course, evident that an overriding factor in model selection must be an evaluation of a model's accuracy in predicting impact and baseline conditions. Most of the existing models have been developed recently and relatively little evidence has accumulated for evaluating their validity. However, given samples of the outputs of model projections for various areas, several types of evaluations can be made quite easily. For example, estimates of economic factors, such as income at the county level and population levels for counties and incorporated areas, are published periodically by the Bureau of Economic Analysis and the Bureau of the Census in the Department of Commerce. These estimates can be compared to those for the various models, and some idea of their accuracy can thus be gained. This approach, which involves a comparison of data from past periods to those projected by a model for such periods, is often termed historical simulation. In addition, it is possible to use dynamic simulation techniques and sensitivity analysis to analyze such models (Pindyck and Rubinfeld, 1976). This involves a comparison of the trends shown in the model output for the projected future periods to those noted in impacted areas in the past. Such comparisons provide a valuable step in model selection. Even though techniques exist for model validation, they have been rarely used (however, see Murdock et al. 1984), and testing for accuracy of predictions remains a weak link in the model development and application process.

Use Characteristics

Additional dimensions that must be considered relate to the use characteristics of such models. Two of these dimensions are the availability and cost of obtaining the input data required for a model's implementation. For instance, many models use input-output economic models that require the use of state or regional input-output interdependence coefficients. These coefficients are available in most areas, but if an appropriate set of coefficients does not exist, then the implementation of such models is likely to be quite expensive and to require extensive data collection. Similar consideration must be given to other data dimensions.

It is essential to note that models that reduce data collection costs by utilizing national data bases may accentuate problems in projecting local-level conditions that depart markedly from national patterns. The tradeoff between the need for locally oriented data inputs and the costs of collecting local data must be evaluated carefully.

The flexibility of use of the model should also be considered. Impact assessments and impact events involve numerous factors that are difficult to evaluate and predict. Thus, it becomes essential to examine the range of potential impacts under widely varying assumptions for such factors.

Models that provide easy alterations of such factors and rapid outputs for alternative development scenarios are desirable. In evaluating models, the options provided for altering key assumptions, such as the number of projects, the size of the project, the location of the project, inflation rates, birth rates, per capita service usage rates, and other factors, should be closely examined.

The size and nature of the impact problem to be analyzed is an all-important factor in determining the appropriate impact model to be used. That is, one should seek to use the proper tool for the job to be done. Much of the economic change occurring in rural areas of the country may be satisfactorily analyzed without the aid of a large, regional simulation model. For this activity, it may be well to examine carefully the smaller, community-specific models, which can usually be more easily adapted to new areas, can be used more efficiently, and can provide faster analytical turnaround for the client.

Indeed, to computerize or not computerize is still a question asked by many people who work with rural communities in their infrastructure development efforts. Why not use the traditional "pen and pad" technique for working through the impacts of economic change on rural communities? The answer is that a good computerized impact model provides the advantage of easy replication and expands the capability of the specialist to provide assistance to a greater number of communities within a given time period. For example, many people would agree that the investment of time and money in developing the socioeconomic impact models in Texas over the last ten years has had a positive payoff in allowing us to serve a larger clientele more efficiently.

IMPACT ANALYSIS IN THE NEXT TEN YEARS

There can be little doubt that major advances in socioeconomic impact models have occurred over the last fifteen years. Models have become much more sophisticated methodologically and their use as an integral part of the planning process, for both large-scale developments and for baseline projections of growth, has increased sharply. As we move into the latter half of the 1980s, all indications are that the demand for socioeconomic impact projections will further increase. However, there may be some dramatic changes in the makeup of our clientele and, as a result, a need to alter existing models or develop new models to address these changes.

During the 1970s socioeconomic impact models were used primarily for state and regional planning efforts, and to satisfy the socioeconomic subpart of environmental impact statements required by the Environmental Protection Agency for large-scale projects--primarily energy developments. Two changes that occurred at the beginning of the 1980s seem to have shifted the demand curve for sophisticated socioeconomic impact models sharply downward and to the left. These were (1) federal agencies that had demanded this type of analysis (e.g., EDA, EPA, and DOE) were early victims of the new federal budget cuts and (2) the turnaround in crude oil price trends caused several large energy companies to delay indefinitely plans for developing large-scale projects that would either produce or use alternative fuels. These two events combined to reduce the development and application of impact models in the early 1980s. However, at least in Texas, there has been a rebound in demand for socioeconomic impact analyses for local decisions and public service planning. A new set of clients now come calling and these include municipalities, county governments, chambers of commerce, industrial groups, and regional and local planning commissions. This seems to indicate that local decision makers have become aware of the availability of assistance and wish to have the impact projections for their planning purposes.

One interesting turnaround has been the nature of the requests for analyses. While most socioeconomic impact models (including those in Texas) have been developed for the purpose of projecting the impact of some specific, and usually large, resource development, more and more requests from local decision makers are concentrated on the baseline projection for their community. Hence, the baseline information that is used for general planning purposes has become just as useful as the analysis of a specific project.

To the extent that the demand continues to grow from this new client group, socioeconomic impact models may be subjected to a different set of stresses in the future. Local decision makers are interested in local problems and are more likely to scrutinize model results in terms of accuracy for very localized areas and specific model dimensions than has been the case in the past. Attempts to serve these clients mean that model development will need to focus on two critical areas. First, the problem of data becomes acute as models move from state and/or multicounty study areas to county and community levels. Data have always been a problem but largely in terms of the cost of maintaining large data bases. State-level data has been fairly complete for most dimensions of socioeconomic impact models (at least we do not know how poor it is). As we move to modeling local economies, much of the data from secondary sources simply disappears. Moreover, we seem to face an era in which the general trend is toward limiting federal and state support for those agencies that have historically provided the data needed. More attention must be given to developing efficient data series necessary for analysis at the local community and county levels. This is a difficult task that is clearly less exciting than the development of more elaborate computer algorithms. The second area of concern is that of model accuracy and validation. If socioeconomic modeling and infrastructure projection is to be a continuing service to local decision makers, there is a need to assess the accuracy of our models. This is a major weakness, and our only consolation is that we are probably no worse off than other economic and demographic forecasters.

Finally, economic modeling of all types, including socioeconomic, is moving rapidly into the mode of the user-friendly, interactive microcomputer. With the growth in microcomputer capacity, most models can be adapted to micros without major difficulty. This opens the possibility of greatly expanding the use of planning models into the offices of virtually every rural county and community with such a need. It also creates the possibility for evaluating different scenarios of impacts with user-alterable coefficients in every dimension of the model. The analytical possibilities presented by this development are astounding. But so are the problems of management and control to avoid the dangers of either deliberate or accidental misuse of models that can precipitate detrimental effects. The question of the extent to which models can be released has been a matter of discussion for some time. The primary problem here is one of user training and education. This obviously presents an opportunity for community resource-development educational programs in all rural areas. It is clear that our electronic hardware and software already far outdistance support data and the knowledge of the users. Perhaps the highest priority for modeling efforts for the remainder of the 1980s should be to concentrate our efforts on improving these two areas as rapidly as possible.

9
Using Fiscal Impact Models in Local Infrastructure Investment Decisions*

John M. Halstead and Thomas G. Johnson

FISCAL IMPACT ANALYSES

Infrastructure investment decision-making involves the commitment of millions of dollars to long term projects with even longer payoffs. The feasibility of the projects are complicated by vagaries of national business cycles, unexpected external shocks, and concurrent public decisions. Furthermore, the feasibility is affected by economic changes created by the projects (induced growth, or the demand which is created by supply, etc.) and by the opportunities forgone when a major project is undertaken.

The conceptual frameworks necessary to take these into consideration are discussed in previous chapters. This chapter outlines, at a conceptual level, the ideal and in some cases, minimum characteristics of fiscal impact models necessary to address these issues.

Local fiscal impact analysis refers to a broad range of studies which consider the government expenditures and revenue impacts of various public policy decisions at the community level. Such analyses are

*This paper is based on research initiated at the 1984 Asilomar Conference on Fiscal Impact Analysis. The research was funded by the Western Rural Development Center. The research project was planned by a committee comprised of Thomas G. Johnson, David L. Darling, Richard Bower, and Larry Deboer.

typically conducted within broader impact analyses including economic, demographic, environmental, and sociological components. This reflects not only the fact that sound decision-making requires information on all of these dimensions, but also that these dimensions are frequently interrelated and must be considered simultaneously.

Impact analyses are usually conducted with the aid of a model or framework. National and state governments typically have access to sophisticated econometric models designed especially for their jurisdictions, frequently for specific purposes. Local governments, except for the very largest of cities, cannot afford the luxury of highly specific models. Instead, they must make do with more generic versions, or with nothing at all. How does the typical local government administrator choose from among the numerous models available?

The next section develops a conceptual framework within which local impact models may be viewed. Then, the results of a survey of practitioners of impact analysis in which twenty-three impact models were identified is presented. Finally, the characteristics of an ideal local impact model for infrastructure investment decisions are outlined.

DIMENSIONS OF LOCAL IMPACT MODELS

Characteristics of local impact models can be divided into six key dimensions for evaluation and selection: temporal, spatial, public service, sectoral, demographic, and operational. These dimensions subsume the three criteria Murdock and Leistritz (1980) proposed for evaluation of fiscal impact models, which were (1) information needs of the user, (2) methodological characteristics of the model, and (3) user characteristics of the model. These criteria consider the dimensions, project phases, geographical units, time increments, total area units, methodological forms, dynamic capabilities, forms of validation, data input requirements, and user and computerization characteristics of the model. Each of these dimensions is discussed in turn.

Temporal Decision

The temporal dimension is arguably, the most important in infrastructure decision-making. It addresses the length of projection and simulation periods, and the model's capacity to separate long-run and short-run impacts and to provide baseline projections. Sound projections of temporal impacts are essential in identifying and anticipating problems which local governments may encounter in growth situations, such as the need for early investment in infrastructure and public services, and prediction of potential cash-flow problems--the so-called "front-end financing" problem (Murray and Weber, 1982; Leistritz and Murdock,

1981). Temporal dimensions also influence the model's ability to provide information for calculation of net present values for benefit-cost analyses.

Spatial Dimension

The spatial dimension addresses the degree of disaggregation in the model, and the level of jurisdiction handled. Typically, a model will identify impacts at the county, city, or town. These dimensions are crucial in determining the transferability of the model to other regions, since they determine multipliers, jurisdictions, and labor market and commuting pattern coincidence (Murdock, et. al. 1979; Winter, et. al. 1981).

Public Service Dimension

Local impact models vary widely with respect to public services identified. Some deal only with specific areas such as housing or education, while others address a wide range of public services. Models can also be differentiated by whether or not specific revenue sources are identified. Those that do identify specific revenue sources can be further categorized by their bases for revenue projection.

The more disaggregated the public service component of the model--that is, the greater the number of specific services identified and addressed by the model--the more useful the model will be to local planning interests (Halstead, et al 1985). Increased disaggregation allows for more accurate determination of infrastructure investment needs (in this respect, this dimension is closely related to the temporal dimension). The benefits of this greater planning ability must be weighed against the added costs of development and other potential costs.

Sectoral Dimension

A model's sectoral dimension determines the extent to which the model can identify differential impacts on different sectors and whether or not the model incorporates a multiplier effect. The most common multipliers are final demand, income, employment, and value-added, based on either economic base or input/output (survey or non-survey) techniques. Economic base multipliers are easier to develop, relatively less expensive, and easier to translate than input-output (I/O) multipliers (Pfister, 1976). However, they lack the specificity (and consequently, also the accuracy) that I/O multipliers possess (Leistritz and Murdock, 1981). Survey based I/O models are commonly considered more dependable than non-survey based models.

Demographic Dimension

The number and characteristics of people moving in or out of a community is an essential input into determination of public service impacts and is therefore crucial to infrastructure investment decision-making. A sophisticated demographic sector is critical for good prediction, especially if the model's public service dimension is disaggregated. Demographic projection techniques which incorporate age/sex cohorts are widely accepted as most accurate (Shryock and Siegel, 1973; Murdock and Leistritz, 1980). In addition, many models project occupational demands and supplies and migration and commuting levels.

Operational Dimension

The final dimension considered is the operational dimension--the actual mechanics of model implementation. This includes type of computer (mainframe or micro), programming language, and software requirements. Sources and costs of data required, time and financial resources needed to run the model, and output format are also important. Finally, documentation available for the model plays a key role in the model's transferability and usefulness. Documentation can be broken down into three levels:

1. Descriptive documentation. This is merely a general overview of the model, describing the nature of multipliers used, capabilities, services identified, etc., which should allow the potential user to determine if the model has the ability to answer the user's questions. Furthermore, it should give some indication of the model's reliability and specificity.

2. Mechanical documentation. This level of detail permits the potential user to run and interpret a setup-calibrated model. It must be very specific about routine data needs, how to develop scenarios, how to run the model, and how to interpret the output.

3. Full documentation. In this case, the potential user is provided with enough information to transfer the model to his/her own area, incorporating region-specific algorithms and characteristics.

These dimensions translate into the user-friendliness of the model: its potential transferability to other states and regions, flexibility with respect to different scenarios, and usefulness for decision-making purposes. Also of importance is the model's potential for abuse --the greater the model's transferability and ease of use, the more likely the model will be misused by parties not familiar with its assumptions and limitations. Training programs for potential users and careful documentation can help alleviate these problems.

IMPACT MODELING SURVEY RESULTS

In 1985, a mail survey (Halstead and Johnson, 1986) was developed to assess different characteristics of impact models currently in use in several states. The most relevant characteristics looked at included: costs of developing the models; costs of running the models; adaptability (transferability) of the models to other areas and/or regions; and data requirements of the models. Also, although the survey was not directly concerned with the accuracy of the models' projections, which relates to model validation, information with respect to this could be obtained from the appropriate model documentation in the reference section.

Potential respondents to the survey were obtained from publications on modeling, various listings, and through recommendations of professionals known to have been active in impact analysis. Forty-five individuals were contacted. Of these, twenty-five responded. The survey identified twenty-three impact models and trend analysis systems used in seventeen states, Scotland, and the Province of Alberta, Canada;[11] some states had more than one fiscal impact model (e.g. Iowa, Texas), while some models were used in more than one state (NEDAM, IIM).

Historical Bases

While the use of economic-demographic models can be traced to the 1960s (Murdock and Leistritz, 1980), all of the models identified were developed in the 1970s or later. The ancestry of these models was principally found in three places: the economic growth impact model (often called the Florida model) (Clayton and Whittington, 1977), the

---

[11] Models identified were the BOOM Series (BOOM, BOOMH, and BOOMR) (Southwestern United States, Scotland, and Alberta, Canada); COALTOWN (Montana, North Dakota); Community Development Impact Model (CDIM) (Kentucky); Community Simulation Model (CIM) (Oklahoma); ENERGYTAX (Minnesota); Fiscal Trend Monitoring System (FTMS) (Iowa); Fort Drum Fiscal Impact Analysis Model (New York); Impact Model for Planning Alberta Communities over Time (IMPACT); Industrial Impact Model (IIM) (Texas, Oklahoma); Iowa Economic and Fiscal Impact Model (IEFIM); Kansas Impact Model (KIM); Local Government Capital Improvement Programming Model (New York); Microcomputer Fiscal impact Model (Nevada); North Dakota Economic-Demographic Assessment Model (NEDAM); Ohio Job Impact Model (OJIM); PAS (Planning and Assessment Model) (Southwestern United States); Socioeconomic Assessment of Repository Siting (SEARS); Social and Economic Assessment Model (SEAM); South Carolina Impact Model (SCIM); Texas Assessment Modeling System (TAMS); and the Virginia Impact Projection Model (VIP). Full reference and documentation information for these models is available from the authors on request.

REAP Economic-Demographic Model (RED) (Hertsgaard, et. al. 1978), and the Shaffer-Tweeten impact estimation procedures (Shaffer and Tweeten, 1974).

The Florida model uses a system of economic base multipliers, while the RED models rely on an I/O module to develop multipliers. The Shaffer-Tweeten procedure is not an impact model per se; rather, it is a non-computerized framework developed for measuring the impacts of new developments on rural communities. These procedures have since been quantified to provide the basis for models in Ohio (Morse and Gerard, 1980), Iowa (Otto, 1984), and Indiana (Darling, 1979).

Comparisons

Responses to the survey related to twenty-three models. Of these, thirteen were designed for use on mainframe computers, eight were for use on microcomputers, and two could be used on either mainframe or micro. Estimated costs of model development varied considerably, but were generally higher for mainframe models. Costs of running the micro-based models were insignificant, while mainframe models cost up to $100 per run. A further categorization could be made based on type of multipliers used in the models--survey I/O, non-survey I/O, or economic base. There is usually an inverse relationship between multiplier complexity and cost of model development, with survey I/O being the most complex. Although the information collected by the survey on data and setup cost is difficult to interpret due to wide variability of possible applications, it appeared that models using I/O multiplier modules are more expensive to develop than those using economic base.

Only eight of the models incorporated age/sex cohorts: TAMS, NEDAM, COALTOWN, PAS, SEAM, IMPACT, SEARS and CIM. TAMS, SEARS, and NEDAM are all direct descendants of the RED I and II models, while CIM's development was influenced by the RED family. Employing age/sex cohorts requires considerable data input on fertility rates, mortality rates, and migration rates, both for present and future generations, making it the most detailed and demanding of the five projection techniques identified by Irwin (1977).[12] The information requirements of this technique may contribute to the fact that the data costs of NEDAM and TAMS are substantially higher than for the other models reporting specific data costs.

---

[12] The five projection techniques Irwin identified were: (1) extrapolative, curve-fitting, and regression-base techniques; (2) ratio-based techniques; (3) land use techniques; (4) economic-based techniques; and (5) cohort component techniques.

Disaggregation by public services varied widely, ranging from no specific public services identified by the IIM (Industrial Impact Model) to 13 public services itemized by the TAMS (Texas Assessment Modeling System). It is difficult to see the number of specific public services identified as an evaluation criterion, however, since some of these models were designed with the intent of looking at development impacts on only one or two areas (for example, the ENERGYTAX model only identified impacts on education). All of the models identified specific public service expenditures.

Eleven of the models had complementary extension programs (several of the models were not expected to have extension programs, since they were developed by consulting firms). Excluding the Fort Drum Model, six of nine models compatible with microcomputers had extension programs, while five of the mainframe-only models had programs. In addition, two of the other micro models--the OJIM and VIP--have been used in conjunction with extension activities, although they currently have no formal programs. This may indicate that micro models are more adaptable to extension uses than mainframe models, and may be well suited for infrastructure planning by small local governments with limited access to mainframe computing services.

CHARACTERISTICS OF AN 'IDEAL' INFRASTRUCTURE INVESTMENT IMPACT MODEL

Based on the preceding discussion, one can describe the characteristics of what could be called an ideal impact model for infrastructure investment decisions. Ignoring for a moment the development costs, this model would involve minimum application expense while providing maximum projection accuracy. It would be flexible and allow for easy transfer to other states and/or regions.

Toward these ends, several features would be incorporated. In the temporal dimension, the model would include variable length of simulation periods, provide baseline projections, and be capable of separating short-run (initial investment) impacts from long-run impacts. The spatial dimension would handle multiple jurisdictions, and identify specific public revenues and expenditures. The model might also identify a maximum number of public services like education, fire protection, highways, and social welfare. The economic sector would use a survey-based I/O module, even though the data and development requirements of this module would have an adverse effect on model expense. The demographic dimension would use an age/sex cohort method; the model would also project commuting levels (using a gravity basis) and migration levels.

On the implementation side, the necessary data would be clean, accurate, and easily and cheaply accessible. Although a model of this size and complexity would likely be developed on a mainframe, adaptations could be made for microcomputer (for example, the Nevada microcomputer fiscal impact model is adapted from the larger Texas Assessment Modeling System, TAMS). Finally, to maximize the model's usefulness, a complementary extension program could be developed.

The characteristics of the ideal model just described which uses a survey I/O module and an age/sex demographic component, and which has a highly disaggregated public service dimension, will likely provide more useful projections than a less complex model. However, its economic and demographic components will also have greater information requirements. In addition, a highly disaggregated public service dimension may incorporate a greater number of specific features, making the model less amenable to transfer. Thus, there is a direct relationship between sophistication/complexity and accuracy, and an indirect relationship between sophistication and transferability and expense, so that this "ideal" model may vary from situation to situation. Thus, decision-makers must prioritize their needs, in terms of information they would require to make a decision, so that the appropriate characteristics are incorporated in the modeling process.

Summary and Conclusions

The impact modeling survey identified twenty-three models varying in size, cost, complexity, and transferability. There appears to be a trend in recent years to adapt impact models to the microcomputer, both through development of new models and modification of existing mainframe models. For example, as recently as 1980, a discussion of twelve impact models by Murdock and Leistritz did not identify one model with microcomputer applications, while ten of twenty-three models in this survey were compatible with microcomputers.[13] Undoubtedly, this is due not only to a wider understanding of the principles and applications of impact modeling, but also to the increased sophistication and capacity (as well as decreasing costs) of the modern microcomputer.

When choosing an impact model for adaptation or development in a particular state or region for infrastructure investment purposes, one should consider the marginal costs of increased complexity. Not every community needs a model of the size and sophistication of TAMS or NEDAM; the relative ease of transfer of a model with economic base multipliers, no age/sex cohort component, and a somewhat aggregated

---

[13] Of these 23 models, the Community Economic Growth Impact (Florida) Model, BOOM, CDIM, and ENERGYTAX are no longer in use or have been transformed into other models.

public service dimension may outweigh the advantages of the larger mainframe models.   As the survey results indicate, there are ample applications and uses for a wide range of models, tailored to suit users needs.

10
Data Needs and Limitations for Public Services Modeling

J. M. (Jack) Whitmer

Major changes are occurring in local governments. In addition to the effects of the "New Federalism", there is also a slow but significant change in the way that local government information is being recorded and reported. To date the principal activity involves instituting Generally Accepted Accounting Principles (GAAP) for the recording and reporting of governmental financial information. Some degree of standardization of the recording and reporting of non-financial governmental data is also being considered.

FINANCIAL DATA OF LOCAL GOVERNMENTS

Elected and appointed local government officials, university researchers, including economic and engineering model builders, may save themselves considerable frustration and possible embarrassment by studying the historical development of the practices of financial managers, investors and government regulators with respect to the recording and reporting of financial data. That experience shows that as the number of people, data entries, and the complexity of the organization increases, the need for standardization of the recording and reporting of the financial data and information also grows, only faster. Only by using consistent and comparable financial information can executives in the private sector make decisions about major investments and corporate policy decisions with any degree of confidence. Consistency and comparability of financial data and information is so important in the private sector that an entire educational subject and profession (accounting) has developed to institutionalize the proper and uniform application of a standardized set of definitions, rules and practices for recording and reporting financial data and information in the private sector.

About twenty years ago financial leaders in both the private and public sector began to emphasize that many of the same needs that lead to GAAP in the private sector are present in the public sector. Their efforts, considerable study, and discussion have resulted in the establishment of GAAP for governmental recording and reporting. The process of institutionalizing this new set of definitions, rules, and principles to govern the recording and reporting of public sector financial data and information has begun.

Although similar in some aspects, governmental or public sector purposes and reporting needs are different than enterprise or private sector purposes and reporting needs. This difference is acknowledged by the financial and accounting profession with the establishment of a Governmental Accounting Standards Board (GASB) to guide the development of rules and standards for governmental accounting just as the Financial Accounting Standards Board (FASB) has done for private sector accounting. Rules, standards and concepts governing the recording and reporting of public sector financial data are now being written and interpreted. Public officials are being trained and instructed on how to use the new information. People who use public sector financial data (investment rating firms, investment sales firms and auditing firms) are very active in this process to insure that they obtain the data and information they need to perform their responsibilities. Public policy-makers, government administrators, and university researchers in non-financial disciplines have not shown a lot of interest in this process. Consistent and comparable public sector financial and non-financial data are valuable and necessary in public policy-making and non-financial models.

Why should local governmental leaders, researchers, including public policy analysts, economic and engineering model builders and management information system professional participate in formalizing the rules for public sector recording and reporting of public sector financial and non-financial data? Non-accounting professionals did not get deeply involved in the process for the private sector.

The answer is in a preceding paragraph of this chapter: Governmental organizations, purposes, activities and data are different than enterprise organizations, purposes, activities and data. Governmental data in records and reports are used in a different manner with different significance than similar data in the private sector.

The nature of enterprise organizations has made the enterprise records adequate to assess the efficiency and effectiveness of the organization in terms of maximizing profits. Thus, financial professions and institutions promoted rules and standard procedures to increase the accuracy, consistency, comparability and thus the validity and reliability of data used to describe financial reality in enterprise funds. For the most part their efforts have been successful. Two recent examples: The E.S.M. governmental securities group collapse and the Continental Bank problem, are proof that enterprise recording and reporting of financial data may still be inadequate at describing the financial reality of enterprise organizations.

Financial data is adequate for enterprise organizations for a number of reasons. First, enterprise organizations are, or can be, artificially separated into single purpose units, each with clear objectives that directly relate to maximizing profits. Traditional Generally Accepted Accounting Principles (GAAP) are designed to provide reliable data to access an enterprise organization's performance in terms of efficiency and effectiveness of maximizing profits. Of course, organizational performance of an enterprise can be expressed in monetary terms. Private sector GAAP data is acceptable for use in the many models developed to analyze and explain enterprise performance because the information from the models is used in terms of assessing the organization's performance to maximize profits. As a result, enterprise data that are reported according to standards developed by financial (accounting) interests work fine in economics, systems and policy models that use profit as the criteria for assessment. This mutual usefulness of data is not necessarily going to be the case with public sector data.

Local government organizations are complex, multi-purpose units with unclear objectives, great variations in organizational structure and interruptable administrative expertise. Local government outputs are delivered in a monopolistic environment that is greatly affected by politics. To date, there are very few, if any, clear objectives available to assess the efficiency and effectiveness of local government activities, functions or organizations. GFOA in its 1984 Intermediate Governmental Accounting manual states that: "Inefficient and ineffective governments do not 'go out of business'; they just raise their taxes" (pp. 2-5).

Governmental GAAP does not make any claim to provide data that is useful as an assessment tool to judge the performance of a local government organization. Local government performance is not usually expressed in monetary terms. Therefore, public sector GAAP data are not likely to be usable in the new models being developed to analyze and explain local government performance. This is because the information from the models is used to determine the organization's performance in terms of social priorities, political policies, tax policies, etc. Using existing local government financial and non-financial data, without substantial validation in public sector models is likely to have very negative effects.

Are rules, standards and specific definitions needed for non-financial local government data? What's wrong with using what's available? The answer is that if a model builder uses existing local government non-financial, and some financial data in its existing form, and without carefully verifying its validity for the purpose of the model, the results are as likely to be completely wrong as completely right. Experiences in Iowa working with local governments is the basis for this conclusion. As attempts have been made to implement improved management practices and policy analysis programs, a very large portion of the time and resources have to be set aside to get a local government unit's data in a form that is usable in the project.

In the ACIR report, Financing Public Physical Infrastructure, (1984a) the source of the information in a number of graphs, tables and narratives was reportedly from unpublished estimates, or unpublished material. A footnote questioned the validity of the information because of omissions, irrelevant enclosures or unclear definitions. This is not a criticism of the commission staff. The information they have provided is as valid as possible, given the availability and accuracy of the data.

Finally, macro-models that report their results in terms of *average costs* can tolerate more variation in the raw data without adversely affecting results than can micro-models that attempt to identify *marginal costs, marginal benefits,* etc., of specific organizations, functions or activities. Invalid and unreliable local government data may discredit the results of all models. If the results of any model, based on invalid data, lead policy-makers to adopt a public policy that is assessed to be counter-productive, the status of all models and model builders will be damaged.

If any model is going to affect a political decision-making process, the information generated by the model must be very defensible. If the data, assumptions, analysis and conclusions are not all openly defensible, the opposition will discredit the entire input and output of the model as unclear and uncertain.

What actions can model builders and users take to improve the validity of the local government financial and non-financial data for models? Possible actions vary from attempts to change the attitude of local government record keepers toward professional status to the formation of a group to establish formal rules for recording and reporting non-financial local government data. Possibly, local government units that conform to the rules and standards should be awarded a Certificate of Conformance for non-financial data as well as financial data.

To initiate the movement for non-financial data in local government, a document needs to be developed that inventories, classifies, and defines/describes the various models that presently exist that use non-financial public sector data. This document should cover all aspects of each model but should emphasize the form, type and nature of the data that are used in the model. The information in the documents should be as complete as possible, including any common assumptions that are made about the data when used in specific models. Information that would be useful to computer users, such as should the value be integer or real, would also be helpful. The purpose of this document would be to provide the basis for a published manual, A Preface to Standard Definitions, Classifications and Assumptions Covering Non-Financial Data in local government records.

NON-FINANCIAL DATA IN LOCAL GOVERNMENT RECORDS

The second phase of this project might be to develop suggested rules, standards, procedures, and structures with detailed instruction on how to record and report data. Once these principles have been refined and survived an informal peer review, they should form the basis for university classes, extension short courses and the like. The purpose of this phase is to initiate the formation of a group of people professionally trained to record and report non-financial data in conformance with Generally Accepted Data Recording Principles (GADRP).

Another dimension of the movement is a general education of government record keepers and policy-makers on the importance and usefulness of models and reliable data. The purpose of this activity will be to inform the record keeper that the data that they work with will be used for very important analysis. Many local government officials presently believe, and for valid reasons, that much of the non-financial data that they record and report will never be checked, validated or used for any purpose. Therefore, the guiding principle of many local government officials when preparing non-financial, and some financial, reports is to get it off the desk and into the mail or file. The quality criteria is one of avoiding rejection for incompleteness. This factor, combined with high turnover of government officials that deal directly with recording and reporting local government data, makes consistency and comparability of data almost non-existent.

Most local government officials could be persuaded to accept new rules and standards for recording and reporting non-financial governmental data if they knew that the resulting data would be put to good use. In some cases the local government officials will make better use of the data if they acquire a complete understanding of the data and what it represents. Retirement and turnover would phase out the resistors. Vacancies left by these actions would be filled by people trained to apply the new rules and standards. The transition will take about the same amount of time no matter when the transition begins. Why not start soon?

Finally, there is no use starting something if provisions are not made to perpetuate in the future. Perpetuation consumes resources, requires personal interest and determination and institutional commitment. Therefore, a Model Data Recording and Reporting Foundation is needed to collect and manage resources. It would be governed by a Model Data Recording and Reporting Board (MDRRB) that would develop and promote Generally Accepted Data Reporting Principles (GADRP). This group could work in conjunction with a National Council in Non-Financial Data Keeping (NCN-FDK), etc. These groups and documents will carry forward the effort suggested here. The goal is to get non-financial data preparation on an equal status with accounting organizations and documents that declare the rules and standards that govern the recording and reporting of financial data. An objective is to achieve the goal with a minimum amount of record keeping and report filing by local government officials. Adding more records and reports to their already heavy load only invites more *questionable* data.

The preceding proposal may be more elaborate than is justified by the present condition. If the incidence of useless or misleading public sector model results were very high and widespread, someone else would have identified this problem before now. However, the incidence of useless or misleading public sector model results is not widespread because the development of these models is just beginning, not because the present non-financial data is valid, reliable and in a usable form. Right now most of the data on local infrastructure are under the control of public works engineers, recorded by construction project and stored in a tube someplace.

The author is fortunate to live in a city that emphasizes accurate records for non-financial data and storing it so that it is retrievable. Using this information, a consulting firm prepared an "Infrastructure Modeling System". An example of this information includes: (1) A detailed map of the complete sanitary sewer system. The inventory data includes line depth, size, slope and material information. This information is in journal or map form and when the project began was not coded for use in computer applications. (2) A detailed map of the storm sewer system is not complete. Approximately 10% of the system will require field work to obtain depth, size, slope, connections and component material. Additional field work will also be necessary to delineate the size and nature of drainage basins. (3) A skeletonized water distribution system, which includes eight-inch or larger water mains, presently exists in a computer model. Similar information is available for transportation, electric distributions and gas distribution. This is an example of the best that a model builder can expect to find.

The author is presently involved in projects in two counties that are referred to as *unsewered*. One project involves 40-50 residences in each of two incorporated communities that have a wastewater management problem. The other project involves over 200 residences in an unincorporated area that also has a wastewater management problem. The similarities in these two situations is that the residences are between 7 and 20 years old and hardly a single owner can even locate his septic tank, much less describe it in the detail necessary to do a complete analysis of the situation. Right now this is an engineering problem, but it could very well be a part of an infrastructure problem. The data in this case would have to be acquired by field work, recorded, coded and validated before it would be usable in a model.

One hundred Iowa municipalities are learning to use the International City Management Association's (1981, 1984) Financial Trend Monitoring System (FTMS). FTMS uses mostly financial data, but it also uses some non-financial data. City officials spend much time getting their data and financial records in a form where the needed information can be input into the computer program.

All these experiences contribute to another conclusion. Many local government officials do not understand the significance of financial and non-financial data, or what aspects of their government the data is intended to describe or represent. Without this intuitive understanding, there is little chance that record keeping officials can or will detect their own errors.

Non-financial public sector data may not be the only form of unstructured, poorly defined and inconsistent data. There are still some problems with public sector financial data that government GAAP does not solve. One is in the area of beginning balances. Some reports include earmarked, reserved resources and others do not. Some include balances of capital projects and others do not. These two differences can greatly affect the apparent financial condition of the unit of government. Government GAAP does not require that depreciation be a part of the governmental fund general ledger accounts. Government GAAP does not cover data relating to the financial dimensions of infrastructure. "ASLGU (Auditors of State and Local Governmental Units) also permitted governments the option of excluding from the General Fixed Assets Group, their public domain or 'infrastructure' general fixed assets -- roads, bridges, curbs and gutters, streets and sidewalks, drainage systems, lighting systems, and similar assets that are immoveable and of value only to the government" (GFOA, 1984). I am sure that presently most government officials will exercise that option and leave the infrastructure data (financial and non-financial) out of all records and reports. Those that do record this data will do so in a variety of ways.

Models can and will provide valuable understanding of complex local government situations if the models are theoretically sound and if they process data that reliably represents the realities of the local government situation and is recorded and reported so that the data are consistent and comparable over time and among units of local government. Each of the two elements, sound models and reliable data, deserve attention if we are to be successful in aiding infrastructure decision-making.

11
New Directions and Challenges for Modeling of Community Infrastructure Analysis

Theodore R. Alter

Chapters 7, 8, 9, and 10 present an overview and critique of important models and approaches for community infrastructure analysis and associated data issues. Chapters 8 and 9 briefly review the development of community impact models, provide a comprehensive, useful set of criteria for evaluating these models, and outline several emerging challenges for community impact analysis. One of these challenges is an apparent growing demand for socioeconomic impact analysis for local, community-specific decisions and public service and facility planning. Chapter 7 reviews the development, use, and future of community service budgeting analysis, one possible technique for addressing community-specific planning issues and decision-making needs. In Chapter 10 we are reminded, with some conviction, that local financial and nonfinancial data are often suspect, and, to the extent such data are used as inputs to community impact and budget analyses, these analyses may also be suspect.

This chapter stresses: 1) the opportunity to assist local decision-makers, especially those in rural areas, with community service and facility planning and decision-making through community impact and budget analyses; and 2) several cautions important in conducting these analyses.

AN IMPORTANT OPPORTUNITY

The opportunity for land-grant research and extension faculty to assist local government officials and other citizens in rural areas with community service and facility planning through community impact and budget analyses is significant. Here are some reasons why.

1. Many rural communities have important community service and facility needs. The needs reflect repair and maintenance problems, but also, and perhaps of greater importance, problems in service and facility development. These needs often translate into demands for planning and analysis assistance.

2. Land-grant university research and extension faculty have established and maintained a comparative advantage, or niche, over time in working with people and problems in rural areas, and many faculty have expertise in and experience working with community service and facility issues and analyses.

3. Helping local government officials and other citizens to more effectively deal with their community service and facility problems has potential for building and enhancing support for land-grant university research and extension activities. This potential is a reality in several states; Oklahoma, Iowa, and Texas come immediately to mind. It is important, before designing research and extension programs around approaches and models used in these or other states, to learn from those who have been successful in building support how they have done it.

4. Helping local government officials and others with community service and facility planning and analysis has potential to open up additional extension education, and perhaps research, opportunities.

A concern sometimes raised from an extension perspective regarding community impact and budget analyses is "won't involvement in these analyses give us too much of a service or technical assistance as compared to an educational orientation in our programming?" This is a legitimate question suggesting a possible outcome that may or may not be comfortable philosophically for certain individuals or state Cooperative Extension Services.

This perspective seems a rather conservative one. Using community impact and budget analyses, as they are used by researchers and extension educators in Oklahoma and other states, involves basic community economics education as well as servicing specific planning and analysis needs.

One aspect of an extension education program associated with community impact and budget analyses, local government fiscal trend monitoring or fiscal distress early-warning systems, and similar approaches might be a special emphasis on the transfer of "technological software." Such an educational program would focus on building the capacity of local government officials and other decision-makers to understand, implement, interpret, and update these approaches and models with little or no outside assistance. A related program might involve helping these decision-makers assess their technical assistance needs and options related to community service and facility planning and analysis. Another audience for such programs would be Extension agents who work with local government and community decision-makers.

These approaches and models can be means of opening up other educational opportunities for extension in the same, related or even unrelated, subject-matters. The educational opportunities are there, constrained only by the programming priorities and resources of individual state Cooperative Extension Services and Agricultural Experiment Stations.

CAUTIONS

While helping local government officials and others in rural areas with community service and facility planning through community impact and budget analyses affords a significant opportunity, carrying out such analyses requires caution. Several important cautions are noted below; there are certainly others that would extend this list.

1. In model conceptualization, development, and implementation, it is important to maintain a user-orientation. This orientation means addressing user planning and decision-making objectives, and helping users better understand all aspects of a model and its application. This is an old saw, but it is crucially important for the effectiveness and decision maker acceptance of community impact and budget analyses. It is easy though to get caught up in theory, methods, data and technology, and forget the local decision-maker.

2. For community analyses, data derived from national, state, or regional data bases must be used with care. Such data are necessary to run the models when local, community-specific data are not available, or not available at reasonable cost. These data make it possible to conduct analyses in many more situations and to respond more quickly to decision maker requests than would be possible using only community-specific data. But, in the context of individual communities and local governments, it is important to determine whether using non-local data provides a distorted picture of local conditions and to assess the implications of any distortions for decision making. The appropriateness of national, state, and

regional data should be checked with knowledgeable community officials and leaders, and community-specific data should be used when possible. Balancing the mix of non-local and community-specific data in light of the needs for reasonable data collection costs, timely response to local decision makers, and accurate projections of local impacts requires careful consideration.

3. Using financial and non-financial data from local resources often poses considerable problems. One problem involves local government record-keeping systems. Are the variables in these systems defined so that available data measure the concepts and variables in our socio-economic models and can be used to operationalize those models? This is not always the case. Another problem involves the local government record-keeping process itself, one of the key issues emphasized in Chapter 10. The great variability in judgments and technical skills of record-keepers, especially in small, rural communities, affects the reliability of data available in local records.

4. From an extension perspective, using a model or approach developed for one state in another state requires great caution, and must not be undertaken lightly. Such transfer and use is going to involve respecifying variables, reestimating cost data, recalibrating coefficients, and other adjustments to make a model usable and useful in a different state context. These activities will require a substantial research effort and commitment of resources, effort and commitment that will also be necessary to update the model over time once it is in use. Those ready to make the extension commitment to community service and facility programming using impact and budget analysis models must be ready to make the research commitment, too.

SUMMARY

Assisting local government officials and other citizens in rural areas with community service and facility planning is an important opportunity. For research and extension faculty at land-grant universities, it is an opportunity to help local leaders address critical community needs and to build support for research and extension activities. Successfully pursuing this opportunity through community impact and budget analyses requires, at a minimum, special attention to user needs; data level, availability and cost, and reliability; and willingness to undertake a substantial, long-run, integrated research and extension effort.

PART III: Infrastructure Investment Decision-Making: Case Studies

12
Local Government Needs for Infrastructure Planning: The Texas Example

Michael D. Woods

The 1980s present a period of challenges for communities in the United States. Infrastructure planning, development, and maintenance often lead the list of challenges and concerns. The purpose of this chapter is to discuss local government needs based on observations and experiences in Texas. The needs will be related to extension/research activities in Rural Economic Development. What are we doing right? What areas for future work should receive the benefit of limited resources? These are important questions concerning a topic affecting all communities.

THE TEXAS ECONOMY AND RESULTING COMMUNITY DEVELOPMENT

Communities in Texas come in many sizes and have diverse economic bases. During the 1970s and early 1980s the growth patterns have generally been upward with some notable exceptions. Of the total 254 Texas counties, 210 (83 percent) gained in population from 1970 to 1980 (Skrabanek and Murdock, 1981). The largest Texas county in 1980 was Harris County (Houston) with a population of 2,410,000. The smallest county was Loving County in West Texas with a population of 91. Counties of all sizes fell between the two extremes. There were 1,195 incorporated and census-designated places in Texas in 1980 (Murdock, et al, 1981). Of the 992 places which existed in both 1970 and 1980, 82 percent (809) increased in population. This growth is occurring in both large and small cities and places. Note that with all this growth occurring there were still 44 counties in Texas that experienced a population decline.

The type of community and existing economic base can have some influence on a local government's planning needs. Several authors have classified communities by economic base or other category (Doeksen, et. al. 1974; Ross, et. al. 1984). The following categories represent many of the communities in Texas: trade center, resource extraction, agricultural base, satellite, recreation/retirement, and other. All types of communities are faced with the challenge of providing adequate infrastructure (services and facilities). In many cases, however, the type of community influences the specific needs or the local governments ability to respond to needs.

Trade centers vary in size and level of services provided. They often have a reasonably diversified economy and are interested in retaining what they have. Sales potential studies, sales leakage and trade area analysis are often areas of concern given they represent potential tax revenues. *Resource extraction communities* generally fall in two categories in Texas: oil and gas and lignite/coal mining. The communities that depend on oil and gas production are at the mercy of forces outside their control. Instability makes planning difficult and of course the present short-term projections show a downward trend for oil prices. These communities are concerned with diversification opportunities and need to understand the cyclical patterns they are experiencing. Large scale coal mines and related power plants present an additional problem. These developments often occur in rural areas and bring large, rapid impacts on the local economy. An understanding of these impacts is essential for the local government entities. *Agricultural based economies* occur most frequently in West Texas. This type of community is of special interest in rural development since there is a strong two-way linkage: many farms depend on off-farm income in the non-agriculture sectors to survive and many communities depend on a strong agriculture sector to remain economically stable. Wide fluctuations in agricultural prices and income directly affect the agri-businesses and local community. In addition, the declining water table in the Plains area has implications for the type of farming activity and level of activity. *Satellite communities* exist in abundance in Texas. In fact, given the tremendous growth of Dallas, Houston, Austin and San Antonio, we now have satellite counties. These are bedroom communities where people reside while commuting to a job in a nearby (or sometimes distant) employment center. Many of these satellite communities are rural areas being impacted for the first time. Local officials are struggling to provide the required services and facilities for the new residents. *Recreation/retirement communities* take on the special characteristics of the immigrating population. The age of the new residents has implications for service needs. The seasonal nature of some residents also presents a challenge for planning. "Snowbirds" from Northern States often spend six months along the Texas Gulf Coast and the remainder of the year in their home state. This affects capacity requirements for local services. The final category listed is <u>other.</u> This includes communities which have a mixture of the above characteristics as many do. Also, there are some communities which are simply dying with no economic base. This brief overview of Texas communities emphasizes the wide range of government needs which result from the diverse types of communities. There are several needs, however, which emerge as important.

LOCAL GOVERNMENT NEEDS

The first need that comes to mind relates to existing historical data at the county and community level. Government officials and employees are interested in utilizing this type of information for planning purposes. Extension specialists and researchers can assist in locating the data, compiling the data from many diverse sources, and interpreting the data.

Another area of government information needs is related to the supply of infrastructure. Cost data for alternative systems is an important area. The computerized budgets used in many states provide a powerful tool for this type of analysis. As federal funds decrease, the issue of financing options also becomes important for local governments.

Governments also need to understand the demand side of infrastructure planning. Projections of future infrastructure needs are frequently requested whether it be for sewer systems, schools, water systems or a combination of service needs. The various impact models discussed in Part II of this book answer many of these types of questions.

A third area of government needs falls in the management expertise category. That is, as population grows and available public funds decrease, the ability to manage resources well becomes more important. Demand estimates and cost estimates are emphasized in economic analysis of infrastructure. However, there is a need to remember that infrastructure must be managed well after construction. Personnel management and record-keeping are examples of government needs in this area.

A final category of need is a complete understanding of financial alternatives. As has been mentioned, local governments are caught in a cost/revenue squeeze. Increased population, regulations, inflation all raise the expense of providing adequate services. Decreased federal funds and a general atmosphere of fiscal conservatism limit available funds. Governments need a good understanding of the implications of user fees, public private partnerships, contracting and other alternatives.

FUTURE NEEDS FROM THE TEXAS PERSPECTIVE

It is apparent that there are many opportunities for the Land Grant System to assist local government. The challenge with limited resources is to maximize output/payoff. The following are needs and opportunities which seem to stand out.

There is much to be done in the area of community economics. Understanding the relationships and forces at work is not only an academic effort but, if delivered properly, greatly aids the local community. In addition, many parameters such as multipliers, demand equations, etc., support the larger impact models used. Hustedde, Shaffer and Pulver (1984) summarized many of the techniques we need to continually refine and convey to community leaders.

The community service budgets provide an excellent summary of need estimates, construction costs and operating costs. The coefficients need to be updated at reasonable intervals. In addition, more research related to regional comparisons needs to be conducted to assist in transfer efforts.

Many types of impact models are also available. Issues to be addressed include use for declining economies, incorporation of risk factors, transfer and adaptation, and micro-computer applications.

After reviewing the many types of communities and associated needs it is apparent that no single model provides answers for all questions. It is also apparent that funding support for these activities is limited. Another point that is driven home is the need for close working relations between research and Extension. Extension's role is very important in providing close contact with the community and as a delivery mechanism. The avoidance of duplication is very important and writings such as this book serve a useful purpose.

SUMMARY

This chapter has summarized the major types of communities found in Texas and their associated needs. There is much that Extension Specialists and Researchers can do (Nelson and Doeksen, 1984). There is a need to listen to the group we are attempting to serve and be sure our product is not only desired by our clientele, but also available in a usable form.

13
Assisting Local Government Needs: The Nevada Experience

Thomas R. Harris

During the decade of the 1970s, Nevada was the fastest growing state in the nation with population increasing from 493,000 in 1970 to 806,900 in 1980 or an increase in population of 63.6 percent in ten years. The two metropolitan counties of Clark (Las Vegas) and Washoe (Reno) realized a population increase of 66.2 percent during the 1970s while the non-metropolitan counties of Nevada had a 52.7 percent increase in population during the past decade. Both urban and rural counties have continued to grow during the 1980s and are projected to continue population growth in the future.

As population has grown, demands for community services in the rural areas of Nevada have expanded. Many of these rural counties are located in sparsely populated areas of the state and have experienced rapid and sometimes cyclical demands upon their community services.

The major activities which have contributed to growth of rural Nevada counties are:

1. Mining Activities;

2. Construction and Operation of Coal-Fired Electric Power Plants;

3. Expansion of the Rural Gaming Industry;

4. Department of Energy Activities; and

5. Department of Defense Activities.

The rural counties of Nevada unlike the metropolitan counties do not have planning staffs and adequate information to determine current and future consequences of economic and population growth or decline. In addition, rural community governments usually lag behind their larger metropolitan counterparts in adopting information technologies which could help decision-makers plan for changes in their area.

With these demands, rural counties in Nevada have requested assistance from the Nevada Extension and Experiment Station in developing plans to meet current and future community service demands. The method used by the Nevada Extension and Experiment Station is to develop community service budgets and use microcomputer spreadsheets to perform "what if" games.

COMMUNITY SERVICE BUDGETS AND TRANSFERABILITY

Public or community service budgets are one tool to evaluate current and future rural community services. In order to develop these budgets, separate demand (usage) and cost data reflecting the situation of each location are required.

In comparison, the budgeting procedures are fairly standard over regions. A public service budget can be viewed as (and in manual methods is actually) a blank form with associated instructions. Once the initial data requirements - blank spaces - are filled, the instructions, entailing certain calculations and a set of formulas, are followed to work progressively down the form until completed.

The construction of community service budgets by hand, however, is very time consuming and is prone to errors. Also to perform sensitivity analysis or "what if" games through hand developed budgets is almost out of question because of time and the probability of errors.

In 1973, the "Great Plains Project" was initiated to assist local decision-makers in the Great Plains region. A major product of the project was the development of computerized community service budgets. Algorithms, analogous to the blank forms in hand budgeting, were developed to estimate costs and returns for selected community services, including water systems (Nelson and Mostafavi, 1981), emergency medical services (Hill and Doeksen, 1981a), rural clinics (Doeksen, et. al. 1981a), fire protection (Nelson and Doeksen, 1982), sewage treatment (Nelson, et. al. 1982), rental apartments (Nelson and Mostafavi, 1982), transportation systems for the elderly (Hill and Doeksen, 1981b), and mobile home parks (Nelson and Gilbert, 1983).

With the success of these computerized community service budgets, other land grant institutions such as the University of Nevada Reno requested copies of these computerized algorithms. However, as these algorithms were requested and applied at other institutions, the issue of transference evolved. In specifically addressing computerized community service budgets, there are at least three dimensions of transferability to be considered: (1) budgeting methods or procedures, (2) data and parameters, and (3) software.

IS THE BUDGETING METHOD TRANSFERABLE?

The use of budgeting as a decision-making tool is widespread in economic and business analyses. The general procedure for preparing community service budgets is simple. On the supply or cost side of a service, one needs to account for the inputs into the process and to apply the prices of these inputs to derive costs. On the usage or demand side, these budgets are typically driven by population delineated by age, sex, or other characteristics. As more detail are specified for either the supply or demand side of these budgets, complexity increases. In general, the method or procedure for conducting community service budgets is transferable.

ARE THE DATA AND PARAMETERS TRANSFERABLE?

Data and parameters are less transferable than the budgeting method. In many cases, data or parameters from other areas should be verified and if deemed necessary, modified before local use. Data peculiar to a region particularly cost data must be collected or estimated by the user. As in the case of Nevada, the cost data in the Oklahoma State budgets were updated through interviews of firms supplying materials to the rural community service and when appropriate through the state Farmers' Home Administration office. Also, certain demand parameters such as in the case of water consumption were revised through interviews of rural water companies and the state of Nevada's Public Service Office.

IS SOFTWARE TRANSFERABLE?

As a general rule, problems with software transferability will exist as long as different manufacturers develop different products and as long as different end users have different goals. As mentioned earlier as the Oklahoma State University computerized community service budgets gained popularity, other institutions requested copies of the programs. However, the Oklahoma State University algorithms were written in PL/1 language compatible to Oklahoma State's computer. If the other institution did not have an IBM computer and/or PL1 interface, the user was faced with either reprogramming the algorithms or not trying to transfer the programs at all.

In sum, the transfer between mainframes is difficult. A few cases may require some modifications, but most will involve considerable resource cost in recoding to the appropriate host language. Another alternative in reprogramming is not to use the mainframe computer at all. Instead use the microcomputer which can fit on the desk top and can be carried to rural areas. This procedure along with using spreadsheet software has been used by the Nevada Agricultural Extension and Experiment Station.

TRANSFERENCE THROUGH MICROCOMPUTERS: USE OF SPREADSHEETS

Like many states, Nevada Extension and Experiment Station requested copies of the Oklahoma State University computerized community service budgets. Since the University of Nevada Reno does not have an IBM mainframe computer, it was decided to reprogram these community service budgets not for use by the mainframe computer but into spreadsheet software such as LOTUS 123.

Spreadsheets make budgeting less transparent because users are able to see and personally create or edit the relationships leading up to the final product. The ability of spreadsheets such as LOTUS 123 to easily edit and derive a final product makes "what if" games possible which is beneficial to the rural decision-makers. Also in using LOTUS 123, graphs of the budget results can be made and presented. The graphics package has proved to be very useful in showing rural decision-makers the costs, returns, and/or subsidies required for alternative community service provision.

14
The Pennsylvania Agricultural-Access Program

William R. Gillis and James G. Beierlein

Maintenance, improvements and construction of roads and bridges is the largest infrastructure investment category for both state and local governments. As dollars available for financing publicly provided goods has become more limited, the importance of targeting investments toward roads and bridges most crucial for the movement of people and products has grown in importance.

In Pennsylvania, an Agricultural Transportation Task Force was formed to: (1) identify the roads and bridges in the state that were most critical to agricultural transportation; and (2) identify the obstructions on that network. The task force included representatives from a variety of federal, state and local government, and farm organizations. The Pennsylvania Department of Transportation was the principal facilitator for this effort.

The task group decided that the most effective way to identify essential rural roads and their obstructions was to draw on the local knowledge of farm and planning organizations in each county. The Pennsylvania Cooperative Extension Service helped arrange a meeting between officials of the Pennsylvania Deartment of Transportation and the agricultural leadership in each of Pennsylvania's 67 counties. Leaders in each county were asked to identify the essential rural access roads, key highways, and the obstructions on this network. This network of key rural roads was dubbed the "Agri-Access Network."

PROJECT RESULTS

As a result of the meetings, nearly 600 obstructions were identified by the agricultural community. The most prevalent restrictions on the network are the 489 bridge obstructions, 312 of which are restricted with weight limits. Prior to the study, 88 of the bridge obstructions were already included on the state's major bridge improvement program. Additional bridges are now being considered for improvement either as future capital projects or as county maintenance projects. As a direct result of the Agricultural Transportation Task Force's efforts, $58 million of the $130 million approved in the latest update of the state's road and bridge improvement program was allocated to repair 49 bridges on the Agri-Access Network.

The study also generated information on the primary agricultural activities in each county. Agricultural representatives identified over 2400 generator locations of heavy truck loads such as dairies, processing plants, feed mills, fertilizer plants, etc. This information is helpful in defining the relationships between the agricultural activities, and the road and bridge network.

ADVANTAGES OF THE AGRI-ACCESS APPROACH

A major positive aspect of the agri-access approach is that it facilitates a good working relationship between agricultural interest groups, local, federal and state governments in jointly solving common transportation problems. The communication links which have been established in each county will hopefully continue and provide for a better understanding between the transportation and agriculture sectors for many years to come.

A second major advantage of the approach is its simplicity. No major data beyond that collected through public input or extensive modeling is required. Consequently, the approach can be implemented relatively quickly and at a low cost.

Third, the model provides substantial flexibility with respect to criteria used in setting priorities among alternative road and bridge projects. This is important because every community faces different situations. For example, isolated rural counties face different problems and solutions than more urbanized areas. Counties dominated by the wood products or mineral industries face special situations due to the temporary nature of hauling routes. Local task groups are able to take factors such as these into account when making decisions about transportation improvements.

Finally, the model is easily transferable to other states. Indeed this was one of the primary considerations in designing the methodology used for the Pennsylvania Agri-Access Network project.

DISADVANTAGES OF THE APPROACH

While the simplicity of the Agri-Access model is a major strength, it can also be viewed as a weakness. In Pennsylvania decisions by local task groups concerning most needed network improvements were based primarily upon their knowledge of problems faced by local agricultural producers and other major rural road users. It is easy to think of a variety of social, economic and technical information which if developed, analyzed and made available to the task group, would aid in their decision-making. The landgrant system, due to its substantial research base is in an excellent position to aid decision-makers by making available relevant research findings through the Extension network. It should be recognized, however, that this would substantially add to the time and cost associated with carrying out the project.

A second concern is that the chairperson of the local task group (usually the county agent) must have effective group process skills in order to ensure the credibility of the groups decisions and recommendations. In particular, he or she must provide opportunities for a wide variety of community interest groups to provide input into the decision and ensure that choices are made in a democratic manner. The agent as leader of the task group must not be in a position of advocating one project over another. The major implication is that Extension Staff education should include training in group process skills as well as technical skills.

EDUCATION ON TRANSPORTATION ISSUES IS COMPLEMENTARY WITH ONGOING COMMUNITY DEVELOPMENT EXTENSION PROGRAMS

Community development extension education programs seek to enhance the social and economic vitality of rural communities. Transportation has played and will continue to play a key role in maintaining business profitability and mobility in rural America. Freight transportation brings production inputs and consumer products into rural areas and carries locally produced products to major markets. Passenger transit provide mobility for rural residents and accessibility to the economic and cultural activities clustered in the downtowns of both rural and urban areas. But that mobility and accessibility is endangered by a plethora of rural transportation problems such as deregulation; rail, air and bus line abandonments; and a road and bridge system desperately in need of repair and replacement.

Extension educators have an important role to play in helping rural communities to remedy transportation needs. The Agri-Access model outlined in this chapter is one of several different educational models which could be followed. However, it is believed that the simplicity and ease of implementing the Agri-Access approach are major advantages.

15
Infrastructure Needs in South Carolina: Factors to Consider in Allocating State Resources to Local Areas

Mark S. Henry

Researchers at Clemson work mostly with state agencies on infrastructure related issues. Recent and current research projects include a statewide assessment of infrastructure needs, a state funded water resources project to identify current and long-run requirements for investment in water systems, and a state funded assessment of the ability of South Carolina communities to finance new investment in sewer and water systems. The relationship between the research faculty and various state agencies and legislative committees has developed primarily because of the history of local decision-making in South Carolina.

"Until the State Constitution was revised in 1975, local governments existed in South Carolina as hardly more than nominal entities. It was said that Columbia (the state capital) was the county seat of every county in South Carolina, and in so far as financial matters were concerned, that statement was particularly true. The county budgets, or supply bills, for each county were enacted by the General Assembly, and the functions that counties could perform were quite limited. Municipalities had somewhat greater autonomy on budgetary matters, but nevertheless were (and still are) constrained with regard to taxing powers and the ability to annex adjacent areas.

The rather severe restrictions on the powers of counties that existed prior to 1975 were the principal factors in the creation of a multitude of special purpose districts. South Carolina counties, for example, were prohibited from spending monies for parks and recreational programs, from providing fire protection services, and from establishing water supply systems. Since urbanizing areas outside the boundaries of established municipalities often had pressing needs for such services, special acts were passed by the General Assembly creating special purpose districts to perform these functions. The home rule Amendment to the state Constitution enacted in 1975 now provides that counties can perform such functions, but the special purpose districts created prior to 1975 continue to exist. Moreover, they have become a significant political force steadfastly resisting any effort to eliminate or restrict their operations" (Hite, et. al. 1983).

This history of top down planning in South Carolina and the lack of county extension activities largely account for the preponderance of infrastructure related work being carried out at the state level. In this chapter a description of one of the infrastructure projects currently in progress at Clemson will be made.

SELECTED INFRASTRUCTURE IN SOUTH CAROLINA

A contract with the South Carolina Governor's Office of Community and Intergovernmental Affairs to help evaluate financial aspects of infrastructure investment in water and sewer systems has been established. The methodology and data base that will aid that office in the evaluation of local requests for water-sewer systems levels is being developed. There are two major characteristics being considered in the analyses; one is the need to assist in the identification of communities with severe water supply or pollution problems (information may be obtained from a related study of water supply systems in South Carolina), and the other is a need to assess the financial condition of these communities.

With respect to the financial end of the problems, the task is twofold: (1) to provide information to the decision-makers regarding the ability of the community to finance its own system and, (2) to evaluate the fiscal effort the community has made in the past.

With respect to task (1), estimation of simple statistics such as total local debt, growth rate of total debt, debt service, and total debt per capita are being looked at to evaluate the likely ability of the community to go to the bond markets and obtain financing. Of course, more detailed analysis of local credit worthiness along the lines of the Standard and Poor or Moody's procedures for municipal bond ratings will be considered. The thrust beyond financial ratios will be to use data already available to assess the prospects for population and economic growth of communities. This will provide an estimate of the long-run per capita debt bond that might be expected.

A related task has been to help the Governor's Office to determine the need for fiscal assistance to local areas through the small cities

Community Development Block Grant (CDBG) program. A measure of fiscal capacity and fiscal effort that is recommended by the Advisory Commission on Intergovernmental Affairs (ACIR) is being used. This representative tax system (RTS) methodology has been used in various forms in six states in the South (TACIR, 1984). Also, it has been recommended for use in South Carolina (Fort, 1985). RTS tabulations will enable the decision-makers to assess the relative effort local communities have been making to raise area source revenues prior to asking for state subsidies.

ADEQUACY OF THEORY, DATA AND INFORMATION DELIVERY IN SOUTH CAROLINA

At this point in time, in South Carolina there is minimal extension programming to provide technical assistance to local officials about infrastructure planning and finance. There are, for example, no educational programs in place to aid small cities in the area of record-keeping and accounting techniques. This is ironic since South Carolina has a good record of training county extension workers on the uses of computer technology and maintenance of records of county extension offices.

There is a need for a data base on local government expenditures and revenues on current and capital accounts that allows valid inter-area comparisons of local fiscal capacity and effort. Because accounting procedures may vary by local jurisdiction such a standardized data base is difficult to obtain even with access to all the records.

There has been some work toward a viable data base via a cooperative research project between the U.S. Census Bureau, the Division of Research and Statistics of the S.C. Budget and Control Board and our department. There are now four years of data on all counties and most cities in the state regarding a wide range of revenues and expenditures.

These data are subject to several verification steps. First, the Office of Revenue Sharing (ORS) of the Treasury Department and the government section of the Census Bureau cooperate to examine the forms for consistency between reporting years. Second, there is now a single audit provision such that any government with more than $100,000 of any federal grants must submit to annual audits (Hogan, 1984-85). If auditors find "auditing exceptions," these exceptions (discrepancy between GRS data and audit data) are reported to Census for adjustments to the data base. Third, ORS does not allow frequent changes in reporting from cash basis to modified accrual, etc. Thus, these data appear to fulfill some of the potential suggested by Peterson in 1977 (p. 308).

Plans for further data consistency tests to assess the reliability of various data elements are being considered. Fortunately, the data are detailed enough to provide some insight into the fiscal capacity and effort of communities. For infrastructure purposes we have an accounting of the current debt position of the communities. By merging these data with local population and per capita income data we can start to provide some answers to the questions posed on our checklist of rules of thumb for credit worthiness of South Carolina communities. This in turn will allow more enlightened judgment on the relative merits of infrastructure grant applications.

IMPACT MODELS

In South Carolina, our impact model work (a Clayton-type model, Henry, et. al. 1981) was partly intended to enhance infrastructure planning by yielding estimates of new resident population required to fill jobs generated by new industrial, commercial or residential development. This hope goes largely unfulfilled to date. However, some of the larger cities (Greenville-Spartanburg) have expressed interest in using the model in their planning departments. Still, most uses of our impact model have been to simulate impacts of rural industrial location or to assess the benefits of new residential developments. Such uses were employed to evaluate proposed legislation and for loan applications for physical infrastructure in an ex post sense.

Perhaps the most effective way to make models more useful to decision-makers, in our area, is to illustrate to state agencies their potential for evaluating current and projected financial conditions for local areas requesting infrastructure subsidies. Certainly the ability to simulate the impact of new infrastructure investment on per capita debt loads under alternative development scenarios is of interest to state funding agencies. (See Henry, 1980 for a discussion of measuring the benefits of more accurate information for such planning.)

THEORY FOR ALLOCATION OF STATE RESOURCES TO LOCAL AREAS FOR INFRASTRUCTURE

At the broadest level, we would like to know the social benefits and costs of public investment in community infrastructure. However, there are complex intertemporal income distribution implications involved in any sort of state financial subsidy of local infrastructure investment. Welfare economics notions of optimality in resource allocation are of limited use once income transfers between individuals, regions, and generations are introduced. This is especially true for evaluating investment in infrastructure designed to prevent pollution externalities in a multiregion setting. (See Cummings and Schulze, 1978 for one attempt to provide an allocation rule for boomtowns.)

   Thus, in deciding the extent of state subsidies of local government's infrastructure, economic theory may be of somewhat limited use. In South Carolina, the political system has decided on an amount of state subsidy for local sewer and water systems investment. Agricultural economists can play a role in helping to direct those subsidies based on a communities ability to raise their own funds, and their needs for physical infrastructure. This in turn implies a continued need to improve our modeling of the physical and financial needs of local areas in South Carolina.

16
Financing Infrastructure in Rapid Growth Communities: The North Dakota Experience

F. Larry Leistritz and Steve H. Murdock

Communities experiencing rapid population growth often encounter difficult problems in balancing public sector costs and revenues and, particularly, in financing infrastructure expansion (Weber and Howell, 1982). Such problems are especially likely to occur when large resource extraction or conversion facilities or industrial plants are located in rural areas with small populations and limited infrastructure (Gilmore and Duff, 1975; Murdock and Leistritz, 1979). Because the work forces required for the construction and operation of such facilities are often quite large in comparison to the economic and demographic bases of the area, such developments present both benefits and problems to the communities nearby. Such projects often lead to long-desired increases in local employment and to general economic growth in the area. However, the total magnitude of economic growth associated with such projects, the rapidity of their development and the fluctuation in their rates of development during the lifetime of the project, the public service demands created by growth, and the uncertainty of the timing and specific location of many of the impacts create severe planning problems for local areas.

Among the community-level problems posed by large energy projects, none is more pervasive than the effect of such developments on the fiscal status of local governments. Such governments must often develop extensive facilities to accommodate future growth with only limited public sector revenues. As a result, programs to assist such governments in accommodating growth are often necessary, and several states have enacted special taxes on large energy and mineral development projects, with part of the proceeds often being distributed to affected local governments. This chapter examines the experience of one such state, North Dakota, in assisting rapidly growing communities in financing needed infrastructure and services. Specifically, it examines the nature of fiscal problems in developing areas, the context of rapid energy-related growth in North Dakota, and the taxation and other fiscal programs implemented to address the financial requirements for local government services.

THE NATURE OF FISCAL PROBLEMS ASSOCIATED WITH RAPID GROWTH

The major fiscal problems relate to the timing and inter-jurisdictional distribution of the local government costs and revenues resulting from the project. The major timing problem arises from the fact that, although service demands and associated expenditures arise immediately during construction of a project, substantial revenues may not be received until operation of the facility begins. This situation is most common for local governments that depend primarily on property taxes, because project facilities often are not taxed until completion and because construction workers often live in temporary housing with low taxable values. As a result, a critical revenue-expenditure squeeze may exist during the first several years of project construction.

Fiscal problems of local government often are exacerbated when substantial project-related growth creates needs for investment to expand schools, water and sewer systems, and other public facilities. Local borrowing capacity often is limited by statute to a fixed percentage of the assessed valuation of a jurisdiction's tax base. In a rapid growth situation, such limitations may severely constrain a community's ability to expand its public facilities in a timely manner (Murdock and Leistritz, 1979; Halstead et al., 1984).

The distribution of project-related revenues and the tax structure of state and local areas also pose problems for fiscal management. In some cases, the facilities and resources that generate new revenues have been located in one county while the bulk of the project-related population is located in a different county, or even a different state. In other situations, the majority of project-related revenues accrue to state and county governments while the bulk of project-related expenditures are borne by municipalities and school districts.

A third factor complicating effective planning for, and management of, growth associated with major projects is uncertainty regarding the extent of local growth that may actually be experienced. Uncertainty regarding whether the project will actually take place, when it will begin, and whether it is possible that it will be developed only to be abandoned later as unfeasible--together with uncertainty regarding the potential impacts at the community level--can have substantial effects on community infrastructure financing decisions. Public officials and voters, cognizant of past boom and bust experiences associated with large projects, have often been reluctant to increase public debt, if it is not clear that future increases in assessed valuation will be sufficient to repay the debt without substantial tax increases. In addition, recent closures and abandonments of a variety of resource facilities (e.g., nuclear power plants, oil shale projects, mines) have led to an increased awareness of such issues and greater reluctance on the part of local officials and citizens to accept the risk associated with extensive borrowing.

THE HISTORICAL CONTEXT OF ENERGY INDUSTRY EXPANSION IN NORTH DAKOTA

Rising energy prices in the early 1970s stimulated considerable development of both coal and petroleum resources in western North Dakota. Between 1975 and 1985 lignite coal production more than tripled, while crude oil production increased 148 percent (Table 16.1). Most of the increased coal production was intended to fuel new mine-mouth electric generating plants; between 1973 and 1980 construction of four new power plants was initiated. In addition, several synthetic fuel projects were proposed for development in the region, and one, the Great Plains Gasification Project, became fully operational in 1985.

Expansion of the energy industry in western North Dakota was both rapid and localized. Coal development centered on the construction and subsequent operation of the four power plants and the synfuel facility mentioned earlier. Each of these projects was a major undertaking, requiring several years to complete and utilizing a construction work force of several hundred to several thousand workers. (The peak construction work force for the Great Plains Gasification Project exceeded 5,000.) Once the facilities were completed, each would require a permanent work force, which was quite substantial in relation to the predevelopment population of nearby communities (typically several hundred workers for a power plant and mine and about 1,000 for the gasification complex). Nearby communities were thus confronted with the need to plan for the influx of a large but temporary population associated with facility construction followed by a smaller but still substantial permanent population associated with project operation.

Petroleum development followed a pattern of rapid growth in exploration activities beginning in the mid-1970s and peaking in 1981. The rig count (number of rigs drilling) rose from 17 in 1975 to 119 in 1981 (Table 16.1). Softening oil prices then led to a precipitous decline in drilling activity beginning in 1982. Oil development activities were also relatively localized. In 1984 the top four oil-producing counties accounted

Table 16.1. Lignite Coal Production, Coal-Fired Electric Generation, Crude Oil Production, and Number of Oil Rigs Drilling, North Dakota, 1960, 1970, 1975, 1980, 1981-85

Year	Lignite Coal Production (million tons)	Coal-Fired Electric Generation (billion KWH)	Crude Oil Production (million barrels)	Number of Rigs Drilling
1960	2.5	NA	22.0	16
1970	5.0	4.0	22.0	9
1975	7.1	5.2	20.5	17
1980	16.8	13.1	40.4	83
1981	17.4	14.2	45.7	119
1982	17.5	15.4	47.5	69
1983	18.0	16.9	50.7	41
1984	20.1	18.5	52.7	57
1985	25.7	NA	50.9	45

Source: Coon et al., 1986.

for 78 percent of the state's total production. Equally significant to state and local planning as the magnitude and localized nature of energy resource development in western North Dakota was the uncertainty concerning its actual extent and timing and the levels of local population growth that might result. Each of the coal development projects mentioned earlier was subject to at least one postponement, and construction work force requirements often differed substantially from those originally projected. (One power plant, for example, required a peak construction work force of about 2,200, compared to a predevelopment projection of 980.) Initial lack of information concerning likely demographic characteristics and settlement patterns of project workers further complicated the problem of estimating likely population growth and resulting infrastructure requirements. In addition, several large synfuel projects that had been proposed for development were first postponed and then cancelled, often after several years of planning.

STATE PROGRAMS TO SUPPORT LOCAL INFRASTRUCTURE DEVELOPMENT

By 1974 North Dakota policymakers had become aware of the magnitude of coal development projects proposed for the state, and many desired that the state adopt a positive, proactive stance in response to both the problems and the opportunities associated with development. As a result, three major programs were enacted by the 1975 Legislative Session to provide a basis for constructively managing the development of large-scale energy facilities. These were (1) a program for special state taxation of energy extraction and conversion facilities and redistribution of part of the proceeds to local governments, (2) an energy facility siting act which ensured that local officials would receive information concerning developers' intentions, and (3) a program to provide projections of anticipated economic, demographic, and service impacts of proposed projects to affected communities.

STATE TAXATION POLICIES

The energy taxation package adopted in 1975 included a severance tax on the extraction of lignite coal and a coal conversion tax that applied to coal-fired power plants and synfuel facilities. The severance tax rate was specified on a per-ton (rather than percent-of-value) basis but was adjusted for inflation using the Wholesale Price Index. The base rate for this tax was initially established at $0.50 per ton in 1975 and was subsequently increased in 1977 and 1979. The effect of these changes was that during the early 1980s, the severance tax rate was slightly more than $1.00 per ton. (For a more detailed discussion of the North Dakota severance tax, see Leistritz and Maki, 1981 or Keller and Luptak, 1983.)

A key feature of the severance tax legislation was the distribution of the proceeds. Since the 1977 Legislative Session severance tax revenues have been apportioned between state and local governments with 30 percent accruing to the state general fund, 15 percent to a state trust fund, 35 percent to a Coal Impact Fund, and 20 percent being returned to the county where the coal was mined. The county's share is further subdivided (by statute) with 40 percent accruing to the county general fund, 30 percent being divided among the incorporated municipalities (in proportion to their population), and 30 percent being divided among the school districts (in proportion to enrollment). The state trust fund was to be administered as a source of loans (at below-market interest rates) for impacted local governments, while the Coal Impact Fund would provide grants (awarded on the basis of need) to the same entities.

The coal conversion facility privilege tax is applied to electrical generating plants and other coal conversion facilities (e.g., coal gasification and liquefaction plants). The tax is in lieu of all ad valorem (i.e., property) taxes except for taxes on the land on which the facility is located. The tax rate for electrical generating plants is 0.25 mill on each kilowatt hour of electricity produced for sale. For coal gasification plants, the rate is 2.5 percent of the gross receipts of the facility or $0.10 per one thousand cubic feet of synthetic natural gas, whichever is greater. For other coal conversion facilities, the rate is 2.5 percent of gross receipts. The revenue from this tax is divided between state and local governments with 65 percent accruing to the state general fund and 35 percent to the county where the facility is located. The county's share is further allocated, by statute, with 30 percent being distributed to the municipalities, 30 percent being divided among the school districts, and 40 percent accruing to the county general fund.

In summary, the taxation program developed by the state of North Dakota was designed to alleviate the most serious fiscal problems typically encountered by local governments facing rapid growth situations. Problems related to revenue shortfalls and needs for infrastructure financing during the early years of project development were addressed by the Coal Impact Fund grants and trust fund loans. The Coal Impact Fund was administered by a Coal Development Impact Office (since 1981, designated Energy Development Impact Office). The Director of this office was authorized to evaluate and approve (or deny) all grant requests and also to review and provide recommendations concerning all applications for trust fund loans. Final approval for loans came from the state Board of University and School Lands, to whom the Impact Office Director reported. The legislation provided considerable flexibility to the administrator of the Coal Impact Fund since grants could be made to any local political subdivision that "demonstrates actual or anticipated extraordinary expenditures caused by coal development and the growth incident thereto." Grant funds also could be used to support almost any aspect of local government services, and so resources could be made available to fund planning studies and to offset unusual personnel or operating costs as well as for building new public facilities or buying equipment.

Problems of jurisdictional disparities of costs and revenues were addressed both by the system for distributing the local share of the severance and conversion taxes and by the grant program. The distribution of the local share of tax proceeds (20 percent of the severance tax and 35 percent of the conversion tax) was designed to provide the major political subdivisions of a county hosting a coal project with a dependable revenue source throughout the operation period.

One obvious problem with the distribution plan was that a town or school district lying outside the county where a facility was located would not be eligible to receive any tax proceeds even though many (even most) of the project's workers might reside within that jurisdiction. The 1979 Legislative Session acted to alleviate this problem by making certain jurisdictions in counties adjacent to coal-producing counties eligible to receive a share of the severance tax collections.[14]

---

[14] The effect of this provision is that, if the tipple (loading facility) of a mine is within 15 miles of another county in which no coal is mined, then the

The risks associated with facility cancellation or closure are addressed in part by the grant program. Because infrastructure expansion is funded partially from state grants, local entities incur smaller debt obligations than would otherwise be the case.

FACILITY SITING

Other aspects of the state's energy development strategy included two efforts to provide decision makers with timely and accurate information. The first of these was the Energy Facility Siting Act. Enacted by the 1975 Legislative Session, this act provided the state Public Service Commission with siting authority over energy conversion and transmission facilities. Energy facilities covered by this act include electric generating plants, synfuel facilities, transmission lines, and pipelines.

The Public Service Commission was empowered to establish siting criteria and procedures for permit application and review for facilities covered by the act. In determining whether to grant a certificate of site compatibility (for plants) or a construction permit (for transmission facilities), the Commission conducts an extensive review and holds public hearings to determine that the construction and operation of the facilities will produce minimum environmental and socioeconomic impacts. Further, the Commission has the authority to impose requirements designed to minimize or mitigate such impacts as a condition of granting a permit. One condition which the Commission has imposed on all major projects is a requirement for regular reporting of current and anticipated work force levels. This information can be very useful in planning for infrastructure needs.

REGIONAL ENVIRONMENTAL ASSESSMENT PROGRAM

A second major effort to provide information to affected entities was the North Dakota Regional Environmental Assessment Program

---

apportionment is based upon 30 percent to the cities in the coal producing county and any city in the non-coal producing county within 15 miles of the mine tipple, based upon population; 40 percent to the county general funds of the two counties based upon a ratio of assessed valuation of all the quarter sections of land which lie in the non-coal producing county within 15 miles of a mine tipple to the assessed valuation of all the land in the coal producing county; and 30 percent apportioned between school districts in the coal-producing county and those in the adjoining non-coal producing counties within 15 miles of a coal tipple based upon the total number of students in the coal producing county and the number of students actually living on the quarter sections of land within 15 miles of the tipple in the non-producing counties (Leistritz and Maki, 1981).

(ND-REAP). This state entity developed a variety of computerized data bases and software to make key information readily available to decision makers. Of particular relevance to this discussion of infrastructure financing was REAP's sponsorship of the development of a computerized economic, demographic, and fiscal impact projection model that became known as the REAP Economic-Demographic Model-1 or RED-1. The RED-1 model was made available for general use by decision makers in January 1977. During the next two years the model was utilized extensively as a planning and policy tool by local governments, state agencies, and legislative committees (Leistritz et al., 1979). As coal development progressed, impact monitoring programs were instituted at three of the four major project sites, and information from these efforts gradually replaced the model projections as the primary basis for funding decisions.

From the standpoint of infrastructure financing, petroleum development received less attention from state policymakers than did coal development. Several factors probably were responsible for this relative lack of attention to petroleum-related growth. First, the oil industry had been present in much of western North Dakota for nearly 30 years prior to the upsurge of activity in the late 1970s, and a taxation program which returned a portion of the oil revenues to the producing counties was already in place. Second, the decentralized nature of decision making in the oil industry (involving literally hundreds of individual firms) tended both to mask the full magnitude of economic, demographic, and service effects associated with its expansion and to complicate the task of predicting future levels of activity. Finally, the effects of oil development tended to be concentrated in regional trade centers (especially the towns of Dickinson and Williston) rather than in smaller communities near the producing fields (Chase and Leistritz, 1983).

Whatever the reasons, it was not until 1981 that the North Dakota Legislature initiated a special financing program for communities affected by petroleum development. This program was essentially the same as the Coal Impact grants program and was initially funded by a special legislative appropriation of $10 million for the 1981-83 biennium. An additional $5 million was appropriated in 1983.

THE ROLE OF STATE-SUPPORTED INFRASTRUCTURE FINANCING PROGRAMS IN ADDRESSING THE IMPACTS OF COMMUNITY GROWTH

Energy resources development triggered substantial growth in some North Dakota communities. Population changes over the period 1960-1985 for eight counties and selected towns are summarized in Table 16.2. The eight counties include the state's four leading oil-producing counties (Billings, Dunn, McKenzie, and Williams) and the three counties where the major new coal mines and conversion facilities were located (Mercer, McLean, and Oliver). The eighth county (Stark) experienced substantial impacts as a result of oil development in adjacent Billings and Dunn counties.

Table 16.2. Population of Selected Counties and Places in North Dakota, 1960-1985

County/Town	Year					
	1960	1970	1980	1982	1984	1985
Billings	1,513	1,198	1,138	1,257	1,300	1,310
Dunn	6,350	4,895	4,627	5,047	5,300	5,007
Killdeer	795	615	790	976	1,005	NA
McKenzie	7,296	6,127	7,132	8,625	8,600	8,703
Watford City	1,865	1,768	2,119	2,329	2,317	NA
Mercer	6,805	6,175	9,404	12,495	13,200	15,137
Beulah	1,318	1,344	2,908	4,752	6,013	NA
Hazen	1,222	1,240	2,365	3,038	3,498	NA
McLean	14,030	11,251	12,383	12,445	13,000	12,479
Washburn	993	804	1,767	1,864	1,987	NA
Underwood	819	781	1,329	1,305	1,346	NA
Turtle Lake	792	712	802	757	766	NA
Oliver	2,610	2,322	2,495	2,555	2,700	2,775
Center	476	619	900	945	969	NA
Stark	18,451	19,613	23,697	28,107	28,000	26,562
Belfield	1,064	1,130	1,274	1,757	1,073	NA
Dickinson	9,971	12,405	15,924	18,950	18,900	NA
Williams	22,051	19,301	22,237	27,590	27,200	27,647
Tioga	2,087	1,667	1,597	1,957	1,983	NA
Williston	11,866	11,280	13,336	16,660	16,188	NA

Source: U.S. Department of Commerce, Bureau of the Census. Census of Popuation, North Dakota. 1960-1980, and North Dakota Census Data Center, Population Bulletin Series, Vol. 2, No. 7, 1986.

Examination of Table 16.2 indicates that North Dakota counties and communities experienced a variety of patterns of population change. Some counties (e.g., Billings, Dunn, McLean, Oliver) had only moderate growth from 1970 to 1985, and for some of these (Billings, Dunn, McLean) this growth was insufficient even to offset the population decreases of the 1960s. Other counties experienced more extensive population growth; in Mercer County population increased 145 percent from 1970 to 1985.

The towns in these energy-rich counties also show a variety of growth patterns. The greatest percentage growth appears to have occurred in towns located near the sites of large coal conversion facilities. Beulah,

Hazen, and Washburn all experienced population increases of more than 100 percent since 1970.

Other towns in both coal and oil areas had smaller, yet still substantial, growth rates. Killdeer, Underwood, and Center all have grown more than 50 percent since 1970, and in each case much of that growth occurred during a few years of intensive development activity. Not all towns located near major energy developments experienced rapid growth, however. Turtle Lake and Tioga are examples of towns experiencing relatively little population change while Belfield demonstrates how a pattern of rapid population growth can be abruptly reversed when development activity lessens. (In the case of Belfield, a precipitous decrease in local oil exploration activity resulted in a rapid population decline.)

The varied patterns of community growth resulting from energy development in western North Dakota posed significant challenges to the administrator of the impact funds. In an attempt to anticipate community growth and provide advance funding for needed infrastructure, the Coal Impact Office made substantial use of the RED-1 model.

The simulation model was particularly useful as an administrative tool because it allowed rapid responses to changes in the development outlook. During the period 1977-1979 three major power plant construction projects were underway in Mercer and McLean counties. These projects experienced frequent changes in construction schedules and labor requirements. The model allowed state and local decision makers to obtain updated impact projections soon after a change in schedule was announced. The extent of correspondence between the distribution of grant funds and the distribution of forecasted population impacts is shown in Table 16.3. Examination of Table 16.3 indicates that grant funds were distributed among counties much as were the predicted population changes. Mercer County, which was projected to experience 56 percent of the population impact, received 60 percent of the impact grants; all together, four counties, which were projected to receive 84 percent of the population impact, received 99 percent of the grants.

The disparities between the impact projections and grant allocations observed in Table 16.3 are primarily attributable to consideration of differences in the capacity of various communities to accommodate inmigrating populations. For example, Burleigh and Morton counties received no grants, although they were projected to experience some population effects. This was the result of a judgment that these relatively populous counties could absorb the impact of a few hundred inmigrants without undue hardship. Similarly, the "other counties" received few grant funds because the number of inmigrants was expected to be small (seldom more than a few dozen people for any community) and their arrival would not strain existing facilities.

The coal impact assistance program ultimately distributed substantial amounts of financial resources. Over the period 1975-1985, the

Coal Impact Fund grants totaled $37.4 million (Table 16.4). The largest expenditures were for education, transportation, water systems, and law enforcement. During the same period $8.8 million in Coal Impact loans were awarded (Table 16.5), and many projects were financed with a combination of grant funds, loans, and local resources. In general, the impact fund administrator seldom funded major infrastructure items solely with grants; he required instead that a portion of the funding should come from local sources or loans.

Table 16.3. Distribution of Coal Impact Fund Grants, 1975-1979, and Distribution of Projected Population Impacts, 1978, Selected North Dakota Counties

County	Distribution of Grants[a]		Distribution of Projected Population Impacts[b]	
	(dollars)	(percent)	(number)	(percent)
Mercer	5,715,301	60.1	3,303	56.2
McLean	3,310,183	34.8	1,613	27.5
Oliver	446,379	4.7	13	0.2
Dunn	30,200	0.3	8	0.1
Burleigh	0	0.0	330	5.6
Morton	0	0.0	198	3.4
Other counties	12,300	0.1	411	7.0
Total	9,514,363	100.0	5,876	100.0

[a]Reflects grants through March 1979. Source: Records of North Dakota Coal Impact Office, State Capitol, Bismarck, North Dakota.

[b]Projected population impacts for 1978. Source: Unpublished printouts, North Dakota Regional Environmental Assessment Program, Bismarck, 1977.

The oil impact program has a much shorter history, but already substantial assistance has been rendered to local governments. Over the period 1981-1985, a total of $15.0 million in grants were distributed (Table 16.6). Almost one-third of the total funding was for transportation functions, reflecting the heavy impacts on roads that often occur during oil exploration and development. Because the grant program was initiated just as oil development activity was reaching peak levels, many grants were made to assist in coping with impacts that had already occurred, and less reliance was placed on forecasts of future impacts.

Table 16.4. Coal Impact Grant Awards by Governmental Function, 1975-85

Function	Total	Percent of Total
Law Enforcement	$ 4,008,269	10.7
Education	10,234,805	27.4
Health	337,580	0.9
Transportation	8,194,802	21.9
Recreation	1,671,468	4.5
Fire Protection	949,660	2.5
Planning	286,308	0.8
Potable Water	5,114,280	13.7
Waste Water Treatment	1,086,891	2.9
Solid Waste	37,500	0.1
Water and Sewer Lines	1,535,166	4.1
Government Administration	2,484,364	6.6
Other	1,472,483	3.9
Total	$37,413,756	100.0

Source: Keller and Luptak, 1983; Vranna and Luptak, 1985.

Table 16.5. Coal Impact Loans Awarded, 1977-1985

Time Period	Total
1977-79 Biennium	$2,910,500
1979-81 Biennium	1,340,000
1981-83 Biennium	3,333,458
1983-85 Biennium	1,202,323
Total	$8,786,281

Source: Keller and Luptak, 1983; Vranna and Luptak, 1985.

Table 16.6. Oil Impact Grant Awards by Governmental Function, 1981-85

Function	Total	Percent of Total
Law Enforcement	$ 2,333,780	15.5
Education	2,529,500	16.8
Health	77,400	0.5
Transportation	4,927,536	32.8
Recreation	416,060	2.8
Fire Protection	1,237,659	8.2
Planning	10,000	0.1
Potable Water	1,299,000	8.6
Waste Water Treatment	772,500	5.1
Solid Waste	74,500	0.5
Water and Sewer Lines	399,000	2.7
Government Administration	721,800	4.8
Other	240,300	1.6
Total	$15,039,035	100.0

Source: Keller and Luptak, 1983; Vranna and Luptak, 1985.

SUMMARY AND CONCLUSIONS

Rapidly growing communities frequently experience problems in financing needed infrastructure expansion. Communities near the sites of large resource or industrial development projects are particularly likely to encounter such problems because of (1) the magnitude of population growth often associated with such development, (2) the rapidity with which it occurs, and (3) uncertainty associated with the extent and timing of future growth.

During the period 1975 to 1985 western North Dakota experienced substantial development of its energy resources. Concern regarding the infrastructure financing problems that might be encountered by communities in the energy region prompted the state to initiate an extensive program of financial assistance to rapidly growing communities. Between 1975 and 1985 more than $61 million of state grants and loans were provided to communities affected by energy development projects.

Evaluating the success of such a program is difficult at best. However, the state program does appear to address the major infrastructure financing problems often reported in rapid growth areas. These are (1) revenue shortfalls during the early years of development, (2) jurisdictional disparities in costs and revenues, and (3) exposure of local residents to inequitable levels of risk should the anticipated project-related growth not materialize. Further, several retrospective analyses suggest that the state's impact finance programs have enabled its energy communities to cope with the problems of rapid growth more effectively than has been the case in many other areas (Gilmore, et al. 1982; Leistritz and Maki, 1981; Halstead and Leistritz, 1983). Specifically, case studies of the effects of energy-related growth in McLean and Mercer counties concluded that the state impact grants and loans had been adequate to fill most cost-revenue gaps for local jurisdictions and that no extraordinary burdens had been placed on local residents (Leistritz and Maki, 1981; Halstead and Leistritz, 1983).

17
Investing in Economic Development Infrastructure: A Decision-Making Framework

Warren Kriesel, Brady J. Deaton, and Thomas G. Johnson

The previous chapter describes the decision-making environment faced by rapid growth communities. Slow growth or stagnant communities face a quite different environment fraught with risk and political and economic uncertainty. Such communities must allocate scarce public dollars so that expenditures on justifiable economic development programs will lead to increases in economic activity. This chapter describes a framework which may be applicable to many areas of the U.S. It is currently being used in Virginia to provide local decision-makers with estimates of the rate of return on investments in economic development infrastructure--roads, industrial sites, water, sewer, fire protection, education, and other public services.

THE NEED FOR BETTER INFORMATION

Many leaders of rural communities are concerned about their perceived economic plight, and they view increased local industrial employment as a basis for economic growth. Their alternative development policies range from community 'booster' programs to the purchase and development of speculative industrial sites. However, while some local organizations have been successful in attracting new plants,

155

others have not and have used substantial resources in this regard. This is due, in part, to shortcomings in the information base of community leaders, and the extreme uncertainty under which they conduct these efforts. For example, in the average year between 1970 and 1982 only 30 new plants located or were otherwise established among Virginia's 91 nonmetropolitan independent cities and counties.

With so few locations occuring, a knowledge of the probability of a particular jurisdiction attracting an industrial plant is essential. However, few communities can afford to collect relevant information about how industries perceive their locational advantages as compared with other towns, and what the most cost-effective means of attracting industry may be. This situation is worsened in rural areas because economic development is promoted primarily by volunteer groups rather than by the professional developers and consultants found in metropolitan areas.

VIRGINIA'S ATTRACTIVENESS-TO-INDUSTRY MODEL

Neoclassical location theory suggests that footloose firms first select a general geographical area in which factor supplies and product market access are optimized. This broad area may encompass all or parts of several states. Secondly, they select a site within that area according to their minimum cost of production criteria. Within this secondary choice level local government actions may have significant effects on the location decisions of private entities. The factors considered by firms include certain locational constants, which communities cannot affect, and certain variables which communities can alter to influence the location decisions of firms. Firms and communities will bargain over the location variables and thus determine the terms of the location transaction; that is, the share of costs for upgrading or adding certain facilities that the firm needs (Wallace and Ruttan, 1961). The net benefits accruing to the community will depend on the importance of the locational constants and the relative bargaining power of the firms and communities.

A logit model of location successes and failures was estimated for Virginia counties and cities (Kriesel, 1985). This model represents an extension of earlier work by Smith, Deaton and Kelch and by Debertin, Pagoulatos, and Smith. Each jurisdiction was assigned a '1' if it attracted at least one manufacturing plant, or a '0' if it did not, during the period 1979-81. This time period was long enough to allow a reasonable number of locations to occur. A manufacturing plant was counted if it had more than ten employees. This lower limit was used because it assumed that, 1) communities had negligible interest in smaller plants and little bargaining occurs, and 2) small plants were more likely to be locally owned and, therefore, alternative communities are not considered in the location decision.

The location factors which a firm considers at the secondary search level are a subject of great debate (Stafford, 1979). Conway (1980) presented a checklist of 300 factors which a community can use to evaluate itself. The overriding consideration was that the selected variables should represent cost factors that apply to all firms. The variables considered in the empirical location model followed these same considerations and are given in Table 17.1. The importance attributed to infrastructure is obvious in Table 17.1. Transportation, industrial sites, education, and fire protection have each been included.

The transportation factor was represented in part by the HWAY variable, because most companies utilize truck shipping today (Stafford, 1979). Railways were accounted for in the SITE variable, along with the land area of the site, and the diameter of water and sewer connections. SITE, an index of industrial site quality, was calculated according to the method proposed by Kelch (1977), where each site receives a score equal to the ratio of settled sites it equals or exceeds in quality on each of these 4 components to the total number of settled sites in the observation set. A "settled" site is defined as one where at least one manufacturing plant has located. This variable was expected to be important in community decision making because it represents a location inducement that lowers firm costs directly. Moreover, the locality can invest in sites in order to become more competitive *vis-a-vis* other communities and, thereby, increase its chances of location success.

The logit model reveals information which will be important for community decision makers who are interested in attracting manufacturing firms. Three of the nine independent variables in the model are directly under the community's control: a) the fire protection rating, FPR, b) the existence of an industrial development group, DEVG, and c) the site quality index, SITE. Two more variables, four lane highway, HWAY, and distance to a college, COLLEGE, are public infrastructure variables. These variables all have positive influences on the probability of location. The SITE variable is especially important, because as noted by Cooksey (1979), high quality industrial sites are location factors that are seldom present in rural areas, unless they have been provided by a public body. Also, it is a variable which may be changed over the very short run by community investments.

A FRAMEWORK FOR VALUING SITE INVESTMENTS

Figure 17.1 illustrates the effects of changes in the site quality index on the probability of location for two different classes of communities. The site quality index will increase as community action is taken to upgrade site quality. The curves were produced by evaluating the logit function at the means of location factors for all places. A separate estimate was made in similar fashion for those communities with location

Table 17.1. Specification of Location Model Variables

LOCATION = '1' if at least one plant with at least 10 employees located in the jurisdiction during 1979-81, and '0' otherwise. Constructed from primary and secondary data.

LABOR = labor force residing within 40 miles of the jurisdiction's center, 1980. Labor availability proxy. Constructed from secondary data. Hypothesized as a positive influence.

WAGES = average weekly manufacturing wages in the jurisdiction, fourth quarter, 1979. Labor cost proxy. From secondary data. Hypothesized as a negative influence.

HWAY = 1-0 presence of an interstate highway in the jurisdiction. Transportation access proxy. From secondary data. Hypothesized as a positive influence.

DEVG = existence of a development group (1-0) prior to 1982. Community attitude proxy. From primary data. Hypothesized as a positive influence.

SITE = site quality index (0-100) during 1979-81. Industrial site quality proxy. Constructed from primary data. Hypothesized as a positive influence.

GRADS = percentage of people older than 25 with high school diploma. Human capital proxy. From secondary data. Hypothesized as a positive influence.

COLLEGE = distance to a college from the jurisdiction's center. Quality of human capital and quality of life proxy. From secondary data. Hypothesized as a positive influence.

FPR = fire protection rating in the jurisdiction, 1980. Higher ratings lead to lower insurance costs for industry and business. It may also serve as a miscellaneous costs proxy. From secondary data. Hypothesized as a positive influence.

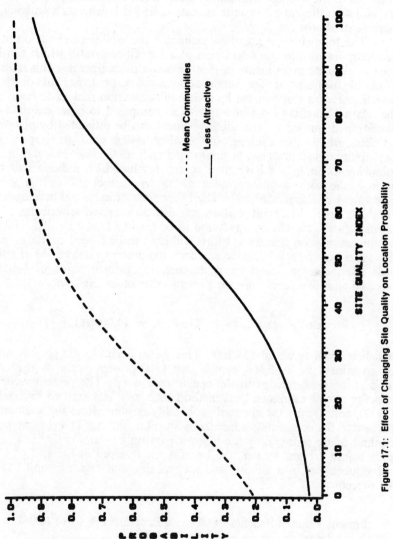

Figure 17.1: Effect of Changing Site Quality on Location Probability

probabilities below .10. The low group is represented by the lower curve. For this group an increase in site quality of 20 points will result in only a three to five percent rise in probability from a point of near zero. On the other hand, the average community starts from a location probability of .21, and with the same 20 points increase in its SITE achieves a probability increase of almost .20.

The following suggests how estimated probabilities of location may be incorporated into the calculation of a benefit-cost ratio which can be used to evaluate investments in plant location inducements. This ratio is a useful measure of the proportionate gains or losses of different investments and can be used by community decision makers to compare the relative benefits of site investments as compared to other community development projects. The site investment can be estimated by planning officials, while the resulting site quality index (and its impact on probability of location) can be approximated from the logit model.[15] In the following example, we have used survey results which indicate that the average site with a quality index of 35 was associated with a mean investment of about $568,500. The other costs of industrial development are those devoted to plant recruitment, such as staff and advertising. The mean annual expenditure was found to be about $11,000 in 1978. Based on the assumption that these efforts will have to be carried on for at least five years before they will have an effect, the present value (P.V.) of a five year effort can be found by subtracting the present value of benefits received after five years from the present value of an annuity:

$$\text{Present Value of Costs} = 11{,}000/r - 11{,}000/r(1 + r)^6$$

which is equal to about $54,100. This value, added to the present value of investment of $568,500, results in a total present value of $622,600. This is the denominator in the benefit-cost ratio. The present value of benefits can be estimated by a method such as that proposed by Shaffer (1972), adjusted by the changed probability resulting from the addition of the site to the community's bundle of location factors. The present value of the benefits is found by the following formula assuming that five years pass before a plant locates, the benefits are received at the end of each subsequent year into infinity, and the real discount rate is assumed to be six percent:

$$\text{Present Value of Benefits} = \text{Annual Benefits}/(1 + 0.06)^6(0.06).$$

---

[15] The logit model has been developed into a spreadsheet template called AIM (Attractiveness to Industry Model). The model is described in Johnson and Kriesel (1986).

The change in location probability is presented in Figure 17.1, where a SITE change from 0 to 34 increases the probability of location by 46%, for the average community. The expected benefits would be:

Expected Present Value of Benefits = Present Value of Benefits * 0.46.

Both of the components of the benefit-cost ratio would now be ready for the final calculation as follows:

Benefit-Cost Ratio = Expected Present Value of Benefits/ $622,600

This ratio can be useful, but only if the community has a reliable estimate of annual benefits to the public sector. Chapters 8, 9, and 10 discuss methods and models available to estimate these benefits. The above calculations represent only one tool which can be used alongside many others in order to enable local decisionmakers to reach more informed decisions about the use of public funds.

The foregoing framework yields valuable information by indicating the annual benefits necessary for the benefit cost ratio to be '1'. Assuming the costs above, the 'average' county or city would need to realize at least $53,000 of value in annual benefits, including social benefits of a nonmonetary type, before considering investment in an industrial site. This figure may be understated because it does not consider the risk of the plant closing at some future date.

CONCLUSIONS

The results of the logit model appear quite useful for localities considering an investment in local infrastructure. These results are most precise for the 'average' community. Statistical inferences drawn from the analysis for jurisdictions with very low probabilities of location should be treated with more caution. However, the analysis reveals that these communities may not significantly enhance their chances of attracting a new industry by making relatively small investments in infrastructure.

The investment decisions of communities should be made with full recognition of the disadvantages they face from unchangeable location constants, such as the distance from a major population center or interstate or four-lane highway. The small predicted increases in probability associated with changes in industrial site quality are due to the poor location characteristics of the low probability communities. This example illustrates that extreme locational constraints are overcome only at very high levels of investment in plant location inducements.

The framework developed here addresses a unique aspect of infrastructure investment--unique, because the payoff is probabilistic and the benefits variable and often must incorporate nonmonetary effects such as the nonpecuniary benefits of reduced unemployment. But because of the importance of the issue, it is critical that the estimates of the costs and benefits are available to local decision-makers so that better decisions can be made.

PART IV: Political Considerations in Infrastructure Investment Analysis

18
Financial Sources for Local Infrastructure Investment

Patrick J. Sullivan

Whether or not rural America is facing a major infrastructure crisis, officials of rural governments undergoing growth will sooner or later face major capital projects. Enlarging schools, upgrading highways and bridges, extending water and sewer lines can all be expected of governments serving communities with growing populations. While these are normal functions of government, they are costly undertakings which cannot normally be financed out of the current year revenues of small rural governments. Therefore, early on in the capital planning process, the question of how the project will be financed will have to be addressed. This chapter attempts to summarize the major financing options open to rural government officials, together with their advantages and disadvantages from the local officials' point of view.

This chapter covers four major options: Federal assistance, State assistance, local revenue and bond financing, and private/public cost-sharing. Current funding levels, and/or financing costs will be discussed for the most important programs within each funding option, together with an assessment of the likely direction of future changes.

FEDERAL GRANTS AND LOANS

The Federal government has a legitimate role to play in financing the activities of local governments. Federal assistance may be warranted when activities undertaken by one jurisdiction substantially benefit the citizens of other jurisdictions (i.e. when externalities exist) or when widespread market failures affect the ability of local governments to provide a minimally acceptable level of public services.[16] For example, economic justification can be made for some level of Federal assistance in the treatment of wastewater because of the benefits enjoyed by downstream (and often out-of-State) communities. Likewise, the presumed failure of private capital markets to adequately meet the capital needs of rural communities has been used to justify Federal credit programs. Whether meant to rectify a capital markets failure, or to encourage a more desirable level of public services, or merely to pump money into a slumping local economy, Federal assistance is often tied to the construction (or more recently, to the rehabilitation) of public facilities.

FEDERAL INTERGOVERNMENTAL GRANTS

Federal assistance is available in several forms. General Revenue Sharing (GRS) funds are often used to finance infrastructure projects. Since the Federal Government places few restrictions on how GRS funds should be spent, local governments retain almost complete control over the projects financed with GRS money. In that respect, the GRS program is unique; most of the other Federal grant programs available for local infrastructure projects come with some strings attached. Matching requirements, safety and performance standards, wage and procurement regulations, and the need to have project plans reviewed and approved by Federal agencies are examples of program requirements which must be met whenever Federal categorical grant funds are accepted. All reduce local autonomy and often increase project costs.[17]

---

16 Other rationales for Federal government involvement in local government finance exist. A desire to reduce interregional disparities in public services and economic growth may warrant Federal involvement to counteract the efficient operation of private sector markets. An argument can also be made for Federal funding of certain merit goods. For example, Federally funded minimum levels of public welfare may prevent interstate "exporting" of welfare recipients. In addition, countercyclical Federal programs have often funded public works projects as a means of reducing unemployment during recessions.

17 The costs associated with Federal grant requirements are difficult to quantify. Muller and Fix estimated a per capita direct cost of $25 for fulfilling the requirements of selected grant programs based on a sample of local governments (Muller and Fix, 1979). The cost of construction delays associated with Federal grants was examined by Choate (1980) and Choate and Walter (1981). In addition, engineering requirements or inappropriate minimum standards may force rural communities to adopt inappropriate technologies, saddling facility users with high construction and operating expenses (Congressional Budget Office, 1983; U.S. GAO, 1980).

Despite these drawbacks, Federal grants are an attractive way for local government officials to build and rebuild public facilities. While in some cases the extra cost and effort needed to qualify for a Federal matching grant is not worthwhile from the local government's point of view, most of the time Federal assistance substantially reduces the locally borne cost of infrastructure projects. As long as Federal program requirements do not raise the future costs of operating the facility sufficiently to counteract savings to the local government in the initial construction cost of the facility, the community should benefit from Federal assistance.[18]

FEDERAL LOANS AND LOAN GUARANTEES

Loan programs, because payment of principal and interest must be borne by the community, will not be viewed as favorably by local officials as grant programs. Nonetheless, there are substantial direct and indirect savings for communities which finance their capital projects with Federal loans or loan guarantees. In general, interest rates on Federal loans tend to be set at levels below market rates, so the interest cost of deferring payment for infrastructure tends to be relatively low. This is particularly true for eligible borrowers participating in the Federal government's infrastructure lending programs. The Farmers Home Administration (FmHA) water/sewer and community facilities programs are designed to assist rural communities that cannot borrow from private lenders at affordable rates. Thus, if left to raise funds on their own, FmHA borrowers would probably face interest rates substantially higher than the average market rate.

In addition to the direct interest rate saving, there may be indirect benefits for smaller communities using Federal loan programs. Rural communities receiving direct loans from the Federal government benefit from the temporary inflow of funds into the community's capital market. The project is financed without drawing down the reserves of local banks and other investors who might otherwise purchase the local government's bonds. These investors are free to loan their reserves to others within the community. In addition, investors should be more receptive to future bond offerings of the aided government since their portfolio holdings would not be as saturated with the government's bonds. As a result, direct Federal loans may indirectly lower private market borrowing costs for the government receiving Federal assistance (and for other borrowers in the "local" capital market).

---

[18] Of course, local taxpayers do bear a portion of the cost of Federal assistance through Federal taxes. In addition, high levels of intergovernmental aid can negatively affect a local government's credit rating and cost of borrowing.

The potential indirect savings associated with Federal guarantee programs would not be as great as those associated with direct loans, especially for small rural governments. To the extent that the guaranteed debt is held by investors in the local market serving the community, no real inflow of funds will occur. While a Federal guarantee generally improves the marketability of a debt instrument, unless the guaranteed bonds are sold to investors outside of the community's local bond market, the indirect benefits of a guarantee program will tend to be relatively low.

While quantifying local benefits may not be a straightforward matter, there is little doubt that many rural areas have benefited from several infrastructure-related grant and loan programs administered by the Federal government in the past. Current proposals and legislation under court review aimed at cutting the Federal budget deficit and consolidating Federal programs may greatly affect many of these rural-oriented infrastructure programs.

THE FUTURE OF FEDERAL ASSISTANCE

Table 18.1 lists several major community development grant and loan programs, together with their proposed 1987 allocations. These proposals include generally discouraging news for rural government officials. If adopted, budget authority for several rural-oriented development programs would be terminated in 1987. These "zeroed out" programs include USDA's rural water and sewer grant and loan programs, its community facilities loans, and the Appalachian Regional Commission development programs. While continuing to receive funding, Interior's payments-in-lieu-of-taxes programs and USDA's rural electrification loans would undergo drastic reductions from their 1985 levels. Federal aid to highways, USDA's rural telephone bank loans, and HUD's small cities discretionary grants program would all take moderate cuts in budget authority.[19] Virtually none of the rural-oriented programs listed in Table 18.1 is scheduled for an increase in budget authority over 1985 levels. Of the programs which are neither urban or rural oriented, GRS would be eliminated after 1986; EPA's wastewater construction grants would be phased out by 1990.

For lending programs, even if the rural infrastructure-oriented programs survive the budget process, it seems likely that the implicit subsidy embodied in their interest rates will be greatly reduced. In recent years, the Federal government has shown a preference for guarantee

---

[19] Currently, 30 percent of the CDBG budget is earmarked for small cities; the Administration has proposed that this be increased to 35 percent in 1987. Despite this funding change, cutbacks in the CDBG program would result in fewer dollars flowing to rural governments.

Table 18.1. Federal Assistance Programs for Community and Infrastructure Development and General Government

Agency	Program	Budget Authority			Met/Nonmet Orientation[a]
		1985	1986	1987	
	Spending Programs:	Millions Dollars			
ARC	Appalachian regional development programs	151	36	--	Rural
HHS	Community service programs	372	172	4	NA
EPA	Wastewater treatment construction	2,400	2,374	1,800	Neutral
HUD	Community development (CDBG)[b] entitlements	2,388	1,703	1,676	Urban
	small cities/disc. grants	1,084	788	949	Rural
	Urban development action (UDAG)	440	109	--	Urban
Interior	Indian area and regional development operations	521	489	509	Rural
	Payments in-lieu-of-taxes	134	6	45	Rural
	Land and minerals payments	538	575	551	Rural
Treasury	Local fiscal assistance (GRS)	4,566	3,425	--	Neutral
TVA	Area and regional development	125	99	58	NA
DOT	Federal aid to highways	14,908	14,684	12,770	Rural
	Airport construction grants	987	973	1,017	Neutral
	Urban mass transport aid	3,549	2,812	1,220	Urban
USDA	Rural water and sewer grants	115	109	--	Rural
	Credit Programs:[c]				
USDA	Water and sewer loans	340	340	--	Rural
	Community facilities loans	115	100	--	Rural
	Rural electrification loans	3,801	3,215	2,250	Rural
	Rural telephone bank loans	168	177	139	Rural

NA: Not available.

[a]Based on estimated distribution of Federal funds for fiscal year 1980 (Reid and Whitehead, 1982). A program is considered urban (rural) oriented if it spent or loaned a disproportionate amount of its 1980 funds in metro (nonmetro) areas, based on population and income indices.
[b]Included here is the Budget's proposal to defer until 1987 $500 million of 1986 funds, and the proposal to increase the small cities program's share of total CDBG funds from 30 to 35 percent.
[c]Direct loan and guarantee level.

Source: Office of Management and Budget, various FY 1987 budget documents.

programs over direct lending programs, and has tended to charge interest rates and user fees more in line with those charged by private lenders. Given concerns over the size of the Federal budget deficit, pressure to reduce interest rate subsidies is likely to continue.

The net effect of these proposals, if adopted, will be a much reduced Federal role in infrastructure finance. The Gramm-Rudman-Hollings Balanced Budget and Emergency Deficit Control Act of 1985, if permitted by the Supreme Court to stand, would further reduce most of these amounts by up to 20 percent. Rural officials will have to look more to their State governments, or to the private sector to finance their infrastructure needs. Even for programs scheduled to continue beyond 1986, rural officials will likely receive funds through their State government rather than directly from the Federal Government.[20] The small cities portion of the CDBG program is already administered by the States in most cases--47 States administered the non-entitlement portion of the CDBG program in 1984. Approximately 43 percent of the funds they obligated were for public facilities projects (State Community Development Block Grant Clearinghouse, 1985). Federal aid to highways is also largely handled by State governments.

STATE ASSISTANCE

For the same reasons justifying Federal government involvement in local infrastructure financing, State governments also have a major role in helping local governments plan and finance the construction and rehabilitation of public facilities. Responsibility for insuring an equitable distribution of project costs when external benefits are associated with locally provided public services, or when Statewide standards for locally provided services (merit goods) are adopted, or when perceived market failures hamper local infrastructure decisions, can all fall to the State government when the localized nature of the problem makes Federal involvement unnecessary. In addition, since local government is a creation of the State, subject to revenue raising restriction and a host of mandated procedures and services, a strong case can be made for State government assistance to cover some portion of the cost of the various burdens it places on local jurisdictions.

---

[20] One major drawback of consolidating Federal categorical grant programs into a few block grants is that the block grants may become tempting targets for future deficit reduction proposals. The proposed termination of the Community Services Block Grant, created in 1981, lends credence to this concern. Nonetheless, it remains to be seen whether the legislative process makes the survival of small categorical grant programs, with their well-defined constituencies, more likely than the survival of large block grant programs.

The varied relationships between the State governments and their local governments has lead to a host of State assistance programs. These include direct grants and loans, indirect financial assistance (wherein the State acts as a financial intermediary for its local government borrowers), and nonfinancial assistance. In addition, States can also assist local governments finance infrastructure simply by removing revenue raising restrictions or by helping to improve the efficiency of local revenue raising measures.[21] Each of these types of assistance will be discussed briefly, with an assessment of the potential benefits to local governments of increasing the State's role in capital finance.

STATE INTERGOVERNMENTAL GRANTS

The State government can provide infrastructure to its citizens either directly, through State built and operated facilities, or indirectly through local governments. Table 18.2 provides some insight into how each State chooses to divide the task of providing infrastructure between the two levels of government. Local governments accounted for 59 percent of the State and local government sector's capital expenditures in 1984. However, in 18 States, direct spending by the State government amounted to over half of the State and local capital expenditures.

In addition to their direct expenditures, virtually every State also provides grants which help local jurisdictions build, rehabilitate, or maintain public facilities (U.S. Bureau of Census, 1984c). While reliable data on intergovernmental revenues is available on a regular basis, the extent to which State aid is used for infrastructure remains unknown.[22] In 1984, 33 percent of local government general revenue was intergovernmental aid from the States.[23] While much of this was used for operating expenses, many State grant programs are restricted to financing the construction and equipment purchases of local jurisdictions; still others include local government capital expenditures in their distribution formulas.

---

[21] This categorization of state assistance was borrowed from a series of legislative finance papers published by the National Conference of State Legislatures as part of HUD's Governmental Capacity Sharing Program (Gold, 1982; Hough and Petersen, 1983; Watson, 1982a and 1982b).

[22] The Council of State Governments, with support from the USDA's Economic Research Service, is currently completing a pilot study of the use of State financial and nonfinancial assistance for rural infrastructure investment.

[23] Bureau of the Census publications classify Federal funds passed through the State government to local governments as State intergovernmental revenues. Thus, the State aid figures reported here include indirect Federal aid as well.

Table 18.2. State and Local Government Infrastructure Investment in FY '84, and State Financial Assistance to Rural Governments in FY '82

State	Capital Outlays: Total State & Local	State Share	Per Capita Nonmetro State Aid, 1982: Local Education	Public Welfare	Other Uses	Share of Local Revenues
	$ Millions	Percent	------Dollars------			Percent
United States	58139	41.4	277.72	27.33	80.66	38.1
Alabama	995	54.5	259.00	10.40	52.42	41.5
Alaska	1038	35.7	904.12	755.60	499.25	46.5
Arizona	1078	27.2	341.63	31.99	128.99	41.1
Arkansas	326	53.0	233.04	6.39	55.42	41.8
California	5253	30.1	434.66	75.34	251.00	46.4
Colorado	972	30.6	278.29	35.30	161.58	29.6
Connecticut	559	44.6	153.99	24.32	36.02	27.6
Delaware	194	67.0	382.30	19.45	5.35	57.2
D.C.	177	0.0	0.00	0.00	0.00	0.0
Florida	3109	35.3	324.52	16.12	65.18	38.3
Georgia	1298	47.4	260.18	6.19	42.71	34.3
Hawaii	377	78.4	0.00	17.46	64.52	12.2
Idaho	265	59.1	277.52	10.93	62.38	37.6
Illinois	2668	46.6	214.00	27.46	54.99	31.2
Indiana	1159	44.8	254.51	26.51	67.18	37.1
Iowa	868	49.7	273.30	40.49	86.15	33.4
Kansas	649	39.4	218.97	12.88	31.68	22.3
Kentucky	931	74.5	277.72	29.04	36.38	58.8
Louisiana	1656	57.3	371.24	16.43	93.00	41.9
Maine	213	44.5	227.14	15.47	23.82	32.4
Maryland	1457	41.2	247.38	45.70	48.50	36.4
Massachusetts	1012	43.0	137.47	18.58	78.11	20.3
Michigan	1539	43.9	127.43	17.06	158.77	28.1
Minnesota	1309	34.9	409.49	116.90	151.55	48.6
Mississippi	464	57.4	276.14	21.06	97.18	43.2
Missouri	977	45.5	206.00	6.77	21.28	32.3

Table 18.2 (continued)

State	Capital Outlays: Total State & Local	State Share	Per Capita Nonmetro State Aid, 1982: Local Education	Public Welfare	Other Uses	Share of Local Revenues
	$ Millions	Percent	------Dollars------			Percent
Montana	337	57.5	233.85	26.77	29.37	23.9
Nebraska	457	49.5	129.45	35.19	80.15	22.1
Nevada	387	30.3	428.47	25.27	237.80	47.2
New Hampshire	183	45.2	45.75	28.87	76.68	16.0
New Jersey	1537	37.1	195.36	41.26	130.89	28.2
New Mexico	687	54.2	495.93	30.06	119.74	59.5
New York	4814	31.1	374.68	31.76	209.69	43.4
North Carolina	891	50.2	351.38	12.35	53.03	50.1
North Dakota	259	55.5	385.40	32.38	95.49	45.0
Ohio	2257	53.9	218.35	16.02	103.24	38.0
Oklahoma	951	35.2	347.24	7.84	87.61	41.5
Oregon	649	43.2	321.81	22.15	102.33	34.5
Pennsylvania	2040	36.0	254.85	18.02	49.56	42.2
Rhode Island	174	71.0	215.54	4.45	24.64	27.1
South Carolina	535	47.4	281.06	9.25	32.92	40.5
South Dakota	227	57.0	180.50	29.86	16.85	24.3
Tennessee	1050	49.2	173.05	7.89	61.31	32.2
Texas	4812	33.3	290.15	3.38	4.39	29.9
Utah	561	50.0	332.13	25.32	32.56	32.9
Vermont	110	59.4	130.48	8.16	23.37	21.4
Virginia	1060	53.4	237.20	33.38	34.47	45.8
Washington	1515	40.4	419.88	53.29	104.92	43.3
West Virginia	401	68.1	345.82	8.59	17.04	48.0
Wisconsin	1216	29.0	245.48	44.37	211.24	41.3
Wyoming	488	46.2	343.82	114.84	197.18	26.3

Source: U.S. Bureau of the Census, 1984a, 1984b, 1985b.

As a source of revenue, State aid tends to represent a larger proportion of rural and small government budgets than for urban and large city budgets. In 1982, the most recent year for which rural figures are available, over 38 percent of nonmetro government general revenues were from the State compared to 33 percent for metro governments (U.S. Bureau of the Census, 1983, 1985a). As can be seen in Table 18.2, for a handful of States, State aid comprised over half of the general revenue collected by rural governments. The bulk of State intergovernmental aid is used to support education -- in 1982, 72 percent of State aid to nonmetropolitan governments was for education. Of the remainder, about $81 per capita went for non-welfare functions of rural governments, with a large share of this used to support capital-intensive public services, such as highways.

From the local government's perspective, grants from the State government have many of the advantages and disadvantages of Federal assistance. State grants represent a flow of financial resources into the community and are often pivotal in helping the local government meet the matching requirements for Federal aid programs. On the other hand, acceptance of State monies often reduces local autonomy and shifts final approval of project plans to the State government.[24]

INDIRECT FINANCIAL ASSISTANCE

In addition to intergovernmental grant programs, most States also offer loans to local jurisdictions for approved capital programs. Consistent information on loan programs operated by State governments is difficult to find, partly because of the complexity and variety of their institutional structures. While some States loan funds appropriated from general revenues, most of the major programs are less straightforward; the State government is involved either as a third party or as a financial intermediary, facilitating the flow of funds from private capital markets to local government borrowers. In some cases this involvement takes the form of a State guarantee; in others the State repackages local government bond issues through the use of a bond bank; in still others, the State sets up a special revolving loan fund, with monies borrowed through the issuance of State revenue bonds.

The objective of these programs is to lower the cost of borrowing for local governments, particularly small governments which tend to be

---

[24] While State government mandates are more often imposed on local governments rather than a condition of accepting intergovernmental aid (as is common with Federal mandates), local government officials still complain about "arbitrary" state regulations associated with State aid (Sokolow and Snavely, 1983).

infrequent borrowers. The extent of State involvement in the issuance process, and State liability in the event of a local government default, varies considerably among programs, as does the implicit subsidy associated with the State's role.

State guarantees generally involve the least amount of intrusion into the debt marketing process.[25] In some cases, the State pledges its "full faith and credit" as payment for locally issued debt should the local jurisdiction be unable to discharge its obligations. Often the guarantee is not unconditional, however, with the State placing an upper limit on its total liability under the program, or specifying that only a certain percentage of the local bond issue is guaranteed. Depending on the bond market's assessment of the value of the State's pledge, a guarantee can reduce the cost of locally issued debt by raising the bond's credit rating.

While not a guarantee per se, debt subsidy grants have some of the attributes of a conditional State guarantee. These programs use the dedication of certain State payments to local governments to strengthen the issuers' credit positions. Typically, some portion of State aid is paid directly to the local government's bond paying agent, for use in retiring the local government's debt obligations. In this way, bond holders are guaranteed a first claim on all State payments dedicated toward debt repayment. If the pledged State aid monies are from programs that are expected to continue over the life of the bond issue, investors often view the bond as more secure than bonds issued without the backing of debt subsidy grants. This additional security lowers the borrowing costs for local governments participating in the program.

In addition to bolstering the credit quality of local bond issues, many States attempt to lower local government borrowing costs through more direct involvement in the issuing process. State sponsored municipal bond banks and State revolving loan funds have the State acting as a financial intermediary--the State raises funds on the bond market and loans the proceeds directly to its local jurisdictions. In its most basic form, the role of financial intermediary does not imply a State guarantee of the bond bank's or loan fund's bonds. Savings associated with economies of size in the bond issuance process and lower risks because of the diversified economic base backing the bonds are counted on to lower the local government's cost of borrowing. However, most bond banks and State loan funds also pledge, at least informally, the State's general revenue as additional security, thus lowering borrowing costs still further.

---

[25] However, the process by which a local government applies for and receives a guarantee generally involves a considerable amount of State involvement in local financial affairs. For our purposes, State insurance funds, wherein the local issuer has to pay a fee for the State guarantee, are treated as synonymous with guarantee programs. See (Forbes and Petersen, 1983).

The potential savings associated with these various forms of indirect financial assistance are generally greatest for small rural governments. These governments tend to have low credit ratings, tend to issue small-sized bond issues (with high fixed issuing cost per dollar borrowed), and often lack the expertise larger units of governments acquire through frequent bond sales. As a result, the potential benefit of having the credit quality of their debt enhanced through State guarantees, or of bypassing the debt issuance process entirely through participation in a State revolving loan fund, can be considerable. These benefits are not without their cost, however, and the cost savings actually realized by participating governments may be smaller than anticipated.

To protect their own credit ratings and to keep program costs reasonably low, few States allow their local units indiscriminant use of borrowing or guarantee privileges. In most cases, the local government must demonstrate a need for the capital project being financed and must be judged creditworthy by the State before it can participate in these programs. This need to provide adequate justification for its capital plans, to meet minimum requirements for recordkeeping, and to manage its resources to the satisfaction of State regulators can place a considerable burden on local government officials.

In addition, the bond market may not value the State's involvement in local finance as much as program proponents believe. Since the State government is often vulnerable to the same economic swings as its local jurisdictions, investors may question the State's ability and/or resolve to bailout financially troubled local governments. Furthermore, as previously mentioned, small rural governments tend to sell their debt within localized markets. To the extent that the State's involvement does not broaden the market beyond this group of local investors, a guarantee may not increase a bond's attractiveness sufficiently to lower borrowing costs much.

All this is not to suggest that indirect financial assistance from the State is of little use to local governments. Rather, it is to point out that there are limits to the savings that can be realistically expected. As Forbes and Petersen state, "None of these approaches can be viewed as a panacea for achieving higher credit quality, improved marketing efficiency, or lower borrowing cost" (Forbes and Petersen, 1983, p. 225).

NONFINANCIAL ASSISTANCE

Because of the nature of the State-local relationship, States have long been involved in the supervision of local fiscal affairs and in the provision of technical assistance to local government officials. In the capital finance arena, these State activities have both positive and negative impacts. Table 18.3 presents a count of the number of States which provide oversight, data collection and reporting, technical assistance, and marketing assistance to their local jurisdictions. According to a survey completed by the Municipal Finance Officers Association in 1977, 41 States were involved in the debt management functions of their local governments. The degree of involvement varied tremendously from State to State, however, with some States limiting themselves to data collection activities while other States provided a range of bond marketing services to local officials.

Table 18.3. State Supervision of and Assistance With Local Debt Management

Activity	Number of States
State supervises or collects data on local government debt issues:	41
Collects and disseminates data	24
Maintains data files	22
Prescribes contents of official statements	14
Reviews local bond issues	19
Approves local bond issues	9
Helps market local bond issues	9
Other	12
State provides technical assistance to local government in connection with debt management:	32
Helps with official statement	14
Provides data to:	
Issuers for use in official statements	15
Bond rating agencies	16
Underwriters and dealers	18
Prospective Investors	11
Helps evaluate bids	7
Issues bulletins, pamphlets, manuals	12
Conducts seminars or conferences	12
Other	7

Source: (Petersen, Cole and Petrillo, 1977, p. 9).

Most States require local governments to follow specific accounting practices and to report budget figures to one or more State agencies on a periodic basis. If correctly designed and administered, these reporting requirements can often help local governments in the debt issuance and grant application process by developing the data base and managerial skills needed to produce accurate and complete financial and socioeconomic information for prospective investors and Federal agencies. By adopting generally accepted accounting practices, and providing the training to insure that proper procedures are followed, the yearly budgets, capital plans, and revenue forecasts of local jurisdictions can be brought into compliance with professional standards. While these measures are not without their costs, they can improve credit ratings for the State's local governments, increase demand for their securities, and increase grantsmanship skills within the State, thus lowering the locally borne cost of infrastructure.

The benefits of standardized accounting procedures have been increased in several States through maintenance of central data files and the dissemination of fiscal data to all parties interested in the fiscal health of the State and its local governments, including bond rating agencies, underwriters, dealers, and major investors. The availability of information whose accuracy has been verified by the State reduces uncertainty among bond market participants, thus increasing demand for the State's bond issues and lowering borrowing costs. Uncertainty can be lowered still further if the State formally approves the bonds of local jurisdictions prior to sale. In some States, approval is mandatory and is accomplished through State supervision of local budget decisions; in others, approval is voluntary and is accomplished through validation of the bond issue by the State's court system (Advisory Commission on Intergovernmental Relations, 1985; Haley, 1979).

Many of the benefits of direct State involvement in the local bond issuing process can be captured through voluntary participation in technical assistance and marketing programs. Providing advice on designing and awarding bond issues, offering assistance in preparing and distributing the bond proposals, and awarding small government bond issues through a centralized marketing procedure are all ways the State government can significantly lower the cost of debt financing for small rural governments. By making these services available on a voluntary basis, the State can greatly assist local officials without threatening their autonomy and flexibility.

REVENUE RAISING RESTRICTIONS

State governments have a legitimate concern for the fiscal well being of their local governments. Not only must the State take steps to insure that its citizens are not victimized by their local officials, but it also has the responsibility of minimizing the effect one government's fiscal crisis invariably has on the other jurisdictions in the State. While this oversight and supervisory role cannot safely be ignored by the State, steps can and should be taken to minimize the costs of taxing and borrowing restrictions, both for the local governments affected and for the State's taxpaying citizenry.

The vast majority of States place some sort of restrictions on the taxing and borrowing authority given to local governments. Most taxing restrictions are directed toward limiting local property taxes through ceilings on tax rates, tax levies, the tax base, or the tax assessment ratio (Advisory Commission on Intergovernmental Relations, 1982). It is also common for States to preclude certain classes of governments from collecting specific taxes. For example, as of 1979, 16 States did not allow local governments to impose income taxes or general sales taxes (Advisory Commission on Intergovernmental Relations, 1981).

A review of State statutes published in 1978 found some type of debt limit imposed in 46 States (Hill, 1978). Restrictions on local government debt usually apply only to general obligation bonds. Limits are placed directly on the amount of indebtedness (with ceilings expressed as a percentage of assessed value of the jurisdiction's taxable property), or indirectly by requiring a local referendum before a jurisdiction issues a bond. A number of States also place ceilings on the interest rate local governments can pay, and limit the period for which bonds may be outstanding. An examination of the interest rate ceilings in effect in 1982 found that, in at least 17 States, the ceilings were below market rates (Hough and Petersen, 1983). Local governments within these States were effectively precluded from issuing debt that year.

Even when there is no statute prohibiting local governments from using a new source of revenue, if authority has not been explicitly granted, local officials are often constrained from taking action.[26] Thus, local governments may not make full use of user charges to finance public services even when their use is not prohibited. Likewise, a recent study of State constraints on local government capital financing found few restrictions that directly prohibited the use of most creative capital financing instruments (Hough and Petersen, 1983). Nonetheless, local officials often wait for the passage of State legislation approving these new financing techniques before they are actively considered.

These explicit and implicit limits on local government discretionary authority may contribute to excess costs or inefficient public service delivery under certain conditions. To the extent that restrictions hamper the timing of capital projects, or encourage "tried and true" financing schemes rather than innovative least cost techniques, the cost of infrastructure projects can be needlessly increased. If restrictions prevent diversification of the local revenue base, they can set the stage for the fiscal crisis they are meant to avoid. For example, heavy reliance on property taxes leaves local governments susceptible to fiscal stress during periods of rapid population and economic growth (Stinson, 1981).

By allowing local governments the maximum degree of discretionary authority that is consistent with the State's oversight and supervisory responsibilities, many States have given their local jurisdictions the political power to resolve their own infrastructure problems. State regulations which foster sound management practices (through the imposition of standardized accounting practices, for example) rather than

---

26 In many States, without a specific grant of authority from the State, local governments are unable to act. The exception is in those States which have granted residual powers to local units of governments. As of 1980, the ACIR reports that roughly half of the States have granted residual powers to some of their local governments, although it is unusual for all jurisdictions within a State to be included (Zimmerman, 1981).

imposing arbitrary limitations and prohibitions on revenues are an important ingredient in the State's role in financing local infrastructure.[27] The potential benefits of local autonomy for small rural governments can be maximized (and the potential costs minimized) by coupling political power with technical assistance, training, and education.

THE FUTURE OF STATE ASSISTANCE

It is difficult to make statements about the prospects for increased levels of State financial assistance for locally provided infrastructure in the future. On the one hand, voters have shown considerable support for capital programs recently, both at the local and State level (Menchik, 1985). This, together with predictions of State budget surpluses through the remainder of the decade, could lead to increased levels of State support.[28] On the other hand, many States are still recovering from budget problems brought on by taxpayer resistance to tax increases in the late seventies, and the economic recession of the early eighties. Predictions of budget surpluses aside, cuts in Federal aid, proposed changes to the Federal tax code, and the constitutional requirement that State governments maintain a balanced budget all tend to dampen prospects for rapid growth in State capital assistance programs.

Proposed budget cuts to many Federal domestic programs will, if enacted, leave the State government as the primary provider of many social services. To the extent that States replace funds cut by the Federal government, they will have fewer resources available for capital programs. At the same time, proposed changes to the Federal tax code may reduce the ability of States to use Federal "tax expenditures" to finance their programs. In particular, the proposed change in the deductibility of State and local government taxes will increase the locally borne cost of these taxes and may reduce voter support for revenue raising initiatives. Proposed changes in the marginal rate structure will also reduce the value of any deductions that survive the tax reform process.

---

[27] It should be noted that the bond market may prefer municipal bonds issued by closely regulated jurisdictions. Investors may view the absence of State regulation as an invitation to local officials to radically alter their spending and taxing behavior, thus adversely affecting the value of long-term debt outstanding. As a result, a balance between complete local autonomy and centralized decisionmaking is probably desirable from an infrastructure finance viewpoint.

[28] The U.S. Treasury has predicted sizeable State government budget surpluses for the next few years. However, questions have been raised about the estimation methodology adopted for the Treasury study (Anonymous, 1985).

Even if budget constraints do not adversely affect the flow of State government assistance to local governments, there remain reasons to expect assistance levels to be suboptimal from a national perspective. Interstate competition for business development will tend to hold tax and spending levels lower than they might be in a closed economy. In addition, undervaluation of capital program benefits accruing to out-of-state residents would normally result in suboptimal assistance levels. As a result, a wholesale shift in funding responsibility from the Federal to the State and local level can be expected to decrease investment in infrastructure.

LOCAL GOVERNMENT REVENUE AND BOND FINANCING

Despite Federal and State assistance, local governments have a significant role to play in financing public infrastructure. While local funding of major capital projects can severely strain a community's resources, it is often the most equitable and efficient means of financing the construction and rehabilitation of infrastructure. This is particularly true when there are few interjurisdictional benefits associated with the project. When a capital project's benefits accrue to local citizens, economically efficient decisions will be encouraged if project expenses are financed through local taxes or user charges, rather than through State or Federal categorical grants. Equity considerations may suggest extending intergovernmental aid to low income communities in spite of an absense of interjurisdictional project benefits, but in general, charging those who benefit from a capital project is considered equitable in most situations.

Even when intergovernmental assistance is available, local officials may find it advantageous to "go it alone." As has already been alluded to, intergovernmental assistance is rarely "free." The need to meet reporting requirements, adhere to restrictions and conditions associated with assistance programs, and the time delays associated with these programs can all raise the cost of infrastructure projects and reduce local control over project design and construction.

This is not to suggest that the absense of an intergovernmental aid program implies complete freedom for local government officials. As has already been discussed, State governments often place restrictions on a local government's options for raising revenues. In addition, both the Federal and State governments mandate certain actions be taken by local officials, whether or not intergovernmental assistance is available. Then too, the existence of Federal standards for certain types of infrastructure, such as highways and bridges, puts considerable pressure on State and local officials to adopt those standards even for locally funded projects.[29] Nonetheless, within externally imposed limits, local officials have considerable latitude in how to finance infrastructure investments.

Along the spectrum of financing options open to local officials, there are two major decisions that must be addressed: (1) whether to finance the capital costs through general taxes or to rely on user related taxes and charges, and (2) whether to rely on current revenues to finance projects or rely on future revenues through the issuance of bonds or using other methods to defer payments.[30] While each of these decisions has implications for the other, it is still useful to treat them separately.

TAXES VERSUS USER CHARGES

The source of local revenues used to finance infrastructure has both equity and efficiency consequences. General taxes are most often imposed on bases which are unrelated to the use and/or benefits the taxpayer derives from public services. Income received, value of goods purchased, value of real estate and personal property owned are all used to assess locally imposed taxes. In an admittedly imperfect sense, these taxes are based on an individual's, household's, or business' ability to pay taxes rather than on its demand for public services.[31] In contrast, user charges and certain targetted taxes attempt to collect revenues from those believed to benefit from the service being provided. Utility charges, parking fees, license fees, motor fuels taxes, and special assessment taxes are each paid by the presumed consumers of public services, more or less in relation to their level of consumption. Each approach to funding local infrastructure has its advantages and disadvantages.

General taxes are relatively easy to administer, can be made responsive to inflation, have traditionally been viewed as a "fair" way of

---

[29] Pressure may be exerted because the expectations of the public are raised for all capital projects by Federally financed infrastructure projects. In addition, the fear of litigation may make local officials hesitant to adopt designs or technologies which do not meet Federal standards.

[30] While the issuance of notes and bonds is the most common method of deferring payment of current purchases, other less direct financing techniques are available to local officials. For example, underfunding public employee pension funds defers payment of current expenses.

[31] In a Tiebout-type world, where households are able to choose the optimal level of taxes and local public services from among a large number of local jurisdictions, the distinction between taxes and user charges loses its relevance except for income-tax deduction purposes. However, this is not likely to be the situation for the typical rural household.

raising revenues, and are deductible expenses for Federal (and State) income tax purposes. In those cases where a public service should be available to all citizens without regard for ability to pay, financing through the imposition of taxes has considerable merit. Taxes may also be the only equitable method of financing public services when beneficiaries cannot be identified or excluded. On the negative side, general taxes do not give policymakers clear signals about the demand for specific public services. They often require voter approval before rates can be altered, and are subject to State limitations and restrictions.

User charges and targetted taxes have gained increasing acceptance as a way of financing public services in recent years. Advocates argue that charging fees to users, when they can be readily identified, improves the allocative efficiency of local governments. Consumers can directly reveal their demand for different services to policymakers, rather than attempting to transmit this information through the political process. In cases where most of the benefits of a service accrue to the user of the service, relying on user charges may also represent the "fairest" way of paying for its provision (Colman, 1983). On the negative side, user fees are generally not deductible expenses for Federal and State income tax purposes, thus making them relatively more burdensome for those who itemize their deductions. User fees and targetted taxes may be difficult to administer, and may require special legislation before being adopted (Vehorn, 1981). For essential services to low income residents, equity questions may dictate that user fees not be relied upon, even when users are identifiable and benefits are targetted.[32]

Local government reliance on user fees to finance both operating and capital expenses has been increasing over the past two decades. Taxpayer resistance to rate increases, concern over government waste, State imposed tax and debt limits, and improved management capabilities have all made user charges and revenue bonds the preferred alternative for raising revenues. Nonetheless, their disadvantages should be kept in mind whenever policymakers are faced with the choice of how to finance a capital project.

CURRENT REVENUES VERSUS BOND FINANCING

The second major decision regarding local funding of infrastructure is how to structure the payments. While many major capital projects are so expensive as to make funding with current revenues impractical, and

---

[32] Proponents of user charges argue that equity objections can be overcome with sliding-scale fee schedules, two-tier services, and the like. They also point out that alternative financing techniques--tax funding or privatization--may be equally inequitable (Colman, 1983).

minor projects may be too small to warrant a special bond issuance, many projects can be handled either through current financing or through the issuance of bonds.[33] Each method can be cost minimizing under certain conditions.

Financing capital projects out of current revenues, especially relatively inexpensive projects, is often the most straightforward and simplest method of funding. As long as tax levies are below State-imposed limits, the process of raising funds can usually be handled through the local government's own administrative office, with few, if any, "outside" reviews. If capital outlays tend to remain fairly constant from year to year, then setting tax rates or user changes at levels high enough to cover operating expenses and "usual" capital costs will minimize budgetary outlays. When infrastructure can be rebuilt or added to through an incremental process--such as with highways--this method of financing is feasible.[34] However, when infrastructure needs go unfilled because current revenues are insufficient, nonbudgetary costs are imposed on citizens which should not be ignored. When the cost of meeting infrastructure needs cannot easily be met with current revenues, bond financing may be preferable to project cancellation--this is likely for "lumpy" infrastructure projects with relatively high costs.

For long-lived infrastructure projects, bond financing allows payments to be stretched out over the useful life of the facility. Not only does this greatly reduce the need for year-to-year fluctuations in current revenue collections, but in a world of imperfect tax capitalization, it may improve the balance between the benefits and costs of capital intensive services. Because interest income from municipal bonds is exempt from Federal (and often State) income taxes, a portion of the interest expense from deferred payment is shifted to Federal and State taxpayers, rather than being borne locally. As a result, in present value terms, tax-exempt bond financing may be less costly for local taxpayers than would be true if project expenses were paid with current revenue.[35] This is particularly true for costlier projects.

---

[33] Theoretically, any capital project can be financed through current tax levies if taxpayers are willing and able to borrow on their own to meet their tax obligations. As a practical matter, there is a limit on how much tax levies can increase before public pressure forces cancellation of infrastructure projects.

[34] A recent survey of rural townships in 4 midwestern States found relatively few relied on long-term debt to finance roads and bridges (Chicoine and Walzer, 1984).

[35] Under certain circumstances, local governments may even be able to earn a profit by reinvesting bond proceeds at taxable rates. However, Federal regulations restrict the legal ability of State and local governments to reap the benefits of interest rate arbitrage.

Bond financing becomes relatively less costly as project expense increases. This is because there are high "fixed" costs involved in designing and marketing a bond issue. These costs may include obtaining voter approval of a bond sale when a referendum is required, purchasing a credit rating and an independent audit, and hiring a fiscal advisor to help with the sale. For almost every bond sale, the issuer incurs the cost of legal counsel, and the cost of printing legal notices, the bond prospectus, and the bonds themselves. In general, these costs do not increase proportionately as the size of the issue increases. In percentage terms, these expenses can be considerable for very small issues, but become relatively unimportant as issue size increases (Fisher, Forbes and Petersen, 1980).

In addition to the budgetary costs of issuing bonds, there are also a number of psychic costs. Bond sales often involve State reviews and may require voter approval. The sale of a bond also requires the involvement of "outsiders" in local fiscal affairs--bond rating analysts, fiscal advisors, bond attorneys, and underwriters. Then too, bond market participants have a rather specialized language to describe a highly technical procedure. There remains the very real possibility that, in spite of expert advice by those marketing the issue, the local official will make a wrong decision which could prove costly for the issuing government. For all of these reasons, local officials may hesitate to issue bonds for capital projects, even when it would be cheaper to do so.

TYPES OF TAX-EXEMPT BOND FINANCING

If the decision is made to rely on bond-financed infrastructure investment, then the local official is faced with a dizzying array of debt instruments to choose from. In general, tax-exempt bonds can be categorized according to their length to maturity (i.e. short-term versus long-term), their security backing (i.e. general obligation, limited tax or special assessment bond, or revenue bond), and whether or not they have other special features (variable rate bonds, zero coupon bonds, etc.).

Particularly for small governments that tend to be infrequent borrowers, the simpler the debt issuance procedure the better. For long-lived capital projects, long-term bond issues are usually appropriate. The choice of whether to issue revenue or general obligation bonds is, in part, determined by whether the public service is paid for with taxes or user charges, but other considerations may also enter into the decision. State regulations are often placed on the issuance of general obligation bonds, but not on the issuance of revenue bonds. As a result, revenue bonds may be quicker and easier to sell. In addition, if a bond rating is important (because of the size of the issue, or the nature of the local market for municipal bonds), it may be easier to convince the rating agencies that a bond backed by specific ear-marked revenues is more creditworthy than is a bond backed the general taxing power of the issuer.[36] These factors may help explain why nonmetropolitan governments have historically issued a higher proportion of revenue bonds than have metropolitan issuers despite the higher marketing and interest costs associated with revenue bonds (Fisher, Forbes and Petersen, 1980; Sullivan, 1983a).

In addition to decisions about what revenues to pledge toward repayment of a bond, issuers also have a number of other options from which to choose--all geared toward making their bonds more attractive to certain groups of investors. These options generally require the bond issuer to shoulder some of the market risk that tax-exempt bond holders have traditionally borne. Variable rate bonds, compound rate bonds, put provisions and warrants all place an added burden on the issuer (if interest rates should move in an unexpected direction) in return for a lower initial interest rate (Table 18.4). They became popular during the volatile market of the early 1980's, but have tended to be used most extensively by large governments and quasi-public agencies borrowing for private purposes (Petersen and Hough, 1983). Since they can involve substantial added risk for the issuing government, these options make projecting ultimate borrowing costs difficult and should be approached cautiously by smaller, infrequent borrowers.

OTHER CONSIDERATIONS IN DESIGNING AND SELLING A BOND ISSUE

While the basic design of a bond issue is being developed, decisions will also have to be made on whether or not to purchase a credit rating and/or external credit enhancements (such as insurance, guarantees, and letters of credit), and how the issue is to be marketed. Each decision will affect borrowing costs.

Only a few nationally recognized independent rating agencies analyze the credit quality of municipal debt and make their judgements known to the public; of these, Moody's Investors Service, Inc., and Standard and Poor's Corporation dominate the field. Both agencies view their ratings primarily as measures of the risk of default. A favorable rating by one or both agencies tends to reduce investors' fear of default and increases the bond issue's appeal as an investment, thus lowering the cost of borrowing.

In the past, many small rural governments have relied on local banks and wealthy individuals within the community to purchase most of their bonds. Within such a localized market, credit ratings were relatively

---

[36] Little analytical evidence exists on this question. However, the distribution of ratings for general obligation and revenue bonds suggest that small governments are particularly disadvantaged in the general obligation bond rating process (Sullivan, 1983a).

unimportant, particularly given the low probability of receiving a favorable rating (Sullivan, 1983c). However, with deregulation of the banking industry, reduced income tax liabilities for wealthy individuals, and the increased availability of tax-exempt bond funds, these traditional investors may be less willing (or able) to purchase the bonds of their local governments. As a result, many rural governments may find it useful to have their bonds evaluated by a credit rating agency to attract a broader group of investors.

Table 18.4. Innovative Bond Financing Techniques

Technique	Description	Risk to Issuer
Compound Coupon Bonds	Semi-annual interest accrues to the bondholder at a compound rate. Interest is paid when the bond matures.	Issuer assumes reinvestment risk. If interest rates decline, issuer ends up paying above-market rates of interest on the investors' accrued interest
Zero Coupon Bonds	Bonds are initially sold at a substantial discount. Interest is paid when the bond matures.	Issuer assumes reinvestment risk. Risk is the same as with a compound coupon bond.
Variable Rate Bonds	Interest rate floats with market interest rate rather than being fixed at the time of sale.	Issuer assumes a share of the investors' market risk. If market rates go up, the cost of the debt goes up.
Put Options Bonds	Bonds which may be redeemed by investors prior to maturity.	Issuer assumes a share of the investors' market risk. If rates go up, bonds will be redeemed and will have to be resold at a higher rate of interest.
Bonds with Warrants	Bonds which give investors the option of purchasing additional bonds at the same interest rate during some period in the future.	Issuer bets that interest rates will not go down during the period covered by the warrant. If rates go down, additional bonds will have to be issued, paying above-market rates of interest.

Source: Derived from Government Finance Research Center, 1983; and Petersen and Hough, 1983.

Both rating agencies evaluate the same basic criteria to arrive at their credit rating: the structure and relative burden of debt for the issuing government and for other governmental units serving the area, the economic base of the area, expenditures and revenues of the issuing governments, and the management capacity and organizational structure of the issuer (Lamb and Rappaport, 1980). Because of their limited economic bases and management skills, relatively few rural governments can expect to receive high credit ratings without some form of external credit enhancement. There are a number of ways rural governments can improve their ratings (both among investors and rating analysts) by using someone else's good credit. Private insurance, pledging timely payment of an issue's principal and interest expenses in the event of a default, can be purchased by qualified governments. Bonds insured by the major tax-exempt insurer--Municipal Bond Insurance Corporation--receive the highest credit rating from both Moody's and Standard & Poor's. Several States have guarantee programs for certain types of local government bonds. In general, these public programs tend to increase ratings that would otherwise be received by small governments on their guaranteed bond issues (Forbes and Petersen, 1983). A third means of raising a bond's credit rating is through the purchase of a bank letter of credit (LOC). Used to assure an issuer's liquidity, LOC's can be purchased which essentially guarantee that the issuer will have a line of credit available with which to retire a bond issue, even if the issuer is insolvent. If the LOC unconditionally guarantees the issuer's right to borrow from the bank, then the bank's credit rating is generally assigned to the bond issue.

While many rural governments can qualify for these services, they are seldom provided free of charge. One-time fees of 0.5% to 2.0% are charged for private insurance, and annual charges for LOC's generally cost 0.5% percent or more of the amount of authorized loan funds (Petersen and Hough, 1983). These charges can easily cancel out much of the interest savings a small government can reasonably expect to accrue from receiving a favorable rating on its bond issue.[37] While the decision on whether or not to purchase credit enhancements is based on simple arithmetic, the arithmetic is seldom simple, particularly when small, infrequent borrowers are involved.

A final concern is over how the bond issue should be marketed. For most public purpose tax-exempt bond issues, the entire issue is sold to an underwriting firm (or syndicate of firms) which then resells the bonds to the investing public. The underwriter can be selected either through a competitive bidding process, or the issue can be awarded through negotiation with a preselected underwriter. Competitive sales generally are accepted to be the cheapest and fairest means of marketing municipal bonds. Nonetheless, a negotiated sale may be the only practical marketing technique for many rural borrowers.

Rural bond issues tend to be small and either unrated or unfavorably rated (Sullivan, 1983a). In addition, rural governments tend to borrow

---

[37] An analysis of interest rates on municipal bonds sold during 1977 found that small governments benefited less from favorable ratings than large governments. While an Aa rating implied an interest rate saving of 106 basis points over a similar bond with a Baa rating for a large government, the interest rate differential was only 43 basis points for small governments (Sullivan, 1983c).

infrequently, so they often lack access to the specialized skills needed to market a bond issue. These characteristics make competitive offerings difficult and potentially expensive. Given these factors, rural officials may find it cost-effective to market their bond issues through a preselected underwriter.

COSTS OF BOND FINANCING

The major component in the total cost of bond financing is the interest costs paid to investors. As already noted, however, there are also marketing and underwriting expenses that issuer's face. For small-sized issues or short-term bonds, these up-front costs can also comprise a significant share of the total cost of bond financing.

The interest rate on municipal bonds tends to fluctuate with general interest rates, but is somewhat more volatile over the interest rate cycle. Due to the exemption of interest income earned on municipal bonds from Federal and State income taxes, the interest rate on municipals is somewhat lower than the rates paid on taxable securities. Historically, the municipal bond interest rate has averaged about 70 percent of the taxable bond rate for Aa-rated bonds (U.S. GAO, 1983). Over the last few years this ratio has been well above the historic level, indicating that the value of the tax exemption to investors has declined somewhat (Table 18.5).

The rate individual governments can expect to pay differs from the prevailing market rate because of investor reaction to the bond issue's and bond issuer's characteristics. Interest rates tend to be higher on revenue bonds, bonds sold through negotiation, smaller-sized bonds, longer-termed bonds and unrated or unfavorably rated bonds. Unique financial, organizational and managerial conditions of the issuing government can also affect borrowing costs, over and above their impact via the credit rating. In addition, unique local market conditions can affect the borrowing costs of smaller governments, either exacerbating or mitigating national market trends.

Based on the characteristics of rural municipal bonds, most observers believe that rural governments probably pay a higher rate of interest on their bond issues than urban governments. However, analyses of bonds sold during 1977 and 1982 fail to support this generally held belief. On average, rural governments paid interest rates roughly equivalent to those paid by urban governments during both the stable market prevalent during 1977 and the highly volatile market of 1982.[38]

---

[38] Analyses were of Public Securities Association long-term municipal bond data. Results for 1977 were published in (Sullivan, 1983b). Results for 1982 are preliminary.

Table 18.5. Average Annual Yields on Moody's AA-Rated Tax-Exempt and Taxable
Bonds, 1950 to 1985

Year	Average Annual Bond Yields on: Municipals	Corporates	Tax-Exempt/ Taxable Yield Ratio
		------Percent------	
1950	1.76	2.69	65.4
1951	1.78	2.91	61.2
1952	2.00	3.04	65.8
1953	2.54	3.31	76.7
1954	2.16	3.06	70.6
1955	2.32	3.16	73.4
1956	2.72	3.45	78.8
1957	3.33	4.03	82.6
1958	3.17	3.94	80.5
1959	3.55	4.51	78.7
1960	3.51	4.56	77.0
1961	3.46	4.48	77.2
1962	3.17	4.47	70.9
1963	3.16	4.39	72.0
1964	3.19	4.49	71.0
1965	3.25	4.57	71.1
1966	3.76	5.23	71.9
1967	3.86	5.66	68.2
1968	4.31	6.38	67.6
1969	6.28	7.20	87.2
1970	6.28	8.32	75.5
1971	5.36	7.78	68.9
1972	5.19	7.48	69.4
1973	5.09	7.66	66.4
1974	6.04	8.84	68.3
1975	6.77	9.17	73.8
1976	6.12	8.75	69.9
1977	5.39	8.24	65.4
1978	5.68	8.92	63.7
1979	6.12	9.94	61.6
1980	8.06	12.50	64.5
1981	10.89	14.75	73.8
1982	11.30	14.41	78.4
1983	9.20	12.42	74.1
1984	9.88	13.31	74.2
1985	8.93	11.82	75.5

Source: Moody's Investors Service, as reported in U.S. GAO, 1983; Moody's Investors
Service, 1986a and 1986b.

Less is known about the other costs involved in marketing municipal bonds. Out of pocket marketing costs per dollar borrowed tend to be higher for revenue bonds, and higher for smaller issues (Fisher, Forbes and Petersen, 1980). Based on this information it seems likely that rural governments might pay slightly higher marketing costs than do urban governments. However, the evidence is far from being conclusive, and the differential is probably modest.

FUTURE PROSPECTS FOR LOCAL FUNDING OF INFRASTRUCTURE

Since local funding of infrastructure tends to be the residual component of the funding formula, its future prospects depend upon the future availability of the other sources of financing--the Federal and State governments and the corporate sector. Looked at in this way, the future for local funding looks good. This prognosis does not imply an absence of problems for local officials faced with infrastructure decisions, however. While local funding provides officials maximum control over capital projects, the locally borne costs of "local funding" are still influenced by Federal and State policies, and by economic conditions.

Federal and State policies affect local decisionmaking by altering the mix of functional responsibilities for providing public services and by altering the legal framework within which local governments, and their citizens, operate. The current retrenchment of its domestic programs by the Federal government is effectively shifting responsibility for many social services back to State and local governments. Since demand for social services competes with other uses of scarce local government revenue dollars, such as infrastructure investments, Federal program cuts may put added pressure on local capital outlays.[39] Local governments already experiencing relatively high levels of fiscal effort are likely to be most affected by these Federal program changes--a group that includes many rural communities (Reeder, 1985 and 1986).

In addition to cutting outlays, the Federal government also affects the cost of locally provided services through Federal tax laws and various regulations. Currently, a portion of the cost of locally funded public services is actually paid for at the State and national level through "tax expenditures"--Federal and State taxes not collected because of exclusions and deductions within their respective tax codes (Advisory Commission

---

[39] In addition, Federal policies mandating the State and local government sector to monitor and correct environmental hazards through clean water, groundwater, solid waste disposal, and asbestos legislation, and court ordered changes in personnel practices have increased the operating costs of local governments.

on Intergovernmental Relations, 1984b). It has been estimated that the deductibility of State and local property, sales, and income taxes reduces the tax price of State and local goods and services by about 10 percent for the average itemizing taxpayer. For New York State residents, deductibility of State and local taxes reduced Federal tax payments by $230 per capita in 1980 (Digler, 1985). Federal and State tax provisions which alter the deductibility of local taxes thus have a direct impact on the cost of locally funded infrastructure. There are currently several proposals being considered which could radically alter the Federal income tax treatment of State and local taxes, eliminating or restricting their deductibility from gross income. However, even if the deductibility of local taxes is left intact, proposals to reduce the marginal tax rate structure could reduce its "value" to itemizers. Thus, the ability of local government officials to shift a portion of their tax bill to the Federal and State governments is likely to be reduced, to some extent, in the near future. Depending on the offsetting income effect associated with lower Federal taxes, the higher tax price likely to face itemizers in the next few years may result in pressure to hold down tax-funded spending, particularly in high tax localities.

These tax-law changes, if adopted, may encourage a further shift away from tax-financed infrastructure investment toward user fees as a source of revenue. As the relative burden of local taxes increases, local officials may find it politically easier to rely on user fees. To the extent that this shift is accompanied by a growth in the importance of special districts, infrastructure investment decisions may be removed, at least partially, from the political arena. It has been suggested that such a development may lead to a more rational infrastructure construction and maintenance program (Advisory Commission on Intergovernmental Relations, 1984a).

The effect Federal tax code changes could have on the cost of debt-financed spending is equally important, but their likely impact on infrastructure decisions is more uncertain. As with the deductibility of local taxes, lower marginal Federal income tax rates reduce the value of the tax-exempt feature of municipal bonds. Thus, tax reform which significantly alters the distribution of the Federal income tax burden among income groups will likely affect the size of the interest rate differential between tax-exempt and taxable securities. In particular, changes which reduce the marginal rates paid by the wealthy should tend to narrow the interest rate differential. Minimum tax proposals might also reduce the appeal of municipal bonds for some investors. On the corporate-side of tax reform, proposals to restrict the ability of commercial banks to deduct interest expenses incurred in holding tax-exempt securities will depress the banking sector's demand for municipal bonds.

Not all of the tax reforms being discussed would adversely affect the cost of local government debt financing. Reforms which reduce the availability of competing tax shelters should make municipal bonds more attractive. Current proposals to restrict the use of Individual Retirement

Accounts, to restrict private-purpose uses of tax-exempt securities, and to restrict the ability of passive investors to apply paper losses on their investments against current income will all tend to make municipal bonds more attractive as a tax-sheltering devise.

The net effect of all of these changes is difficult to estimate. What may emerge is a municipal bond market that serves the public infrastructure needs of the country much more efficiently than does the current system. Certainly a flatter marginal tax rate structure coupled with much tighter restrictions on alternative tax shelter has the potential of reducing Federal income tax losses without adversely affecting the cost of debt-financed infrastructure. Whether or not the tax law, as eventually adopted, will attain this goal remains to be seen.

As important as the tax law is to the cost of municipal bond financing, the condition of financial markets is probably more important. This is one area where current trends clearly favor debt-financed funding of infrastructure investments. Currently, yields on tax-exempt securities are approximately 7 percent--this represents a drop of 4 percentage points from average market yields recorded in 1982 (Moody's Investors Service, 1986a and 1986b). The current condition of financial markets is particularly beneficial to smaller government borrowers that lack the experience and skill to undertake the "creative financing" techniques needed during periods of increasing interest rates.[40] Whether current rates will continue beyond 1986 is impossible to predict with any certainty. However, while interest rates remain low, they greatly facilitate infrastructure financing.

A further development which may help rural borrowers is the introduction of State-specific tax-exempt bond funds in many States. Tax-exempt bond funds have grown in importance as the municipal bond market has moved toward retail sales of bonds. Generally, these funds have not been too interested in the bond issues of small, infrequent borrowers because of the absense of a viable secondary market for these bonds. Recently, bond funds have been introduced which specialize in the issues of a particular State to maximize the tax benefits of their portfolio. While empirical evidence is scarce, it seems likely that these State-specific bond funds might be more willing to purchase and hold bonds issued by

---

[40] On a related matter, proposed changes in Federal bank regulations may reduce the appeal of many of the creative capital financing techniques popular at the beginning of the decade. Several of these techniques relied upon commercial bank letters of credit (LOC) to allay investor fears of liquidity problems by the issuing government (Petersen and Hough, 1983). Recently, the Federal Reserve Board of Governors has proposed changes to its minimum capital regulations which would discourage banks from issuing LOC's.

some of the State's rural government, thus broadening the market for rural issues.

PUBLIC/PRIVATE FINANCING

In addition to relying on its own and other government resources to build, maintain, and operate public infrastructure, local government officials also have the option of involving private sector institutions. The degree of private sector involvement can vary tremendously. The advantages of private sector-assisted financing depend upon the method and degree of private sector involvement, but all approaches share a common characteristic--they all reduce the budgetary costs of capital projects from the local government's point of view.

The public/private partnership concept encompasses a range of economic development activities. At one extreme, the term refers to government assistance to private firms to foster job growth and local economic development; at the other, the term refers to private sector support for public activities (Weiss, 1985). Since our concern is with public infrastructure, we will concentrate exclusively on techniques used to tap private sector support for government activities. This subgroup of public/private partnerships can be further categorized into three broad approaches: (1) private sector contributions which are conditions of development, (2) private sector contracting, and (3) complete privatization of "public" services. While the distinctions between these three approaches are not always clear, the underlying relationships between the public and private sectors tend to be different.

SUPPORT AS A CONDITION OF PRIVATE SECTOR DEVELOPMENT

A wide variety of arrangements have been used to insure that new housing and economic development projects come with at least some of the public facilities required to service the developed areas. In some cases, the developers are required to construct roads, water and sewer lines, public school buildings, recreational facilities, and other facilities before housing or office units can be occupied. In others, developers are required to pay development fees which can be used to finance the construction of public facilities. Kirlin and Kirlin list 16 variations on the developer-jurisdiction relationship, each of which calls for a different pattern of planning, financing, constructing, and owning infrastructure projects (Kirlin and Kirlin, 1985).

While developers often bemoan the need to pay "exorbitant" fees for the right to develop private property, direct assistance can be beneficial to the developer. Developers willing to internalize the costs of providing public infrastructure for their projects can greatly reduce political opposition to development, increasing the probability of timely and satisfactory project completion. In addition, developers who take part in the planning and construction of infrastructure can often avoid construction delays, can maximize the value of infrastructure to their properties, and may be able to reduce the ultimate costs of infrastructure to property owners.

From the jurisdiction's point of view, developer-funded infrastructure results in lower budgets and debt levels than might otherwise occur. By insulating established residents from the costs of adding to the jurisdiction's capital stock, development fees can relieve political pressure against growth. Their distributional impact can be viewed as synonomous with a special assessment district, without the associated tax and debt increase that special assessment bonds entail. Since funding is "off-budget," state restrictions can often be avoided, and bond ratings are unlikely to be affected.

While useful in many situations, developer assistance has its limitations and drawbacks, particularly for small rural jurisdictions. Since the benefits and costs of infrastructure tend to be unique for each housing or economic development project, determining what type of support is appropriate has to be done on a case-by-case basis, often with face-to-face bargaining between the jurisdiction and the developer. Such interaction can easily lead to charges of favoritism and misuse of public authority. Furthermore, small governments which lack in-house capacity on zoning and economic development issues may not bargain very efficiently with developers. A lack of these specialized skills could retard economic growth in the jurisdiction, and even with expert advice, development fees may not be a viable financing option for jurisdictions in a poor bargaining position.[41] Finally, in jurisdictions which have a substantial amount of debt outstanding, relying on developer fees raises equity questions. These fees force new residents to pay for the infrastructure that serves their development, while their taxes and user charges help pay for the infrastructure serving the rest of the jurisdiction.

---

[41] The extent to which developers can afford to pay for infrastructure development depends upon their ability to pass the added costs on the eventual property owners. If a jurisdiction lacks the qualities which make it uniquely suited for a development project, then the developer may be unable to pass along infrastructure-related costs, and will therefore be less willing to incur these costs.

CONTRACTING WITH THE PRIVATE SECTOR

A second, more generally applicable method of tapping the private
sector for assistance with the construction and operation of infrastructure
is through contracting--that is, paying the private sector to provide
facilities or services to the public. Such arrangements can take two basic
forms: a lease, where a privately-owned facility or piece of equipment is
rented by a governmental entity; or a service contract, where a range of
services are provided to the government by a private concern. Both leasing
and service contracts became very popular at the beginning of the decade
in response to record high interest rates and favorable Federal tax
provisions. However, the Tax Reform Act of 1984 substantially reduced
the tax-advantages for most government leasing arrangements, so their
popularity has declined somewhat in recent years. Nonetheless, both lease
and service contracts remain an attractive financing alternative for certain
types of infrastructure.

There are several types of leasing arrangements possible for acquiring
the use of long-lived infrastructure (Quinn and Olstein, 1985). For Federal
tax purposes, these can be categorized into three general types:
lease/purchase agreements, safe harbor leases, and true leases. The first
two types of leases are financing schemes which allow the government
effective ownership of a facility, with the private sector providing the initial
financing. Under a lease/purchase agreement, the government rents a
facility from a private investor with ownership transferred to the
government at the end of the lease period. Since the government is
considered the owner for Federal income tax purposes, the private investor
cannot claim investment tax credits, depreciation allowances, or other
investment-related deductions for Federal income tax purposes. However,
the investor can treat part of the rental income as a tax-exempt interest
payment (analogous to interest paid on municipal bonds), thus lowering
the cost of the lease.

Under a safe harbor lease, a lease/purchase agreement is entered into
which preserves many of the tax advantages associated with private
investments. In essence, the government receives a cash payment in return
for "selling" these tax benefits to a private corporation. Such an
arrangement is currently legal only for leasing mass transit vehicles.

Unlike the lease/purchase and safe harbor lease, under a true lease
the private investor retains effective ownership of the facility and rents it
to the government. Under current law, private investors cannot claim an
investment tax credit on property that is leased to a governmental entity.
In many cases, however, investors can still depreciate property leased by
a government under the accelerated cost recovery system (ACRS).[42] Thus,

---

[42] If the facility was financed with tax-exempt bonds, or if the arrangement
involves a sale/leaseback or lease/purchase agreement, then the property must

the investor can take advantage of tax breaks not available to tax-exempt entities, and can pass along a portion of these savings in the form of lower lease payments for their government customers.

If the government is willing to purchase a service, rather than just the use of a facility or piece of equipment, then more liberal tax provisions can be used. Under current law, investors who have a bona fide service contract with a government can still claim all of the tax advantages available on private investments generally, even if tax-exempt financing is used. However, the rules which the IRS applies to determine whether an arrangement is a service contract or a disguised lease agreement require that the government clearly not own, control, or have a significant economic interest in the facilities and equipment associated with the service. Fewer restrictions apply for service contracts associated with solid waste disposal facilities, energy facilities and water treatment facilities (Hough, et. al., 1985).

While the Federal tax advantages available to private investors are the chief source of lease and service contracts' appeal, there are other potential advantages of having the private sector produce government services. In many instances, leasing from the private sector allows local jurisdictions to avoid State procurement regulations. Avoidance of voter approval requirements, competitive bidding requirements, project design and engineering requirements, quality standards, union wage regulations and the like can save time and money.[43] In addition, relying on the private sector to provide the initial financing preserves the government's debt capacity and isolates the government, and its taxpayers, from the risks of project performance problems. If one believes that the private sector can produce goods and services more efficiently than the public sector, because of the profit motive, greater flexibility in providing performance incentives, etc., then contracting with the private sector could lower the cost of public services even without the benefit of "tax expenditures."

As with other financing alternatives, there are a number of disadvantages associated with private sector contracting, particularly for small rural governments. The principal disadvantage with true leases and service contracts is that the government loses control of the facility and may lose some of its flexibility. For service contracts, it also loses the power to hire employees to manage and staff the facility. There are also State regulations and political pressures which often make reliance on

---

be depreciated under the straight-line method, thus significantly lowering the tax advantages of the arrangement (Quinn and Olstein, 1985).

[43] While avoidance of regulations may be beneficial in some cases, it is not without its risks. Regulations are generally meant to insure that well designed facilities are constructed at competitive cost. Disregard for such regulation could result in poor facility design and high construction costs being passed on to the government lessor.

private sector contracts difficult. For small rural governments, the lack of private sector providers in the area may severely limit contracting opportunities. A lack of in-house capacity, coupled with the complexity of many leasing and service arrangements, may also make contracting for small-scale projects impractical.

COMPLETE PRIVATIZATION

A final option which involves reliance on the private sector is to completely "privatize" the service. While this term covers a variety of public/private service provision arrangements in the literature, it is used here to refer to the divestiture of a government's responsibility for paying for a service. That is, for a select group of services, governments have the option of leaving responsibility for service provision entirely up to the private sector, with consumers purchasing services directly from the provider rather than channeling payment through their local government.

Services which lend themselves to this approach are those with few public-good characteristics. Such services may be governmental responsibilities in some locations because they can be provided most efficiently as monopolies. However, it is possible to regulate monopolies without requiring public ownership, as privately owned power companies, cable television firms, telephone companies, and water companies demonstrate. Since regulated monopolies are still treated as private corporations for Federal and State tax purposes, they are eligible for the full range of tax incentives. Whether the tax advantages accruing to privately owned facilities are large enough to offset the advantages reaped by tax-exempt entities is open to question. Thus, arguments for complete privatization are generally based on philosophical grounds (i.e. a smaller government role is preferable), or on the presumed efficiency of the private sector.

FUTURE PROSPECTS FOR PUBLIC/PRIVATE FINANCING

The future importance of public/private partnerships as a method of providing infrastructure depends importantly on changes in the Federal tax code, and on the ability of the two sectors to devise schemes which are mutually advantageous (Quinn and Olstein, 1985). Current proposals to reform the tax code, and the increasing complexity of IRS regulations, raise serious questions about the future attractiveness of private sector contracting, and to a lesser extent, other public/private financing techniques. Proposals to repeal the investment tax credit, lengthen depreciation periods, and reduce the corporate tax rate will all tend to raise the effective cost of capital for private investors. Proposed restrictions on the ability of passive investors to use investment losses to offset other income will dampen the appeal of leveraged leasing arrangements. Further restrictions on the use of tax-exempt financing for privately owned facilities will increase the financing costs and recordkeeping requirements for projects which continue to rely on industrial development bond financing.

While the eventual outcome remains uncertain, in all probability, the ability of local governments to benefit from Federal and State tax expenditures through private sector contracting will be reduced in the near future. As a result, the cost of many types of contracts will undoubtedly increase, but contracting will likely remain as a viable approach to infrastructure provision. For certain types of facilities, under certain circumstances, local governments will continue to find lease agreements and/or service contracts the most economical method for acquiring the use of needed facilities and equipment.

The extent to which tax reform will affect the usage of developer assistance and privatization efforts is unclear. While Federal tax reform may alter the economics of certain approaches, the relative bargaining positions of developers and jurisdictions is as important as are the costs and benefits of each approach.

Perhaps more important to the continued use of developer assistance and privatization is the recent passage of the Local Government Antitrust Act. The bill prohibits awarding monetary damages against local governments and their officials for anticompetitive or monopolistic behavior. The bill does not, however, give local governments immunity from Federal antitrust laws (Golonka, 1985). Thus, developers and potential competitors of "privatized" facilities can bring suit against local governments and request court injunctions prohibiting local officials from anticompetitive behavior. Fear of litigation, more than tax reform impacts, may dampen local government enthusiasm for public/private schemes.

CONCLUSION

The 1980's have brought significant changes in the ways public infrastructure is financed. Changes in the relationships between the Federal, State, and local governments, coupled with volatile financial markets, deregulation of financial institutions, and cyclical shifts in the economy have all contributed to rapid changes in infrastructure finance.

At the Federal level, functional decentralization, deficit reduction, and tax reform have all drastically affected the financing options available to local governments. Federal court decisions and Federal agency regulations have also affected the costs and benefits of certain financing techniques. Since many of these Federal activities are still evolving, the ultimate impact of Federal decisions on the cost and availability of funds for local infrastructure projects remains uncertain. However, it seems likely that Federal intergovernmental aid will play a smaller role in local infrastructure finance than it played in the late 1970's for the foreseeable future. In addition, actions to reduce "tax expenditures" will likely raise the locally borne costs of many other financing techniques.

Activities by the State governments can partially offset some of the adverse Federal impacts, but the ability and willingness of State governments to play a larger role in local infrastructure finance varies considerably from State to State. Economic factors may preclude massive increases in State intergovernmental aid, but as was pointed out, there are a number of ways States can make local infrastructure investment easier, quicker, and cheaper through nonfinancial assistance, particularly for small rural governments. It seems likely that political pressures will grow, encouraging States to take steps to relieve the financial and regulatory burden placed on local governments trying to address their infrastructure problems.

In all likelihood, local governments are going to have to play a larger role in arranging for the financing of local infrastructure in the future. Reliance on debt financing and public/private partnerships should tend to increase as intergovernmental assistance becomes harder to find. At the same time, these local financing techniques may become more expensive as tax loopholes are closed at the Federal and State levels. On the brighter side, current low interest rates and inflation rates could easily offset any tax-induced increases in financing costs if they continue for the remainder of the decade.

Until the impacts of all these changes can be estimated, there will continue to be a pressing need for expert legal and financial advice for local officials faced with infrastructure investment decisions. Unfortunately, this need for up-to-date information on a constantly changing tax and regulatory environment puts many rural governments at a distinct disadvantage. Lacking both in-house expertise, and easy access to private consultants, local officials may find their financing options reduced to the most basic "tried-and-true" methods. All to often in the past, by the time rural officials learned how to play the development game, the rules were changed. This situation is not likely to become less prevalent in the near future.

19
Political and Organizational Considerations in Infrastructure Investment Decision-Making

Beverly A. Cigler

"Infrastructure"--the word for this nation's vast and vital network of public works facilities necessary to produce and deliver public services--including streets and bridges, sewers and water systems, and installations such as schools and prisons--came into prominent use in the early 1980s. Alarming articles in the popular press aroused public concern (*Business Week*, 1981; *Newsweek*, 1982, *U.S. News and World Report*, 1982). Studies by professional and municipal associations, research institutions, and consulting firms have documented the problems resulting from the deterioration of existing facilities and the difficulties of new development (American Public Works Association, 1981; Associated General Contractors, 1983; Choate and Walter, 1981; CONSAD, 1980; Government Finance Officers Association, 1984; National League of Cities and U.S. Conference of Mayors, 1983; and Peterson et. al., 1983.)

National attention to the infrastructure problem has been heightened by a series of additional studies and suggested policy options by the national government (Advisory Commission on Intergovernmental Relations, 1984a; Congressional Budget Office, 1983; Joint Economic Committee, U.S. Congress, 1984a, b, and c; U.S. Department of Commerce, 1980; U.S. Department of Housing and Urban Development, 1982; and U.S. House of Representatives, 1983). A Congressional Budget Office's 1983 study highlighted three sets of problems related to declining investments in infrastructure: deterioration, technological obsolescence, and insufficient capacity to serve future growth. The report also suggested the adverse effects of declining investment: (a) higher costs borne by users of inadequate or deteriorated facilities; (b) higher life-cycle construction costs for facilities which are not properly maintained; and (c) potentially significant constraints on economic development.

A variety of "how-to-do-it" books, addressed primarily to state and local officials, has proliferated (Gitajn, 1985; Peterson and Hough, 1983; Peterson and Miller, 1981; Thompson, 1983; Vaughan, 1983; Vaughan and Pollard, 1984; Watson, 1982; and Weiss, 1985). Most of what has been said and written about the nation's infrastructure problems has been related to finance, with "big bucks" solutions in vogue. But, the estimated price for dealing with the problems of the nation's infrastructure has ranged from $470 billion to three trillion dollars within a twenty year period, with most studies at the high end of the range. While doomsayers bemoan the "disinvestment" of America's public infrastructure, advocating more capital spending, others suggest that current analyses of trends are misleading (Kamensky, 1984). Despite the disagreements over defining the problem, little has actually happened in the decision-making bodies at the national, state, and local government levels. And, media attention is no longer focused on the problem. There is a need for some restructuring of the debate and development of guidelines for local government infrastructure decision-making strategies.

This chapter focuses on the nature of local decision-making to understand the prospects for addressing the infrastructure problem at the local level. A neglected area of the debate--the political and organizational conditions associated with local infrastructure decision-making--is highlighted. It is argued that "nuts and bolts" concerns at the local level--primarily organizational and management issues-must be addressed before the broader questions can be successfully examined.

The chapter examines: (1) factors related to infrastructure that facilitate decision-making; (2) factors related to infrastructure that inhibit policy development; and (3) ways to influence the local environment and organizational process to ease the dilemma posed by decision-making constraints.

FACTORS FACILITATING INFRASTRUCTURE DECISION-MAKING

The numerous studies of the nation's infrastructure conditions and needs highlight eight factors that can serve to structure future debate and policy options in ways that may facilitate decision-making. Each of these eight positive factors will be outlined briefly in this section, along with their relevant drawbacks.

The first concern is the status of the infrastructure issue on political agendas. In the 1980s, "infrastructure" issues clearly were placed on the "systematic agenda" of the nation, its states, and local governments (Cobb and Elder, 1983). This means that the topic was commonly perceived as meriting public attention and as involving matters within the legitimate jurisdiction of existing governmental authority. On the other hand, a second type of agenda, the institutional, governmental or formal agenda, is what must be reached for topics of concern to receive explicit active and serious consideration by authoritative decision-makers. Clearly, this occurred at the national level, with a number of Congressional hearings, studies, and proposals. However, to date, no major legislative actions have occurred. In addition, it does not appear that most local institutional agendas have either considered infrastructure as a key priority and/or achieved much policy success.

Despite infrastructure policy reaching both the systemic and institutional agendas in the 1980s, then, not much has happened. And, because the lag between the two agendas is great, as well as the lack of correlation between the priorities of the two agenda types, the failure to achieve policy initiatives to date may mean that another round of widespread attention-building is necessary for infrastructure concerns to once again achieve a place on societal and institutional agendas.

The fast pace of information development on the topic yields a second optimistic observation. Estimates now suggest a more manageable problem than previously presumed. Recent studies offer the positive news that revenue shortfalls may not be as serious as previously presumed. More important, the average individual infrastructure project is estimated to cost between $1 and $5 million dollars, figures that are not so high as to cause local officials to have a doomsayer attitude. This also means that dealing with basic problems may be accomplished in piecemeal fashion rather than attempting to shape truly rational, comprehensive approaches to "the infrastructure problem."

The recent optimism, however, is guarded. The initial projections help shape public and local official behavior and are difficult to erase. And, cost estimates depend on how "infrastructure" is defined. Basic public infrastructure refers to highways, transit, water facilities, and so forth. Human services public infrastructure includes at least educational, medical, and correctional facilities (Christopherson, 1983). And, quasi-public development infrastructure refers to civic centers, parks, and hotels, among other projects. One observer has included housing as an infrastructure issue (Tuchfarber, 1983).

If cost estimates are disaggregated among infrastructure types, it is argued here, reasonable approaches may be planned for dealing with problems for which institutional, legal, and financial responsibility is highly dispersed among separate government entities. Because institutional and political settings affect the nature of the infrastructure problem and the options available for dealing with it, mismatches between responsibilities and fiscal capacity are more easily uncovered and addressed when costs are disaggregated.

The third positive factor is related to the dispute about the actual costs of the infrastructure problems--including unraveling the causes for long-term disinvestment and whether that trend has negative effects. This is the fact that there has been a decreased demand for public infrastructure investment itself. Demographic shifts (e.g. less school age population, movement to rural areas and the sunbelt), the use of better pricing mechanisms (which reduce demand) such as users fees, and changes in service delivery (e.g. privatization) are examples (Kamensky, 1984).

While all of the effects of these trends on demand are unclear, many effects are obvious. Less school age children means reduced investment demand for school buildings. Population shifts to rural areas translate to demands for new construction, making it possible to link infrastructure concerns to economic development needs, and suggest stronger political coalition-building possibilities than for financing rehabilitation, the greatest need in urban areas. Privatizing capital facilities, such as hospital construction, shifts responsibilities from the public to private sector, making "needs" estimates unclear. A recognition of these changing demands means that the widely varying aggregate cost estimates mentioned in point two above are misleading. Efforts to reverse the much discussed declining infrastructure investment trends must be tempered with an understanding of the real causes of declining investment.

A fourth factor that facilitates infrastructure decision-making is that it is truly a "national" problem affecting every region. This helps to eliminate traditional rivalries between east and west, sunbelt and frostbelt, and urban and rural, for examples. On the other hand, while the problem exists nationwide, there are vast differences in both degree and kind. Most attention to date has been placed on how to finance the repair of deteriorating facilities, but the immediate problem for many rural areas, for example, may involve building facilities for the first time (Reid and Sullivan, 1984; Reid, et.al., 1984) This suggests the need for examining entirely different issues in conjunction with the infrastructure concern, such as the capacity of some communities to plan and implement infrastructure projects.

Fifth, because infrastructure includes such a broad array of physical and human resource concerns, its very comprehensiveness demands attention. Its comprehensiveness ironically also makes possible the use of piecemeal and fragmented options, linking issues to each other. A drawback, however, is the tendency to look for single approach options to deal with what are considered pervasive problems, making success less likely. And, the considerable variation across types of infrastructure and, within types, across facilities owned and maintained by different government agencies, complicates coherent political action. The diversity of problems and needs highlighted by a comprehensive definition of infrastructure, moreover, shows the necessity for local solutions.

Sixth, because there are already highly developed political coalitions in existence for some components of the infrastructure "problem" (e.g. highways) the potential for political action is increased. On the other hand, the existence of infrastructure is often unseen and so is taken for granted. As a result, those responsible for developing the physical infrastructure especially are hampered by the lack of public awareness, political support, and resulting necessary fiscal resources. The lack of strong coalitions for certain infrastructure types, and in certain areas, such as rural areas, turns this positive factor into a very negative one for many concerns, and raises equity issues as especially meriting attention.

The seventh facilitating factor consists of federal grant cutbacks to local governments. Diminishing financial resources result in local governments cutting back on operating budget allocations for maintenance and repair of existing infrastructure and greatly limit capital investments made for expansion and rehabilitation (Peterson, et .al., 1983; Peterson and Miller, 1982; Jump, 1982; and Choate and Walter, 1981). Lost funding moves agenda-setting responsibilities more clearly to the local arena, forcing the realization that limited resources and unlimited demands must be faced with good information, leadership, and innovation. Not able to ignore deteriorating facilities and/or the need for new facilities, local governments have been forced to examine their existing management systems, especially financial systems.

While it is too optimistic to argue that local officials will cast aside "pork barrel" concerns and turn to "invisible" infrastructure matters lacking a constituency, a shifting of more responsibilities to one level for decision-making, funding, and implementation may, in the long run, have positive effects in motivating local decision-makers to exert the political "will" necessary to deal with problems. State laws and practices that inhibit local governments' abilities to solve their infrastructure problems have already received increased attention. These include statutes that place legal restraints and controls on local revenue raising and spending capacity laws in some states that prevent local government from creating capital reserves to finance future capital expenditures (Rosenberg and Rood, 1985).

The eighth and last infrastructure decision-making facilitating factor also relates to the comprehensiveness of the topic, as discussed earlier. This is the fact that infrastructure can be linked to many topics. A very promising linkage is to local economic development, possibly projecting an often unseen and neglected issue to prominence. The linkage also increases opportunities for public-private sector cooperative ventures.

Still, the linkage of infrastructure to positive economic development is largely unexamined. While Choate and Walter (1981) argue that one-half to two-thirds of the nation's communities are unable to support economic development until major new investments are made in basic facilities such as wastewater treatment plants, Peterson and Miller (1982) claim that the actual reliance of business on public infrastructure has not been adequately researched. Business location decisions are extremely complex and include at least the following factors: plant or site availability, access to and cost of transportation, quality and cost of labor, proximity to markets, cost of utilities, proximity to supplies, proximity to other company facilities, state taxes, the regulatory environment, educational quality, housing cost, level of public services, and a range of other amenities that can be described as the general "quality of life" offered (Schmenner, 1982; Vaughan, 1979).

FACTORS INHIBITING INFRASTRUCTURE DECISION-MAKING

The previous section discussed facilitating factors related to the climate for infrastructure decision-making at the local level. Unfortunately, each of the eight characteristics also has drawbacks that could place them in the policy-inhibiting category. This section deals with twelve more political characteristics of the infrastructure decision-making environment, those that explicitly inhibit policy making. Each, however, can be manipulated to positive advantage, with skillful approaches to the local political environment and organizational process. All of the factors considered in this section serve as background for developing a set of conditions that should be met for achieving successful approaches to local infrastructure policy development, an issue which is treated in the last section of this chapter.

The first inhibiting factor is that the local agenda is perceived to be crowded, with citizens and their elected officials viewing other problems more pressing than vaguely defined "infrastructure," a word not well understood. When a community's financial capacity is limited, and competition among program alternatives is great, capital investment, maintenance, and rehabilitation are the first to be cut or delayed in local budgets.

On the other hand, the very comprehensiveness of infrastructure means that, for decision-making purposes, it can be linked to other issues, especially the central concerns of local government. Infrastructure maintenance is a key factor in the health, safety and welfare of a community. Expanded public facilities are sometimes essential to maintaining the health, safety, and welfare of communities as part of overall growth management strategies.

With limited resources and unlimited demands, local officials need to tie their infrastructure needs explicitly to other community issues. Poorly maintained roads and bridges cost drivers more to drive, with operating costs for the average car climbing 35% when routes rated poor rather than good are used. Unsafe dams bring tragedy in lost lives and property. Deteriorated drinking water systems threaten health and are costly. Inadequate wastewater facilities destroy watercourses and flood basements with sewage. Aquifers on which some communities rely for raw water are contaminated by chemicals seeping from disposal sites.

A second drawback that often inhibits local decision-making of any type is that elected officials "share misconceptions" about the attitudes of other elected officials. When an individual thinks he or she is alone in holding concern for a particular issue, no individual action may be taken on that issue. If each individual thinks he or she is alone, there can be no collective action. The policy literature repeatedly uncovers the need for "fixers" or "policy entrepreneurs" (Eyestone, 1978). Someone must take on the responsibility of translating issues into proposals and then marshall their cause through the formal policy process. If policy entrepreneurs do not emerge inside of local government, they may be needed from outside, including the private sector and/or other levels of government and professional associations. Small and/or rural governments may hold a special need for outside policy entrepreneurs due to their relative lack of expertise and staff availability.

The third major inhibiting factor to local infrastructure decision-making relates to the type of political controversy involving most infrastructure problems. Infrastructure usually involves "low visibility" issues (e.g. sewers and water lines that are unseen and other seemingly "invisible" issues). As such, most citizens do not become concerned until after a problem is too neglected. Low visibility/low salience politics are characteristic, then, of the infrastructure decision-making environment. With no political constituency for most infrastructure issues, elected officials may adopt what they perceive the public wants. Capital investment is delayed, and maintenance and rehabilitation overlooked. It requires attention to detail--good information to document problems and needs. It requires leadership, civic leaders, and wise timing.

Two other constraints related to the quality of information available to decision-makers further complicate the issue of political visibility. Factor four is that infrastructure decision-making appears to be beset with problems of underestimation, especially regarding the condition of existing structures. "It's important, but it's not going to happen to us" has probably been said about suggested rehabilitation before a bridge collapsed, a dam broke, drinking water became corroded, and sanitary sewers crumbled in more than one community. The fifth constraint is the complexity of infrastructure decision-making itself, with uncertainty the norm. It is often difficult to know, for example, what level of government is responsible for which facility or how various levels are related.

A sixth decision-making constraint relates to fact/value issues. As implied earlier, "public infrastructure" is a catchall phrase with no consistent definition. While usually used to describe fixed, physical assets, the term may involve social investment also. Regardless of the definition used, fact questions regarding "need" are unclear due to an array of measurement problems. Too little thought has been given to developing standards by which "need" is measured. Construction standards, for example, contribute significantly to perceptions of demand for capital investment. As Peterson noted (Odell, 1982; p. 8), however, "Capital standards are not needs in any literal sense, but are merely policy objectives which must be balanced against their costs of achievement."

Of course, the "costs" include not just financial but all costs, raising concerns for equity. Before adequate solutions are posed for financing infrastructure, an array of difficult equity issues must be addressed, complicating the decision-making process. Capital development benefits future generations as well as the present population. How should costs be distributed among generations? What is an equitable distribution of cost and a fair price for construction and maintenance of local infrastructure? Cost and affordability must be considered with equity in the fact/value dimension of the infrastructure decision-making debate.

Seventh, while infrastructure needs are a "national" problem, they demand local solutions. While the national and state governments have many roles and responsibilities to perform regarding infrastructure, the major responsibilities are at the local level. Instead of one government (national) or fifty-one governments (national plus all states) in the decision-making arena, there are likely more than 80,000 governmental units involved (national, state, regional, local units). And, there is often a serious mismatch between a governmental unit's responsibilities and its fiscal and/or management capacity. Moreover, as noted earlier, there is also considerable variation across types of infrastructure and, within types, across facilities owned and maintained by different government agencies.

The eighth inhibiting factor is the large category of administrative inadequacies within local government itself, though varying in degree and kind among governments. These shortcomings include: poor data generation, insufficient planning capacity, weak policy and program coordination, fragmented organizational responsibilities, poor financial management, and other "nuts and bolts" management and organizational concerns.

Most local governments, for example, budget on a line-item, object of expenditure basis. Despite advantages, that approach does not provide accurate analysis of infrastructure investment decisions. Maintenance and repair costs are generally not systematically included in typical operating budget allocations. In addition, capital improvement plans--the basis for analyzing public facilities in terms of need and priority, fiscal capacity, financing strategy, timing, and growth management--are not commonly used by local governments. And, the conclusion holds for the use of capital budgeting and life-cycle costing. Few local governments, in fact, have developed even an inventory of their infrastructure as cost accounting is not used to measure public assets for depreciation purposes as in the private sector.

It is difficult to plan for the future, in terms of new infrastructure, rehabilitation of existing infrastructure, and/or general maintenance of all infrastructure without first knowing what government owns, its value, and its maintenance history. Even overlooking the relatively sparse use of many sophisticated financial management tools, poor financial management in general is costly to local governments when attempting to finance infrastructure. Unfortunately, the smaller, especially non-metropolitan, governments are most likely to possess a wide array of administrative inadequacies (Sokolow and Honadle, 1984; Weinberg, 1984; Stinson, 1981; Honadle, 1983; Dillman and Hobbs, 1982; Browne and

Hadwiger, 1981; Bryce, 1979; and Cigler, 1985b, 1984). Research on the topic itself is fraught with many difficulties (Reeder, 1984). Because there are more small governments than any other type, the category of administrative inadequacies looms as a significant set of obstacles to local decision-making of any type.

The barriers posed by the lack of use of sophisticated financial and planning techniques (e.g. capital budgeting, capital improvement planning, strategic planning) are increased when the structural barriers to infrastructure decision-making posed by the state and national government are realized, the ninth category of constraints on local government infrastructure decision-making addressed here. The Congressional Budget Office study (1983) suggested, for example, that federal programs and funding created a bias toward construction rather than maintenance and repair. And, state and local governments receive almost forty percent of all their public works funds from federal grants, with regulations and matching requirements largely defining how the balance is used.

As pointed out earlier in this chapter, state laws have placed legal restraints and controls on local revenue raising and spending capacity. Many states also prevent local governments from creating capital reserves to finance future capital expenditures, especially impacting negatively on small communities that are otherwise unable to enter the bond market or operate on a "pay-as-you-go" approach (Danzinger and Ring, 1982; Florestano, 1981; MacManus, 1981; Ladd, 1978; and Rosenberg and Rood, 1985). The first means that local governments must turn to alternative financing and service delivery arrangements (Florestano and Gordon, 1980; International City Management Association, 1984; Peterson and Hough, 1983; Savas, 1982; Stevens, 1985). The second has led many communities to "hide" capital reserves within the operating budget for financing future capital needs in the form of contingency reserves. This results in a risk that such reserves will be depleted and funds used for non-capital purposes.

All of these structural barriers to local government action must be addressed by other levels of government, complicating the decision-making process at the local level. Until such basic questions as "who does what, when, where, and why?" are examined at the national and state levels, the local decision-making environment is blurred. It may be that local governments will have to utilize creative financing techniques to obtain capital for infrastructure needs (Foster, 1982; Stanfield, 1982). State involvement, such as the creation of infrastructure banks, may also be forthcoming (Vaughan, 1983; Watson, 1982; and Peterson and Hough, 1983).

The tenth inhibiting characteristic related to decision-making for local infrastructure investment is related to political reward systems. Good roads, water and sewer facilities, and sanitation services are taken for granted by constituents. Elected leaders are eager to cut ribbons for new projects but know that their constituents reward them less for "invisible repairs" to existing structures. Only in office for two to four-year terms, in addition, officials can easily defer concern with maintenance and rehabilitation of existing structures and let the next in office be responsible. Of course, the next and the next office-holders may similarly defer concerns and take only reactive stands when major problems arise. And, even new projects are too often "pork barrel" in nature, not necessary, but the products of success by certain coalitions and decision-making processes of a log-rolling nature. Similarly, the mass media take an interest in the ribbon-cutting ceremonies, rarely reporting on long-term infrastructure needs unless a crisis occurs.

These political constraints to decision-making are not peculiar to infrastructure but are especially characteristic of low visibility/low salience issues of which infrastructure decision-making is a key example. This factor highlights the need for administrators to accept greater responsibility for documenting and reporting the condition and need for public works facilities to elected leadership. It is especially necessary that such information be incorporated into local government budgets so that elected officials and the public know the true costs of infrastructure.

Just as responsibilities for infrastructure are scattered among various levels and types of governments, public vs. private responsibilities are becoming blurred, the eleventh inhibiting factor. This makes data generation and interpretation more difficult and complicates decision-making due to constantly changing conditions. Some categories of infrastructure, especially capital facilities, are privatizing. This includes hospital construction, streets, water and sewer lines. Creative methods of providing and financing capital infrastructure include such mechanisms as developer fees, user fees and charges, sale-leaseback arrangements, and leasing of public facilities.

The blurring of public and private roles and responsibilities, in addition, differs across regions of the nation. Utilities in some areas are publicly owned and, in other areas, they are private. Shifts in responsibilities between sectors make trend analysis difficult, complicate projections of need, and pose particularly difficult problems for smaller governments not possessing the monitoring and evaluative capabilities necessary to making adequate decisions to financing infrastructure.

The twelfth and final major inhibiting factor is the continuing data problem that complicates all planning and decision-making. This factor is so basic that it has appeared in most of this chapter's discussion. With changes in demand for infrastructure, its financing, governmental and private sector responsibilities, responsibilities among levels of government, and widely varying capabilities to generate, interpret and use data, this drawback remains as a central obstacle to infrastructure investment decision-making.

INFLUENCING THE LOCAL DECISION-MAKING PROCESS

The discussion of characteristics of the local infrastructure decision-making process has highlighted several factors that, in part, facilitate decision-making and a long list of those that inhibit it. While it is difficult to generalize on ways to achieve success in infrastructure investment decision-making, knowledge gained from studies of program development and implementation processes suggest several common factors that dominate. These may be called the "pre-conditions" for policy development (Cigler, 1985a). This section offers some conclusions about the types of conditions necessary to produce policy change. These are separated into two broad categories: local environmental characteristics and organizational process factors.

A key set of pre-conditions relates to the local environment: (1) the occurrence of a disaster or emergency; (2) the presence of a political constituency for infrastructure maintenance and/or development; and (3) supportive programs by external agents, such as state government, the USDA's Cooperative Extension, and professional and municipal associations.

The first pre-condition for decision-making success is limited to those rare occasions when the disaster moment can be seized to push for greater decision-maker, general public, and media attention to infrastructure problems. This usually occurs in relation to deteriorated infrastructure, but may happen when an industry does not choose a site for development because of inadequate public infrastructure.

The second pre-condition is rare, given the low visibility/low salience nature of most infrastructure issues. Without the "push" of public opinion, or the "pull" of other incentives, including funds from the national government, it is unlikely that local officials will give most infrastructure concerns high priority. It may be that public work administrators will have to take the initiative in developing and disseminating adequate information on infrastructure condition and need for elected officials and the public. Infrastructure's relationship to issues perceived to be most important must be explained.

Third, patterns of support for building the capacity of local governments, either through technical assistance programs or direct or indirect regulatory efforts, are important. Given the wide array of administrative inadequacies within government, especially smaller, non-metropolitan units, "capacity building" (Honadle, 1981, 1982; Newland, 1981) looms as very important in establishing pre-conditions for policy-making success.

The USDA's "Great Plains Project," initiated in 1973, and its follow-up, "The Local Decision Project," along with related spin-offs are outstanding examples of capacity building efforts that can offer small governments help in developing their financial and planning capacities. Budget studies of alternative delivery systems, project and impact studies, and locational studies, such as those formulated at Oklahoma State University, all facilitate local decision-making capacity. With approximately 54,000 rural governments and 318,000 rural elected officials, systematic capacity building is clearly necessary. These and other efforts by Cooperative Extension can have significant capacity building impact and mitigate the effects of the relative absence of all three key local pre-conditions.

In addition to capacity building, the third pre-condition related to the local environment suggests the need to rethink the structural limitations imposed by states on local governments, including enabling legislation for revenue-raising and expenditures as well as mandates. All this would enable local governments to partake of creative financing mechanisms.

The other category of pre-conditions for successful local decision-making relates to the local organizational process, with the following factors: (1) early and continued support by local officials, especially elected mayors, council members, and managers who set local agendas and are empowered for action; (2) a clear linkage of infrastructure issues to the economic self-interest of community leaders and citizens; (3) an early focus on implementation and selected activities that are highly visible and cost-effective; (4) skillful program management; (5) an emphasis on building existing programs or activities that support agreed-upon community objectives; and (6) personnel with the capability of implementing plans. In addition, many of these imply more intergovernmental cooperation.

These pre-conditions appear to be generic to local decision-making. For infrastructure concerns, they suggest that greater attention be paid early to the "nuts and bolts" of local governance. This means a clear focus on budgeting and financial management systems, development of staff with expertise, information dissemination to those with authority to act, and "developing" constituencies by linking infrastructure policy to economic self-interest, among other concerns. Again, the capacity building efforts of recent USDA Cooperative Extension projects address all of these concerns. Handbooks, technical assistance, circuit riders, and other options are worth additional consideration. Of course, much more research needs to be performed relating to all of the pre-conditions.

Local infrastructure investment decisions involve far more than finance. As a result, "megabucks" solutions will not necessarily solve problems. First, basic organizational and management issues need to be addressed. Local infrastructure investment decisions involve complex institutional relationships, political traditions (pork barrel), technological innovation, regulatory and tax policies, and a wide array of agricultural and management inadequacies.

While current disjointed decision-making processes are ill-prepared to deal with the problems, there exist a vast array of pragmatic approaches for helping local communities shift to more strategic planning and management modes. Vaughan (1983), for example, has offered an eight-point strategy for public works renewal. Many others have offered worthwhile approaches to various aspects of the problem (Porter and Peiser, 1984; Walter and Choate, 1984; and Olsen and Eadie, 1982). Central to all of the suggestions is the conclusion that comprehensive public investment strategy requires much more sophisticated planning and budgeting procedures and the design of more effective management techniques (Vaughan, 1983).

If someone or some organization wants to help small communities with infrastructure decision-making, the best approach may be to improve their ability to manage money and projects. The necessary public support for dealing with the revenue-raising necessary to support projects is unlikely to occur unless local governments prove their competence by improving their management skills. Increased governmental competence, in turn, may help change the political reward systems that built unnecessary projects, neglected existing infrastructure, and missed opportunities for wiser development.

20
Needed Institutional Change to Provide Local Infrastructure

Glen C. Pulver

Institutions associated with the provision of local infrastructure in the United States have grown out of the form and character of the times. Problem solving mechanisms (laws, regulations, organizations, bureaucracies and other devices) created by either public or private act, are essentially designed in response to the physical, political, philosophical, and economic realities of any given period. Perhaps the only consistent characteristic of these institutions is their resistance to change.

Those who create the mechanisms of development and control of local infrastructure generally do so out of a sense of need or expectation for a public good or service. They may wish for a convenience such as a sidewalk so that they might be more comfortable walking to church or they may expect a high quality water purification system to assure an adequate supply of drinking water. Mechanisms are likewise developed using a political structure acceptable to the combined value systems of the decision-makers and their constituents or contemporaries. The specific mechanisms chosen will vary widely depending upon currently accepted local views regarding self reliance, government involvement, tax burdens, external resource availability, and individual power.

For purposes of this chapter, local infrastructure is defined as including a wide spectrum of capital facilities associated with services generally provided for the benefit of the public as a whole either through fees or taxation. This includes streets, sewers, water, airports, parks, hospitals, fire protection, public protection, telephone systems, hospitals, libraries, public housing, industrial parks, etc. (Rogers, et. al. 1981;

Committee on Agriculture, Nutrition and Forestry, United States Senate, 1977; Reid, et. al. 1984).

Any useful examination of the institutional changes and developments, responsibilities, and realignments necessary to assure adequate local infrastructure must carefully consider the form and character of the concerned community at that time. Institutional reality grows out of the needs, expectations, values, and political environment of the community (local, state, and nation).

INFRASTRUCTURE INSTITUTIONS OVER TIME

The evolution of infrastructure institutions might best be understood by looking at the relationships between local infrastructure and four specific characteristics of the United States over a series of time periods. The four characteristics are: 1) the distribution of human population; 2) the income producing base of the economy; 3) the personal expectations (e.g. material goods, health, security); and 4) general political perspectives (e.g. individual vs. collective). The time periods might be titled: Period I - the agricultural era; Period II - the early industrial era; Period III - the advanced industrial era; Period IV - the service era; and Period V - the early information era.[44]

Period I - Agricultural Era

Farming was the dominant occupation and source of economic well-being on the North American continent until approximately 75 years ago. As a consequence, most of the homes of residents of the United States were widely dispersed throughout the countryside with a few relatively small cities with growing populations. Self-reliance characterized nearly all households including rural and city residences where backyard gardens, chicken houses and barns abounded. In those days, there was little demand for public services other than protection from other countries and domestic scoundrels, a bit of education, and the U.S. mail. Federal

---

[44] In his presentation at the 1983 annual meeting of the American Agricultural Economics Association, Leroy Hushak described four time periods: a) Pre-Depression (before 1929); b) New Deal and Post-World War II recovery (1929-60); c) the Great Society (1960-75); and d) the New Federalism Era (1975-?) (Hushak, 1983). His time periods are approximately the same as those chosen here except that it is useful to divide the 1929-60 period into two (1929-45) and (1945-60). The expectations and politics of the periods are quite different. The descriptions Hushak uses are also totally acceptable with the appropriate separation of the New Deal and Post-World War II periods.

and state government roles were limited. Early roads were built and maintained by shared effort and private capital.

Period II - Early Industrial Era

It was in the 1930s and 40s that the United States began to perceive itself as a nation of manufacturing. An increasing portion of its population earned a living in the steel mills of Pennsylvania and automobile factories of Detroit. People began to move out of rural areas of the north and south and into urban concentrations. The huge machines needed energy; the people needed transport, sewer and water systems. People began to replace their sense of self reliance with values of mutual support and cooperation. Labor unions and farmer cooperatives took root. The shocks of depression, drought, and war justified public action beyond the individual community level. Huge electric power projects, major port and river systems, and national airports were built, largely by federal investments. Income taxes became a fact of life.

Period III - Advanced Industrial Era

Rolling out of World War II the people of the U.S. felt themselves to be invincible goods producing geniuses. Together they could do anything. People continued to flock to the cities to feed the human capital hopper of the great production machine. Economic expectations were high. If the U.S. could produce the war machinery it had, surely it could provide well for everyone in a time of peace. The federal government was now a full partner with state and local governments building roads, streets, transit systems, educational institutions, and hospitals; the bricks and mortar of our traditional economic system.

Period IV - Service Era

The tremendous increase in U.S. goods production efficiency convinced the entire nation that it could afford the new luxury of improved health care, higher education, police and fire protection, legal services, recreation, tourism and a wide range of new services. Furthermore, the people supported major growth in social services (e.g. Social Security, Medicare, and remedial education) aimed at helping those less well off. The perspective was one of great national wealth and public capability. Individual expectations were high and everyone expected to participate. The migration to the suburbs and beyond began. Need at the local level was fed by aids from both national and state governments. Local governments caught the spirit as well.   Government expenditures burgeoned.

Period V - Early Information Era

Some have chosen to call this the New Federalism Era (Hushak, 1983).   Others have suggested this time period be called the "Me Generation." In any case, large metropolitan areas dominate the U.S. population. The broad service producing sector provides over 70% of the employment opportunities. Smaller employers are the primary generators of new employment.   Entrepreneurship has once again gained great credibility.   Large national budget deficits, substantial commitments to income maintenance, national security concerns and high individual economic expectations when combined have led to disenchantment with all big institutions (government, industry, labor) and the massive communication industry can instantly disseminate the necessary fuel for this fire. No one knows how long Period V will last.

The vital point in this brief history is that those institutional changes with any prospect of surfacing in response to the immediate concerns of the local infrastructure, are wholly dependent upon people's needs, expectations, values, and the political realities of the moment. If we could be as confident of our ability to predict these elements in the future as well as we can in retrospect, then we could feel more comfortable in predicting the institutional change which might be expected.

LOOKING AHEAD

In spite of the risks associated with "gazing into the crystal ball," at times it becomes necessary. The fundamental question is, how long will the current era, sometimes called New Federalism, last? Will it end with the current presidency in 1989, or will it continue into the future?

If we look at the present state of the four characteristics used in examining past periods we may gain some insights into likely institutional prospects of the future.

Population Distribution

Although the early 1970s were characterized by an important migration of people to rural areas, the largest increases in absolute numbers of people continue to be in major metropolitan areas. The concept of "megalopolis" remains valid and of ever increasing importance. While some continue to drill their own wells, build their own septic systems, drive the backroads and live the country life, most share the fundamental need for collective sewer, water, transportation systems, etc., which simply cannot be provided independently. There appears to be little likelihood of lessening need for group action in the future. As a matter of fact, growing population concentrations lead to increasing concern for air and water quality, personal security, and general human development. Although there will be some private sector role, it seems certain that there will be mounting pressure for continuing collective action in dealing with these societal requirements. The question remains open as to whether the growing metropolitan areas will be able to accept the fiscal burden of immigrants from other communities, states, and nations or if they will demand state and national assistance. The latter appears more likely.

Income Producing Base

The United States has already entered what might best be called the Internationalization Era. Tremendous improvements in world communication associated with air travel, microprocessors, satellites and other technology have made instant international commerce a reality. The ability to talk immediately, understandably, and at low cost with colleagues and customers nearly anywhere on the globe has provided the critical underpinnings for multinational banking and industry. International offices and outlets, formerly only within the purview of nations and large corporations, have now become a possibility for small and medium sized firms as well. The economic well-being of even the smaller firms is tied closely to international trade issues (e.g. exchange rates, tariffs).

In the past, streets, highways, railroads, ports, industrial parks, and water systems were the critical infrastructural needs tied to income production. Current locational analysis tells us that technology generating institutions (e.g. universities), airports, and communications systems are the critical factors in location and growth of production and service producing industries and government (Premus, 1982). All three elements of infrastructure are large and very expensive. Once again some form of collective action is necessary if this infrastructure is to be developed and maintained. The action may be by public governments or corporate combinations. In any case, national control and regulation will be required to maintain order and security.

Personal Expectations

Major improvements in the distribution of information, both public and private, almost always result in the raising of individual expectations. Persons who see repetitively a good, service, or "way of life" which is perceived as better than the one they have, soon adjust their expectations upward. Increasing skills and commitments in advertising and merchandising present an excellent example of massive efforts targeted at making this happen. Fortunately, the increased efficiency in both the goods and service sector feeds the higher expectations.

People in all parts of the U.S. have come to expect the prospect of a reasonably secure old age with nearly unlimited access to health care. The public judgment has declared repeatedly that even complex medical care (e.g. bypass surgery, liver dialysis) should be available to all. Recreational facilities are in growing demand as individuals have more leisure time. The current debate over federal support to student loans for higher education is a good example of how difficult it is to lower human expectations once established. It is highly unlikely that a large number of American people are going to accept a return in any significant degree to the earlier era of expectations. On the contrary, the magic of television and more advanced transportation and communication technology will cause them to want more.

Political Perspective

As has always been the case in the democratic and private enterprise U.S. society, the political pendulum swings back and forth. At the moment, the rhetoric of "let the private sector do it," "get the government off our back," "cut social spending," and "lower taxes" dominates. The fundamental question is, does this represent a total disenchantment on the part of the American people with the public government as a useful tool in meeting its demands and expectations which require collective action? The answer to this question will strongly affect the changes in the institutions necessary to support needed local infrastructure.

The United States has a long history of increased reliance on governmental participation in the provision of complex goods and services requiring collective action. This history includes more frequent interaction on the part of federal, state, and local units of government over time. In more recent years the private sector has joined with the public sector in mutually beneficial economic partnerships. Housing development is perhaps the best example. The American people have grown accustomed to the presence of government. A high percent of them gain their living from it. How disenchanted can they be? To quote Pogo, "We have met the enemy, and they are us". The political pendulum may already have reached its zenith in the direction of the self reliance and independence from government which characterized the earlier agricultural era.

The major conclusion reached when looking ahead using the historical perspective of the influence of factors such as population distribution, income producing base, personal expectations, and political reality is that the predominant institutions utilized in financing infrastructure in the past are apt to carry the biggest load in the future.

The American people are continuing to huddle together and are experiencing the irritations resulting from the demand they are placing on the infrastructure. They derive an increasing proportion of their incomes from industries requiring massive communication and transportation facilities. They expect more goods and services such as social security and health care requiring multi-community, multi-state, and national infrastructure. And, they are accustomed to an active relationship including taxation, with a wide range of governments. In short, the people are demanding more joint action (public and private) and have developed a value system which for the most part is accustomed to paying for it.

CHANGES IN INSTITUTIONS

The problems associated with the rebuilding and maintenance of current local infrastructure are well documented (Reid et al. 1984; Dawkins, 1984; USDA Office of Rural Development Policy, 1983; Markle et al. 1982). Less well understood are the development and construction requirements of facilities and services to meet future needs. In nearly all cases the total costs involved are great. Lenders in government and the private sector throughout the United States are seeking alternative ways of providing the funds to meet local needs.

The provision of the major portion of the infrastructure is the responsibility of local units of government. Municipal governments are the most frequent form of local government in the United States. Counties are responsible for an increasing share. Township governments are acquiring new duties and funding sources. Special districts which cut across other units of government and perform specific functions are increasing in numbers (Sullivan et al, 1981).

In the past, local units of government received substantial funds from state and federal government. These funds were frequently used by joint agreement for infrastructure-capital purchases. Historically, the local share of investment in infrastructure declined as first the states and then the nation extended their commitment. More recently this has been reversed. In any case, less attention was paid to the maintenance of the systems. With real and proposed cutbacks at the federal and state level, at least in the short run, there is intense fiscal pressure on local units of government to find new ways of financing the maintenance of deteriorating physical structures and at the same time build the new facilities necessary to keep pace with economic change (Wisconsin Department of Development, 1985).

In previous times of local fiscal crisis, suggestions for solution have included mergers of local governments, more regional planning and control, greater state and federal aid, local tax increases and economic development. Now the search seems to be for institutional change including alternatives providing longer run solutions. Three general

categories might be used to encompass most of the current suggestions:
1) planning, 2) privatization and 3) financing. They are obviously closely
interrelated.

Planning

Local infrastructure development often suffers planning shortfalls.
Plans are generally short run in perspective. A few examples will make the
point. Decisions regarding street and other improvements are made on a
year to year basis. Investments in water treatment plants are often made
years after environmentally safe capacity is reached. Facilities are planned
and built hurriedly in response to short term state or federally funded
programs. As a consequence little thought is given to financing their
maintenance or long run adequacy. Consequently, they may be underbuilt
or overbuilt and/or poorly maintained.

Little recognition is given the relationship of the community and its
need to those of neighboring communities or the broader region. Local
governments are often provincial. In many rural areas there are significant
opportunities to share or exchange facilities. The capacity to make wise
purchase decisions, and for utilization, maintenance and repair are not
uniform. Sharing may allow more up-to-date services and better
maintained equipment at lower cost.

A wide range of interlocal cooperative mechanisms is possible.
Mutual aid in health care, police and fire protection, highway repair, and
special education are all useful examples. Joint purchases and user
agreements of specialized and/or seldom needed equipment could also
lower the cost per unit of government. Joint effort in purchases of
computer-equipment, software and advanced programming may improve
both management and cost effectiveness. The use of shared circuit riders
for specialized management and technical assistance has possibilities, but
to this point little practical experimentation has taken place as a cost
sharing mechanism. The highly organized cooperative purchasing systems
of school districts in the United States provide a working model for other
government units.

Broad regional solutions are of limited success. The infrastructure
problems are often quite community specific and when several
governments are involved, efforts at agreement almost always lead to
controversy (Markle et. al., 1982). Efforts aimed at improving local
planning require great sensitivity to local and regional similarities and
differences and a good deal of flexibility.

A number of institutional shifts should be considered:

1.   *Expansion of public knowledge regarding the technology and
      economics of contemporary infrastructure.* Local governments are
      constantly pressed to respond to demand for new capital investments

which will supposedly encourage economic development or otherwise improve public well-being. Facilities are apt to be built serving the private interests of a few powerful individuals or as the misguided means of a broader group of well-meaning people. Private sector consultation is useful and available, but not always free of conflicts of interest. Planners and grant writers are often directly connected to architectural, engineering and facilities management firms. Knowledge in the hands of the public sector is critical.

2. *National, state and local support of the study of infrastructure need, capacity and cost across a broad region.* This could include the capacity to assist varying combinations of local governments in the analysis of organizational possibilities. No attempt should be made to establish the ideal combinations of communities or a rigid definition of region beforehand. These efforts seldom generate more than the heat of disagreement. National and state support of infrastructure funding might then follow this analysis with some measure of reward to those local governments making real effort at developing infrastructure most efficiently.

3. *Reexamination of public works standards.* In an effort to assure safety, construction and performance standards are often uniform across broad regions and states and higher than necessary in specific cases. Demand pressure on infrastructure varies. Significant economies may be possible through the tailoring of requirements to need. One best system of planning and regulation should be abandoned.

4. *Introduction of more aggressive competition in the analysis of need for infrastructure, its design, construction and operation.* All too often, the analysis of need and design of infrastructure is simply granted to a consulting firm with little assurance of real design competition. Effort might be made to assure the preparation of alternative solutions to a specific problem. The same goals might be accomplished in creative and less costly ways. Likewise, service providers might be encouraged to propose several response mechanisms rather than simply to bid a previously specified contract. Reduced cost and joint effort could result.

5. *Limitations on the creation of new units of local government.* The formation of new units of local government including special districts is apt to encourage provincialism rather than cooperation. States might establish regulations which discourage the incorporation of new units of government and inefficient infrastructure. This might be accomplished by requiring a community proposing incorporation to prove an ability to demonstrate the tax capacity to build and maintain its infrastructure in the long term.

6.   *Introduction of small scale technology.* There will continue to be a large number of local governments with small economic bases for a long time to come. Increased research on the economies of size in infrastructure and the development of new technology more appropriate to smaller communities could be of vital assistance.

7.   *Require "life cycle" costing for new infrastructure.* Funding the maintenance of infrastructure has been a major problem. State and federal funding at the local level has focused primarily on building infrastructure with little concern about its upkeep. Planners might be required to determine long range maintenance and operating costs as well as construction costs. National and state policy might also be modified to place greater emphasis on funding the maintenance of existing infrastructure.

Privatization

Advocates of the "New Federalism" often suggest that any necessary new local infrastructure might be better provided by the private sector rather than the public sector. They also suggest that private corporations, development groups and chambers of commerce be asked to assume responsibility for services such as street maintenance. The argument is that these institutions will be more efficient in their operation than the public sector since the provision of quality infrastructure is more directly in their personal interest. "Use of government contracts to do this work would foster small business, foster community cooperation, control costs, and make the clear beneficiaries of services most responsible for paying the costs" (Markle, et. al. 1982). Privatization focuses on the techniques whereby the private sector participates in the provision of public infrastructure and associated services.

A few institutional variations might be considered without necessarily accepting the basic premise of greater private sector efficiency:

1.   *Private construction, ownership and operation.* One option would be for the private sector to build, own and operate a specific piece of infrastructure with some form of public protection. Those who advocate this alternative ask if there is any fundamental reason why snow removal, waste collection, health care, etc., should not be entrusted to private enterprise accountable to the community (Jequier, 1984). They make the point that this already occurs in specific sectors in many communities in the U.S. and elsewhere. Of course, if the private business fails for any reason, the local government is apt to have to pick up and operate the enterprise.

2. *Special tax advantage to private sector providers of infrastructure.* A few tax credit options already exist which provide advantages to private investment in public institutions. These might be expanded to include options such as increased investment credit, the right to buy and sell business losses, and tax free income for businesses that build and operate community infrastructure.

3. *Sale-leaseback arrangements.* Local governments might sell portions of their infrastructure to private business. They could in turn leaseback the specific property for a period of time at a reduced cost. This might be possible if the private enterprise could realize tax or other cost advantages. At the end of the lease, the public entity might then take the property back for a small fee. Uncertainty regarding the long range tax policy of broader governmental units generates some risk in this option (Wisconsin DOD, 1985).

4. *Public ownership and user fees.* There is nothing especially innovative about the general concept of user fees for publicly owned services. User fees are common throughout the U.S. Of course, they raise a series of questions regarding equity, such as, will critical education and life support infrastructure be provided only to individuals having the ability to pay? Nonetheless, this concept offers some interesting opportunities for privatization. For instance, a system might be generated which identifies the user of specific streets and accounts for the seriousness of that use. Fees and maintenance funds might be allocated accordingly. Developers who open up a new area might not only be asked to build new streets in the development, but assessed a reconstruction cost for public infrastructure which will receive additional population pressure (Markle, et. al., 1982).

5. *Public-private partnership.* Little explanation of this option is necessary. There are numerous examples, such as, combinations of subsidized and nonsubsidized housing and retail establishments in single developments, hotel and conference facilities, public and private communication satelites. There is a great deal of opportunity for wider exploration with other types of infrastructure.

Financing

There are a variety of institutional changes which might be useful in aiding local governments to finance the creation and maintenance of critical infrastructure. The national and/or state government would continue to be a partner in many of them. There are precedents for most. A few examples of institutional possibilities will suffice:

1. *Loan guarantees.* Federal and state governments could provide major assistance to local governments by assuming a contingent liability for local debt obligation associated with specific infrastructure investments. In the case of default, the federal or state government would take over the debt service. This would be especially useful to high risk local debt issues which might otherwise be denied access to financial markets. Guarantees might be limited to those cases where no access to financial markets is available. In any case, the cost of debt service would likely be less. The greatest danger might be that a local community's inability to service its municipal debt obligation is apt to coincide with general weakness in the state or national economy.

2. *National and state financial intermediaries.* Small local governments often find their debt issues too small to take full advantage of price advantages associated with large issues in national financial markets. Broader units of government might assist by combining a number of local issues. The process also allows a spreading of the risk across several higher risk local issues. Reserves might be built into the system to protect against losses from higher risks.

3. *State bond banks.* States might go directly into larger financial markets and sell general obligation bonds which they in turn could lend directly to local units of government. The funds might be used for new capital investment or repair of existing infrastructure. Local units of government could save through lower interest rates and reduced administrative costs. The state would be at some risk, but with the proper distribution of the package across a number of local governments and an appropriate reserve this could be minimized.

4. *Creation of special funds.* States might also require the formation of special sinking funds at the local level where new infrastructure is built. This might be used for maintenance. Or the state could provide funds for local investment using fees or other income from an activity requiring expanded local expenditure. For example, logging a state forest or mining might cause additional school expenditures in a nearby community. Income from the forest or mining severence tax could provide the necessary financial support (see Chapter 8).

Summary

These few examples of institutional innovation in planning, privatization, and financing of local infrastructure represent only the tip of the iceberg of change. In the next few years, creativity in providing financing for capital plant investment and maintenance will be critical.

The short run retreat from federal participation in the financing of vital local facilities and services will create the kind of pressure which leads to creativity. The pressure for increased collective action will mount as the consequence of population growth and concentration, the need for massive communication and transportation technology, and the expectations of greater individual wealth and well-being throughout the United States. It is unlikely that the American people will accept the reduced role of the federal government for long. Nonetheless, the old ways of doing things will be changed. New knowledge will be at a premium. The great challenge for those in research and education will be simply to run fast enough to stay ahead of it all.

21
Reflections and Directions

Ron E. Shaffer

This book reviews the state of the art of theory, tools, and data that extension and research faculty can use to assist local units of government in their infrastructure decision-making. Infrastructure is broadly defined, although for the most part we are talking about physical capital (e.g. roads, ambulance service) - not human capital. The purpose of this chapter is to reflect on what has been said up to this point, and make some suggestions about gaps and needed focus. With that as background, three general themes will be emphasized: the first is decision-making capacity; the second is model/data validation; and the third is appropriate questions.

DECISION-MAKING CAPACITY

Earlier discussions and pervasive public sentiment suggests that the private decision-maker is much more rational and knowledgeable than the public decision-maker. Therefore, the results of private decisions are more efficient and the public sector is less efficient and less rational. This is a myth that we tend to perpetuate by not speaking out forcefully about the reality of the situation. First, public decision-making often requires the need to respond to multiple goals which are not necessarily complementary. Second, many of the issues that the public sector is forced to deal with (e.g. pollution, crime, school systems) are public issues because the private sector has consistently chosen not to deal with them. Third, the literature of private corporate management is replete with examples of seemingly irrational and inefficient decisions by private decision-makers, even though they are presumed to be pursuing a profit motive.

A serious problem in much of the discussion concerning public decision-making is the tendency to expect part-time local officials to implement relatively complex strategic planning or decision-making models. It is easy to forget that these individuals often expend much of their creative energy and enthusiasm earning a living or addressing such mundane topics as leash laws or zoning variances, leaving them little time to understand complex strategic decision-making methods. Thus, it is very important for Extension professionals to synthesize the various decision models and to adjust them to the context of local officials in small communities without a professional staff.

The new federalism places an increased premium on local decision-making capacity. Regardless of one's political views, this phenomenon cannot be overlooked. The use of categorical grants and the heightened involvement of state and federal agencies in the delivery of local public services happened because, from an economic perspective, many of these decisions and standards were better made at a more aggregated level. One implication of declining federal involvement is that decisions which had previously been made further up the federal chain are now back at the local level. Thus, local officials must use a different creativity in solving their own problems. An important thing to remember in this new era is that not all local issues lend themselves to local level solutions (e.g. equal opportunity, environmental standards).

MODEL/DATA VALIDATION

Concerning model and data validation, we now have enough experience to start the exercise of determining if our projections were correct. The author knows of very little work measuring the accuracy of environmental or social impact projections. There is a need to start asking ourselves how accurate our past estimates have been and how effective we have been in alerting decision-makers about potential problems. No doubt there are many examples of successes, and failures, but no one knows to what extent these exist.

The second form of data validation relates to public service delivery. There is a need to start compiling economic budgets of the various services reflecting such factors as population densities, social economic characteristics, and management capacities. This is analogous to the farm enterprise budgets which emerged in the 50's and 60's. The current use of engineering budgets presumes above-average management skills and ideal technology. The work done in Oklahoma (see Chapter 7) is definitely a step in the right direction. Those individuals are to be commended for taking that step and making the intellectual investment.

However, the need remains, given our years of experience with this type of effort, to determine the precision of our initial estimates.

There are indications in this volume that some excess infrastructure capacity may exist in rural areas. The difficulty in making these judgments is that we lack adequate measures of infrastructure capacity. It may be that there is excess capacity in those services required by economic activity (e.g. industrial parks), but none in services to households (e.g. schools, health care). There is need to answer the questions, "How do we measure the output and the capacity to produce output from our infrastructure?" and "What is the real economic demand for public output?" While we may deal with needs and standards we must recognize that these are quite different from demand.

Appropriate Questions

The state of Pennsylvania (Chapter 14) is to be commended for its support of the Agri-Access project. The state responded to a definite need and responded in a fashion that has encouraged client involvement. However, economists also need to step back and ask, "Were the appropriate economic questions asked?" For instance, was the purpose of that project to bring people together to identify deficient bridges, or would that project have done more public good for the Commonwealth of Pennsylvania if they had asked, "How can we best move people and/or agricultural products about rural Pennsylvania?"

The example of a business buying equipment that is too big or heavy for the bridges that in effect surrounded the business, leads one to question whether it is appropriate for the public sector to continually rectify the irrationality of private decision-makers. In the case of milk, might not an alternative collection system using smaller, lighter trucks and a collection point have been just as efficient (when both public and private costs are considered)? Perhaps it would have made sense to buy out that dairy herd and shift that farm to alternative enterprises. These questions need to be raised before attempting to repair and/or replace every bridge in rural America.

There is a tendency to perceive agriculture as the driving force of rural economies. Farming is a significant component of rural economies, but the economy of rural America is rapidly being transformed. While some parts of this country are still heavily dominated by production agriculture, the vast majority of rural area economies are no longer dominated by farming. The dominant forces are manufacturing, trade, recreational activity, and in many cases, nonlocal passive income (e.g. retirement funds, dividends, interest, and rent). To the extent that infrastructure decision-making is driven by the historical importance of agriculture, rather than the emerging forces of rural economies, we do rural America a disfavor.

Part of this disfavor appears as a failure to recognize the implications of the economy-wide transformation from goods production to service production, and in particular the importance of information. The production of goods will continue to be important to the economic vitality of rural America. Yet, rural America will find itself at a relative disadvantage in terms of future economic activity if it does not provide infrastructure that moves data and information as well as physical goods and people. What types of infrastructure investments are municipalities making to move information? The alternatives range all the way from local telephone switching equipment that permits data transmission to the use of fiber optics or communication dishes, etc. To the extent that rural areas do not make these investments, they will be at an even greater disadvantage in the competition for the emerging economic activities.

Finally, economic theory fails in its inability to respond to the types of decisions that local public officials must often make. Their decision is -- how do we choose between repairing a bridge or investing in a water and sewer system, or building a school? We really cannot provide local decision-makers with the guidance that would help make that trade-off and understand the implications of their choices. This constraint is, perhaps, the most frustrating aspect of the work we do. We can generally provide excellent counsel on partial solutions to complex investment decisions. Yet, our inability to resolve the more important trade-off issues remains legendary.

Progress in understanding local infrastructure decision-making is the common element of our recent efforts. Our extension programs have improved substantially. Yet much remains to be done to help local decision-makers understand their options, as well as the consequences of their choices.

22
Rural Infrastructure Research Needs

Beverly A. Cigler

This chapter highlights two broad areas of research need for rural infrastructure policy: (1) data generation/classification and (2) analyses that sort out the relationships among the allocation of governmental responsibilities for infrastructure, alternative financing mechanisms for service delivery, and rural management capacity.

DATA GENERATION/CLASSIFICATION RESEARCH NEEDS

The literature on "infrastructure" condition reveals a wealth of descriptive studies by professional and municipal associations, research institutes, and consulting firms, but little attempt at the kinds of taxonomies necessary for policy relevance.[45] Some studies by the national government offer a greater specification of policy options.[46] New proposals

---

45 See: American Public Works Association, 1981; Associated General Contractors, 1983; Choate and Walter, 1981; CONSAD, 1980; Government Finance Officers Association, 1984; National League of Cities and U.S. Conference of Mayors, 1983; and Peterson, Humphrey, Miller, and Wilson, 1983.

46 See: Advisory Commission on Intergovernmental Relations (1984), Congressional Budget Office (CBO) (1986, 1985a, 1985b, 1983); Joint Economic Committee, U.S. Congress (1984a, b, and c); U.S. Department of Commerce (1980); U.S. Department of Housing and Urban Development (1982); and U.S. House of Representatives (1983b).

may increase the amount of information available to Congress and others interested in the condition of the nation's infrastructure. The Public Works Improvement Act of 1984 established a National Council on Public Works Improvement and instructed it to report annually on the nation's infrastructure--its age and condition, its maintenance and financing needs, and its capacity to sustain growth. Other parts of the bill require that the President's budget submission identify and project public capital investment levels.

Possessing information describing the nation's infrastructure does not necessarily advise decision-makers about what to do about the situations described. Knowing that roadways are in poor shape, for example, does not inform decision-makers whether the roads should be resurfaced, minimally repaired, or, maybe not repaired at all (i.e., when traffic is sparse). The inventories and needs surveys that have been completed, however, do point out some of the major infrastructure problems faced in the U.S.

In 1983 the Congressional Budget Office (Congressional Budget Office) highlighted three key sets of problems related to declining investments in public facilities in general: deterioration, technological obsolescence, and insufficient capacity to serve future growth. Also suggested were the adverse effects of declining investment: (a) higher costs borne by users of inadequate or deteriorated facilities; (b) higher life-cycle construction costs for facilities which are not properly maintained; and (c) potentially significant constraints on economic development. These categories help focus research efforts directed toward studying community facilities problems that differ in kind, suggesting that alternative policy approaches for financing, management, and allocating responsibilities may be necessary. The many "How-to-do-it" books, addressed primarily to state and local officials, offer useful first steps in structuring such research.[47]

Several studies specifically addressed to rural community facilities are important in demonstrating that rural needs are considerable and changing (Beale, 1981; Reid, 1982; Stinson, 1981b). (For example, although plumbing equipment has increased, water supply and sewage disposal now may pose greater immediacy since deterioration of facilities is severe.) Under contract with the Environmental Protection Agency, Cornell University's survey (Francis, et. al., 1982) of 2,654 households (representing 22 million rural households) found that almost two-thirds of all rural households had water judged unacceptable for at least one major contaminant. This suggests that residential sewage disposal capability is inadequate. More than two-thirds of rural households, for

---

[47] Examples include: Gitajn, 1985; Marlin, 1984; Peterson and Hough, 1983; Peterson and Miller, 1981; Thompson, 1983; Vaughan, 1983; Vaughan and Pollard, 1984; Watson, 1983; and Weiss, 1985.

example, rely on septic tanks and cesspools for sewage disposal; many others use means other than public sewers, septic tanks, or cesspools (U.S. Bureau of the Census, 1980). Two-thirds of the land area in the U.S. does not meet the minimum requirements for soil absorption systems, as much of the land area with severe soil limitations is in the areas where septic tank-field absorption systems are most concentrated.

The National Rural Community Facilities Assessment Study (NRCFAS), profiling the availability and condition of public facilities in rural America in 1978, was conducted by the U.S. Department of Agriculture (Reid, et. al., 1984; Reid and Sullivan, 1984). It reinforces the findings of the Cornell study and offers benchmark descriptive data on a broader range of rural public facilities. The data base includes inventories of hospitals, fire protection, local roads, streets, and bridges, and public water supply.

Of special importance is the NRCFAS's demonstration of regional variations in community facilities. The data show that fifty-nine percent of the nonmetropolitan communities in the North Central region and forty-five percent of those in the Northeast have no public water supply, whereas most of those that do have public systems serve less than two-thirds of their year-round households. Moreover, while fewer Northeast communities are served by wastewater treatment plants, the South's proportionately greater number of facilities are used less by the local population. The South, then, has the largest portion of people using on-site disposal methods, with more than 13 million people located within the various plants' service areas but not connected to them. Such wide variations in regional facilities suggest that something other than aggregate data collection is necessary in order to correlate the availability and condition of public facilities with variables related to local environmental factors, governmental organization, and other key regional characteristics.

Existing inventories have measurement problems that limit their utility. Scant attention has been devoted to the use of common definitions and concepts, with most studies "reinventing the wheel." It makes little sense to replicate such research until the necessary first step in developing a widely agreed upon set of definitions and conceptual framework is established. Community facilities problems are complex, complicated issues that impact communities in both the short and long run.

Existing data are scattered in many areas, across many disciplines, and are not always in the most usable form for developing, implementing, and evaluating policy options. There is need for research in at least the following five areas:

1. Basic data needs should be identified for each type of community facility, entailing considerable effort in taxonomy building.

2. Once data needs are known, research should be conducted to identify data available to meet those needs, judge their usefulness and, perhaps, transform some existing data into usable form.

3. Of particular concern is the need to dovetail what has been learned about infrastructure and community facilities with more narrative policy comment about rural problems in general (Block, et. al., 1984; U.S. House of Representatives, 1983a; U.S. Senate, 1977; U.S. Senate, 1979). One suggestion is to review all of the infrastructure reports by agencies of the national government, including Congressional testimony, organize it into categories of policy suggestions, and assess the availability of empirical research data to evaluate those policy suggestions.

4. By comparing data needs, availability, and policy prescriptions, gaps in the data base will be identified. Well-focused, systematic research can identify these gaps and devise a plan for obtaining missing data.

5. The availability of data does not ensure that technology is available for researchers to utilize them efficiently in analyses. More attention should be paid to ways to centralize, analyze, and present complex data in usable forms. Linkage to other data base systems is of key importance, considering the necessity to deal with the range of variables related to finance, management, and governmental organization and responsibility as related to public facilities.

The greatest data problem stemming from existing research is a lack of attention to "need," based on measures of the adequacy of facilities. While most of what has been said and written about the nation's infrastructure problems has been related to finance, price estimates for dealing with problems have ranged from $470 billion to three trillion dollars within a twenty year period, with most studies at the high end of the range. Doomsayers bemoan the "disinvestment" of America's public infrastructure, advocating more capital spending, while others suggest that current analyses of trends are misleading (Kamensky, 1984). Better assessments of "need" would help restructure the policy debate. Widely varying cost estimates on infrastructure needs make the rural infrastructure problem seem intimidating. More attention should be paid to highlighting the costs of the average individual infrastructure project (perhaps ranging between $1 and $5 million dollars). That is, research is needed on costs by specific project type.

There are many problems, however, with using the device of needs estimation. Typically, studies list physical flaws or deficiencies in infrastructure, compared to some technical standard. Then, a price list of remedies is developed and compared against projected program levels. For decision-makers, such needs estimates pose problems in making budgetary choices. Some potential remedies do not require capital spending, for example, and some deficiencies may not be worth addressing. Project designs and costs can vary widely according to local conditions. Needs lists cannot lead to informed choices among projects and across programs, nor ascertain priorities. In addition, true benefits are not measured by needs assessments. Another research need is derived from the relationship between standards and the measurement of "need." Construction standards, for example, contribute significantly to perceptions of demand for capital investment. As Peterson noted in a recent article by Odell (1982, p. 8) "Capital standards are not 'needs' in any literal sense, but are merely policy objectives which must be balanced against their costs of achievement."

In addition, more research could be directed toward the choice between design specifications and performance standards for meeting program goals. Two federal programs in which managers have switched from project design specifications to project performance are pollution abatement and transit for the disabled. Research determining whether performance standards achieve program goals more quickly, more efficiently, or at lower cost than under technology-based specifications could be used to help determine more accurate infrastructure need and cost assessments.

More research must be addressed to development of an infrastructure management system that recognizes the diverse possibilities for satisfying the demands for infrastructure, evaluates them realistically, and implements the best options. The Congressional Budget Office (1986) recently issued a report that outlines these three key activities that together can help guide budgetary choices toward providing careful infrastructure investments. Researchers can devote more attention to the examination of noninvestment choices and options for alternative investments. Relieving congestion, for example, does not always mean the need for new facilities or improvement of those that exist. Manipulation of demand for service through prices is a noninvestment alternative. Needs estimation research must incorporate such alternatives.

A related factor is that cost estimates depend on how "infrastructure" is defined. Basic public infrastructure refers to highways, transit, water facilities, and so forth. Human services public infrastructure includes at least educational, medical, and correctional facilities (Christopherson, 1983). Quasi-public development infrastructure refers to civic centers, parks, and hotels, among other projects. One observer has included housing as an infrastructure issue (Tuchfarber, 1983). The sufficiency of the nation's infrastructure cannot be measured in the aggregate. Adequacy must be measured by the characteristics of the projects undertaken. Cost estimates must be disaggregated among infrastructure types if policy options are to be seriously addressed.

A background study (Abt Associates, 1980) for the National Rural Community Facilities Assessment Study by the U.S. Department of

Agriculture is clearly the most comprehensive classification of categories of infrastructure to date. Thirty-seven categories under two major headings (service and production facilities) were identified. While actual existing inventories of availability and condition focus primarily on water and sewer systems, streets and highways, and mass transit and bridges (Dossani and Steger, 1980; Holland, 1972; Reid, et al. 1984; U.S. Department of Commerce, 1980) common use of the 37 categories developed by Abt Associates can help structure replicable research that compares infrastructure type to institutional arrangements, financing, and management responsibilities. Upon determination of cost estimates for public facilities in greatest need for rehabilitation and/or development, focused research can examine environmental and legal arrangements to sort out feasible service delivery options.

Another research priority also relates to the actual costs of the infrastructure problem. More information is needed regarding long-term disinvestment and whether that trend has negative effects. Demographic shifts (e.g. less school age population, movement to rural areas and the sunbelt), the use of better pricing mechanisms (which reduce demand) such as user fees, and changes in service delivery (e.g., privatization) are examples of factors that have reduced overall demand (Kamensky, 1984).

While all of the effects of these trends on demand are unclear, many effects are obvious. Population shifts to rural areas translate to demands for new construction, making it possible to link infrastructure concerns to economic development needs and suggesting stronger political coalition-building possibilities than for financing rehabilitation, the greatest need in urban areas. Privatizing capital facilities, such as hospital construction, shifts responsibilities from the public to private sector, making "needs" estimates unclear. A recognition of these changing demands means existing aggregate cost estimates are misleading. Basic research is needed on the real causes of declining investment.

The linkage of infrastructure to positive economic development is still largely unknown. While Choate and Walter (1981) argue that one half to two-thirds of the nation's communities are unable to support economic development until major new investments are made in basic facilities such as wastewater treatment plants, Peterson and Miller (1982) claim that the actual reliance of business on public infrastructure has not been adequately researched.

Business locational decisions are extremely complex and include at least the following factors: plant or site availability, access to and cost of transportation, quality and cost of labor, labor climate, proximity to markets, cost of utilities, proximity to supplies, proximity to other company facilities, state and local taxes, the regulatory environment, educational quality, housing cost, level of public services, and a range of other amenities that can be described as general "quality of life" offered (Schmenner, 1982; Vaughan, 1983). Since limited resources and unlimited demands result in the need for local officials to tie their infrastructure needs explicitly to other community issues, research on the economic development linkage should receive high priority.

Finally, the linkage between communications technology and the measurement of "need" for public community facilities is necessary to uncover, since improvements in communications technology are likely to exert increasing influence on transportation and other policies. As new forms of communication become less expensive, physical travel will become unnecessary for many purposes. Similarly, the continuing revolution in communications offers the promise of lessening the effects of isolation, low population density, mobility disadvantages, and other rural characteristics (Honadle, 1983). Also, decentralization of activities and staggered work shifts, among other changes in the work environment, lead to reduced transportation and infrastructure demand. There is a need for research that categorizes the areas in which new communications technology might reduce the adverse impacts of some distinguishing characteristics of rural areas.

INTERGOVERNMENTAL RELATIONS, MANAGEMENT CAPACITY, AND ALTERNATIVE FINANCING

Honadle (1981, 1982, 1983) defines a government's capacity as its ability to anticipate and influence change; make informed, intelligent decisions about policy; develop programs to implement policy; attract and absorb resources; manage resources; and evaluate current actions to guide future actions. The general capacity of small governments to undertake their responsibilities is weak. Research has found generally low levels of usage of innovative expenditure reduction, revenue enhancing, and management techniques (Banovetz, 1984; Brown, 1980; Cigler, 1986; Green and Reed, 1981; Howitt, 1978; Newland, 1981; Sokolow, 1981).

Organizational and management issues, then, deserve careful consideration when assessing public policy for rural infrastructure (Cigler, 1985b). Institutional, legal, and financial responsibility for public community facilities is highly dispersed among separate government entities and, often, within each local government. Any mismatches between responsibilities, management capability, and fiscal capacity can influence both the nature of infrastructure problems and options for dealing with them. No single approach or packaged set of options is likely to help local communities. The considerable variation across types of infrastructure and, within types, across facilities owned and maintained by different government agencies complicates coherent policymaking and the design of appropriate research.

Intergovernmental transfers offer a reasonable starting place for examining local financing, as well as the ability to plan and implement projects. Diminishing financial resources result in local governments cutting back on operating budget allocations for maintenance and repair of existing infrastructure, and severely limiting capital investments made for expansion and rehabilitation (Choate and Walter, 1981; Jump, 1982; Peterson, et. al., 1983; Peterson and Miller, 1982).

While resource scarcity presents a major obstacle, lost funding has moved agenda-setting responsibilities to the local arena, meaning that limited resources and unlimited demands must be faced with good information, leadership, and innovation. Unable to ignore deteriorating facilities and/or the need for new facilities, local governments have to examine their existing management systems, especially financial systems.

Several research priorities for public facility policy in rural areas emerge from these intergovernmental shifts. State laws and practices that inhibit local governments' abilities to solve their infrastructure problems deserve attention. This includes statutes that place legal restraints and controls on local revenue raising and spending authority as well as laws in some states that prevent local governments from creating capital reserves to finance future capital expenditures (Rosenberg and Rood, 1985). This especially impacts negatively on small communities that may otherwise be unable to enter the bond market or operate on a "pay-as-you-go" approach (Danzinger and Ring, 1982; Florestano, 1981; Ladd, 1978; MacManus, 1981; Rosenberg and Rood, 1985). Smaller governments must increasingly turn to alternative financing and service delivery arrangements, partly because of these state laws (Florestano and Gordon, 1980; International City Management Association, 1984; Peterson and Hough, 1983; Savas, 1982; Stevens, 1984; Vehorn, 1981). Also, since many communities are forced to "hide" capital reserves within the operating budget for financing future capital needs in the form of contingency reserves, there is a risk that such reserves will be depleted and funds used for non-capital purposes. Research on the existence of such local practices, as they relate to state practices, is essential.

Existing barriers posed by the lack of use of sophisticated financial and planning techniques (e.g., capital budgeting, capital improvement planning, strategic planning) by small governments are increased when the structural barriers to infrastructure decision making posed by the state and national government are recognized. The Congressional Budget Office study (1983) suggested, for example, that federal programs and funding created a bias toward construction rather than maintenance and repair.

The key federal role in infrastructure provision is as a source of finance. It provides over half of the nation's gross investment in infrastructure, yet determines only 20 percent of the actual infrastructure project choices (Congressional Budget Office, 1986). Research that examines federal eligibility limits would lead to more understanding of the search process used at the local level to develop the most efficient and necessary infrastructure projects. Any relaxation of federal rules in favor of guidelines that recognize differences among communities and that encourage a wider scope in local choices for improvements are key research targets for understanding differences among localities.

Similarly, research that examines the incentive structure offered to state and local governments by the national government through its grant programs is necessary for understanding the role of pricing and infrastructure costs. Possible changes in allocation rules or management policies themselves could be studied to assess impacts at the local level. The Congressional Budget Office (1986) has suggested six possible changes:

1. Reduction of federal aid,

2. Development of sunset conditions for some programs,

3. Alteration of matching shares,

4. Use of broader financing categories and block grants,.

5. Use of innovative financing techniques, and

6. Restriction of aid eligibility by performance targets.

The first three areas of possible change focus on the idea that state and local governments might make more efficient choices among infrastructure options if faced with greater shares of costs. Items 3, 4, and 5 would also encourage greater competition for funding among potential projects, possibly influencing infrastructure choices. The first five potential changes listed encourage wider searches for and better appraisals of options. The sixth item would encourage the same end and reward agencies using preferred management practices.

As the changes listed above become reality, research that helps sort out inadequacies in rural area management practices becomes all the more important. Small, rural communities, especially those with constrained resources, might have difficulty competing against other units that can provide higher matches as a leverage for federal aid, for example. Reduced federal funds would make local agencies more reliant on local budgets for investment and operating resources. Without help in developing better management techniques, already hardpressed rural areas would be more disadvantaged. Financing very large projects would be especially difficult. In summary, research on the effects of both federal and state funding practices and mandates in general on rural public facilities policies is needed.

In order for states and localities to keep up with infrastructure demands, they must make increasing use of creative financing techniques to obtain capital for infrastructure needs (Foster, 1982; Stanfield, 1982). These new financial mechanisms, including greater reliance on user charges and special dedicated revenue sources, as well as earmarking to ensure that funds are available to meet infrastructure construction and repair needs (Joint Economic Committee, 1984c; Urban Land Institute, 1983;

American Planning Association, 1980) are attracting interest. A new concept in infrastructure finance is that of an infrastructure revolving fund or bank. At the federal level, several proposals are currently being considered, as well as proposals for a fund to finance wastewater treatment plant construction. Some states have established or are about to establish similar institutions, some for multipurpose assistance and some targeted for the neediest counties (Peterson and Hough, 1983; Vaughan, 1983; Watson, 1983). Research that classifies existing legal, institutional, and financial arrangements across the fifty states is a prerequisite to understanding how alternative financing may be used by local governments.

In addition, since fund administrators would want assurances that loan repayments could be made, the need for research assessing the financial condition and financial practices of rural governments is heightened in importance. Since local officials would be more likely to pay increased attention to proper pricing of their services, the development and uses of user charges, especially pricing decisions, is a key area for research.

The major responsibilities for infrastructure are at the local level, with rural governments alone numbering nearly 54,000 units, comprising 318,000 elected officials. Much of the discussion in this section has highlighted the need for research relating to possible administrative inadequacies within local government itself. Rural responsibilities may exceed the ability of management. Possible shortcomings to examine include: poor data generation, insufficient planning capacity, weak policy and program coordination, fragmented organizational responsibilities, poor financial management, and other "nuts and bolts" management and organizational concerns. Comprehensive public investment strategy requires more sophisticated planning and budgeting procedures and the design of more effective management techniques (Devoy and Wise, 1979; Olsen and Eadie, 1982; Porter and Peiser, 1984; Vaughan, 1983; Walter and Choate, 1984), both key research needs.

Most local governments, for example, budget on a line-item, object of expenditure basis. Despite its advantages, this approach does not provide accurate analysis of infrastructure investment decisions. Maintenance and repair costs are generally not systematically included in typical operating budget allocations. In addition, capital improvements plans--the basis for analyzing public facilities in terms of need and priority, fiscal capacity, financing strategy, timing, and growth management--are not commonly used by local, especially rural, governments. The conclusion holds for the use of capital budgeting and life-cycle costing.

Few local governments, in fact, have developed even an inventory of their infrastructure since cost accounting is not used to measure public assets for depreciation purposes as in the private sector. It is difficult to plan for the future, in terms of new infrastructure, rehabilitation of existing infrastructure, and/or general maintenance of all infrastructure without first knowing what government owns, its value, and its maintenance history. This type of information is essential to understanding one set of privatization alternatives--asset management-related options. This involves the sale of surplus assets and sale and lease-back options.

Poor financial management in general is costly to local governments when attempting to finance infrastructure. Unfortunately, the smaller, especially non-metropolitan, governments are most likely to possess a wide array of administrative inadequacies (Browne and Hadwiger, 1981; Bryce, 1979; Cigler, 1985a; Cigler, 1984; Dillman and Hobbs, 1982; Honadle, 1983; Sokolow and Honadle, 1984; Stinson, 1981a; Stinson, 1981b; Weinberg, 1984) and research on the topic itself is fraught with many difficulties (Reeder, 1984).

Small and/or rural governments may hold a special need for outside policy entrepreneurs due to their relative lack of expertise and staff availability. Possible roles to be played by the national and state governments in helping local communities achieve adequate management capacity loom as important as research on measuring "need" relating to physical structures.

Public vs. private infrastructure responsibilities are also blurred, complicating data generation and interpretation. Some categories of infrastructure, especially capital facilities, are privatizing. This includes hospital construction, streets, water and sewer lines. Creative methods of providing and financing capital infrastructure include such mechanisms as developer fees, user fees and charges, sale-leaseback arrangements, and leasing of public facilities. The blurring of public and private roles and responsibilities differs across regions of the nation. Utilities in some areas are publicly owned and, in other areas, they are private. Shifts in responsibilities between sectors make trend analysis difficult, complicate projections of need, and pose particularly difficult problems for smaller governments that lack strong monitoring and evaluative capabilities.

Given the wide array of administrative inadequacies within rural governments, "capacity building" (Honadle, 1981, 1982; Newland, 1981) is very important in achieving policy successes. More needs to be known about rural organizational change and the role of external change agents. (See Anderson, 1979; Beyer, et. al., 1983; Bullock and Lamb, 1984; Jones, 1977; Mazmanian and Sabatier, 1983; Montjoy and O'Toole, 1979; Nakamura and Smallwood, 1980; Pressman and Wildavsky, 1973; Rich, 1981; Sabatier and Mazmanian, 1980; Van Horn and Van Meter, 1976; Van Meter and Van Horn, 1975; Williams, 1967).

The U.S. Department of Agriculture's "Great Plains Project," initiated in 1973, and its follow-up, "The Local Decision Project," along with related spin-offs are examples of capacity building efforts that can offer small governments help in developing their financial and planning capacities. Budget studies of alternative delivery systems, project and impact studies, and locational studies, such as those formulated at Oklahoma State University, presumably facilitate local decision making capacity. (e.g., Doeksen, et. al., 1981c; Goodwin, et. al., 1979; Goodwin and Nelson, 1981; Nelson and Doeksen, 1982; Nelson and Fessehaye, 1981; Webb, et. al., 1980.) Evaluations of these capacity building efforts are another research need. Without research on the current state of the practice, future policy-making is hampered.

CONCLUSION

This nation faces a serious, but manageable, problem with the condition and adequacy of its infrastructure. With uncertainty about the federal role in funding infrastructure, state and local governments are assuming primary responsibility for infrastructure management, financing, and development. Rural governments, with limited expertise, financial resources, and other conditions necessary for sound programs, are especially hardhit by changes in the condition of their infrastructure system and its management.

This chapter reviewed the key rural infrastructure research needs. An examination of the data generation and classification of research needs highlighted a wealth of descriptive information on deteriorated rural facilities, conflict about how to measure "condition" and "sufficiency" of facilities, and the linkage of infrastructure to economic development policies, new communications technology, and other factors. A key concern is the need to consider alternative infrastructure investment decisions.

A review of likely changes in the intergovernmental system, especially in financing infrastructure development and maintenance, was linked to the realities of rural management capacity. The institutional, legal, and financial arrangements at the local level emerged as key research foci. In effect, rural government ability to anticipate and influence change; make informed policy decisions; develop programs; attract and use resources; and evaluate actions relating to any policy area is in need of clarification. Research that explains the "nuts and bolts" of rural management capacity can increase understanding of the likely rural response to the infrastructure dilemma.

23
The Role of Cooperative Extension, USDA, Land Grant Universities, and Rural Development Centers

Russ Youmans, Bruce A. Weber, Glenn Nelson, and J. Norman Reid

INTRODUCTION

The preceding chapters identify the state of our knowledge, and its gaps and weaknesses.   Next we, as representatives of institutions responsible for helping localities make the best possible infrastructure decisions, must critically examine our resources and determine their adequacy. Each institution's comparative advantages must be identified. Improved arrangements among the institutions, and between the institutions and their clients must be developed.

Today's institutions are the products of yesterday's conditions, and the forces acting upon those conditions.   Ideal institutions, like finely suspended automobiles, are unaffected by short term shifts in external forces and yield only to the greater, secular trends. The challenge is to distinguish between the temporary and permanent changes and to adjust appropriately.   Unlike the automobile, there are tangible benefits to institutions that anticipate the changing forces and obstacles, and make the appropriate changes as they occur.

Among the many public institutions which effect local infrastructure decision-making, three are of particular interest because of their close relationship and interdependence. These are the Cooperative Extension Service, the Federal Government, and the four Regional Rural

Development Centers. What are the roles of these institutions, and can we anticipate how they must change to meet our emerging needs?

COOPERATIVE EXTENSION SERVICE

The State Cooperative Extension Service is an important point of contact between nonmetropolitan local governments and the public institutions designed to provide aid in infrastructure decision-making. Extension is currently facing unprecedented pressure to establish priorities and to scale down those programs which are least cost-effective. On the other hand, this process of introspection offers an ideal opportunity to assess the relative importance of the most pressing infrastructure-related needs.

This section addresses the gaps between what could or should be done in Extension programs and what is actually being done.

Opportunities

There are at least three ways in which Extension can provide useful education with respect to local infrastructure decisions. First, Extension can give perspective to the context and the constraints within which this local decision will be made. It can do this by putting the local social and economic changes in a regional, national or global context. Programs to assist local governments with financial trend monitoring are an example. Understanding the constraints within which these decisions are made is also a part of this perspective: the economic, political, social, cultural and historical factors which shape the infrastructure decisions of local governments.

Second, and perhaps more important, Extension can provide guidance for communities in considering policy alternatives. That is, it can encourage communities to consider a wider range of options and sensitize them to a broader range of their possible impacts. Extension can help communities to ask the "right" questions.

Finally, Extension can assist communities in finding answers to their questions. Extension programs (such as the Texas A&M Impact Analysis Program) can help communities predict the likely social and economic results of alternative decisions. Extension can train local officials to use the tools of economic analysis, and to improve the design of mechanisms for financial investments. Extension educational programs in various states will combine these opportunities in different ways according to the perceived needs in their communities and the resources available in Extension to address them.

Gaps

Four types of gaps in Extension education programs on local infrastructure investment are (1) staff education, (2) linkages between Community and Rural Development (CRD) Extension and other institutions with similar goals, (3) staffing levels, and (4) research.

1. Staff Education. In staff education there is a perceived need to define and articulate to agents and administrators what Extension can offer to local officials and community leaders. Extension has not been effective in communicating what it can do.

Secondly, in many cases neither administrators nor extension agents understand why Extension should be actively involved with local government investment decisions. Although most agents and administrators do understand how the support of county officials is important to the continued strength of Extension at the local level, it is not clear that they always view the efforts of CRD as positive, particularly given the sensitive political nature of many of the CRD issues.

Third, specialists need help in understanding the local decision-making process, both in its mechanics and from the perspective of decision-making theory. Finally, specialists and agents need instruction in the advances in communications technology which could increase their effectiveness, such as training in microcomputers and the use of video tape equipment.

2. Linkages. Strengthening linkages both within and outside the Land Grant System could considerably increase its effectiveness in dealing with infrastructure decisions. Linkages should be strengthened between the county agricultural and natural resource agents, home economics and 4-H agents; faculty in other departments of the University, both in research and Extension; research and Extension faculty at other Universities; the regional rural development centers; and between those in Extension at the Federal level.

Also, it is especially important that linkages be made with those outside the Land Grant structure, including local government organizations (such as the National Association of Counties and the National Association of Towns and Townships); state agencies, particularly those involved in finance and infrastructure decisions; professional organizations (such as those of government accountants and engineers); and with researchers and consultants with expertise not found in the Cooperative Extension System. All of these outside resources are particularly important as potential collaborators of the Extension programs in states with small CRD staffs. The pools of expertise both within and outside Extension are important sources to be tapped in Extension efforts.

3. Staffing. In many states, the above two issues are compounded by inadequate levels of staffing. Do all states have the critical mass necessary to mount and sustain an effective program with regard to infrastructure issues? In those states where the answer is "no", additional staffing is needed even to begin such a program, or to make the linkages within or outside the universities, or to mount staff education programs associated with local infrastructure investment. This is something of a "Catch 22" situation: without the staff resources Extension can not credibly offer additional programming but without an adequate programming track record, CRD Extension cannot make an effective case for additional staff.

4. Research. In order for Extension to have an effective program in the area of infrastructure investment, additional research is needed. Research is needed both to help frame the right questions and to find answers to these questions. With regard to research which could enable Extension specialists to help communities frame questions, two types of research can be identified: research about the scope of the infrastructure investment problems; and research about local, regional, national and global economic trends which form the context around local economic changes and the constraints within which they are operating.

With regard to research which would assist Extension in answering questions, several kinds of research gaps can be identified:

a. Research is needed to measure the implications of changes in infrastructure with regard to growth, stability, decline, and income distribution.

b. There is a need for better data (often mentioned in this book) and better specification of the impact and budget models. The work on financial management at Iowa State (Chapter 10) is an example of the former, while programs like the budget analysis program at Oklahoma State (Chapter 7) are examples of the latter type of research.

c. There is also a need for better understanding of the relationship among different types of infrastructure investments (for example, trade-offs among roads, bridges, and schools), and between different types of investments and economic development, particularly development in the agricultural sector. There is a need for more research looking into the relationships between agriculture and other sectors in the rural community and the effects of changes in these sectors on local infrastructure needs.

Institutional Responses

Extension could fill the gaps identified above through some mix of increased research, staff education, increases in staffing levels, or shifts in educational responsibilities within the existing staff. Clearly, the appropriate mix of these is dependent upon the mix of objectives in a state's CRD Extension program: the extent to which a state wishes to (a) educate communities about the context of local decisions, (b) help communities address the right questions, and (c) assist communities in analyzing and answering these questions.

Within a given state the decisions about objectives and the response to perceived gaps will depend on a number of things, particularly the size and expertise of existing staff, leadership within the CRD program and within Extension, the fiscal condition of the state, support for rural development activities from the regional rural development centers, and from the Federal level. States with bigger staffs, better leadership, and more financial resources can provide more assistance in training local officials and helping them analyze the questions. All states, however, should be able to assist with the framing of the questions, and with helping communities to understand constraints, and the context within which they operate.

RESEARCH: LAND GRANT UNIVERSITIES AND THE USDA

While some advances have been made since 1960, little progress is apparent in the eight years since the National Conference on Nonmetropolitan Community Services Research in Columbus in January, 1977. Within the Land Grant System, a small and diminishing amount of research effort has been devoted either to community services or capital infrastructure. Despite individual successes in specific cases (e.g. the Great Plains Project at Oklahoma State University and the Local Decisions Project at that university and at the University of Missouri), the overall judgment must be that the Land Grant/USDA System has failed to yield many significant contributions to knowledge in this field during the recent period. Some advances outside the Land Grant/USDA system have occurred, but these have not been spectacular and also have often not been integrated into work by the Land Grant/USDA researchers.

Problems

This lack of progress is undoubtedly due to a variety of factors but some general observations seem appropriate.

1. Research resources not concentrated. For the most part, no "critical mass" of researchers exists at any one location and most research efforts are undertaken by single individuals. As a result, researchers tend to generalize in a wide range of community services and facilities, rather than specializing as is typically the case in some other disciplines. The result is the inability to concentrate resources to the extent necessary to tackle and resolve key theoretical questions. Given this allocation of scientific resources, future theoretical breakthroughs are less likely.

2. *Little theoretical focus.* Much of the work on facilities and services has had a pragmatic focus and has not attempted to identify or resolve gaps in existing theory.

3. *Insufficient exposure to outside ideas.* The Land Grant/USDA research network tends to be a closed system, with principal communication occurring among individuals within the system. As a result, Land Grant/USDA researchers tend to have little communication with knowledge advances occurring outside.

Need for Leadership

Thus, there is a need for a national leadership which could help stimulate the Land Grant/USDA System to increase its efforts on infrastructure investment issues and guide it in fruitful directions. The Economic Research Service (ERS) can contribute to this leadership. Particular areas to consider would include:

1. *Research conferences.* Conferences along the lines of the 1977 Columbus Conference should be held to assess in detail the present state of knowledge on public services and facilities. There is consensus that the time is right for such a session. Such a conference should involve presenters and attendees from outside the Land Grant system.

2. *Cooperative research.* ERS should sponsor cooperative research on public facilities and services designed to pursue innovative ideas and support attempts at theoretical breakthroughs.

3. *Thesis support.* ERS could sponsor Ph.D. theses on topics related to public services and facilities, where these attempt to attack theoretical questions and problems of measurement, rather than case studies or practically-focused projects of principally local interest. The purposes are to sponsor innovative research and to attract new researchers to public service and public facility issues.

4. *NRCFAS data.* The data from the National Rural Community Facilities Assessment Study (NRCFAS) should be released for public use.

Needed Conceptual Advances

Based on discussions in previous chapters, there are several areas of infrastructure investment and public services provision research which can be improved upon in order to enhance social welfare. Among those with respect to theoretical gaps which inhibit our ability to achieve further advances in those areas of research are:

1. *Risk.* Understanding and measuring variable and systematic risks in making infrastructure investments.

2. *Causal variables.* Understanding and measuring systematic trends that have causal effects on infrastructure and public decision-making.

3. *Externalities.* Understanding and measuring externalities from public facilities and services.

4. *Outputs.* Conceptualizing and measuring public service outputs.

5. *Distributional issues.* Understanding and measuring the effects of initial endowments and income streams on income distribution is imperative to prioritize investments.

Needed Empirical Research

Other more empirical areas of research can provide information and knowledge. That is the basis for better policy recommendations. These include:

1. Exogenous variables. Major causal factors that affect the national system of public services and facilities; these need to be understood, measured, and monitored.

2. Endogenous variables. Elements of the decision-making process of producing and consuming public goods and services. Improved conceptual clarity and theoretical understanding of these factors and their interrelationships is important.

3. Institutional roles and responsibilities. Choices about the appropriate roles of public vs. private sectors, Federal, State, and local levels of government, and general vs. special purpose types of local government should rest on valid research findings. Relevant areas of research concern the relationship between institutional arrangements and equity, externalities, the attainment of socially optimal service levels, and the dependence of a decentralized system on information flow and local management capacity.

4. Making locally optimal decisions. Specific information, based on economic research, can help assure that local investment decisions are optimal from a community perspective. Local choices involve the following dimensions (among others): what projects to undertake, when to undertake them, what technology to apply, what mix of inputs to use, what location, what level of output is desired, what type of output (mix of alternative outputs and outcomes) is desired, and what method of financing should be used? Economic and other research can clarify financing options; their costs; the effects of alternative rate structures; the effects of alternative service-production technologies on costs and other values; risks involved in making specific investments; tradeoffs involved in each choice; changes in causal conditions facing the community and the likely impact of these changes on future community investment decisions; the present condition of facilities and services; future needs; the costs and benefits of maintaining, repairing, and replacing facilities; practical measures of outputs, outcomes, quantity, and quality; options for alternative input mixtures; and tools for estimating service demand.

5. *Factors that confound rational decision-making.* Research leading to improved understanding of the political benefits of services and facilities to politicians, and research that clarifies their time horizons and the framework within which they decide, can help yield strategies for avoiding local decisions that are economically inefficient. Research could also clarify the extent to which authority allocations produce locally-undesirable decisions.

6. *Values affected by public choices.* Among the important values affected by public choices about facilities and services are the following:

a. costs and efficiency;
b. equity in the distribution of benefits and costs (interregional, intercommunity, intracommunity); social justice;
c. quality and appropriateness of services;
d. quantity and sufficiency of services;
e. impacts of services on quality of life and community economic development potential.

Research is needed that will assist in conceptualizing and operationalizing these values for use in practical decision-making.

OPPORTUNITIES AND RESPONSIBILITIES OF THE REGIONAL RURAL DEVELOPMENT CENTERS

The four Regional Rural Development Centers (RDC's) were created to encourage cooperation between researchers and extension agents in their rural development efforts. They sponsor research and extension projects with a multistate, regional focus, disseminate information, and sponsor conferences and workshops. This section evaluates their efforts and searches for opportunities to play a greater role.

As regional institutions, the RDC's have a responsibility to conduct activities which transcend statewide and local institutions. The first important area relates to data quality. The RDC's should stimulate additional effort to increase and improve local government data by promoting guidelines and standards. Some standards already exist but there is still a lack of conformity. The need for this data is covered elsewhere in this book.

A second issue pertains to evaluation of the quality of the models and budgets developed. How useful are the models and budgets and in what ways? How transferable are they? Are there ways that such models can be shared?

A third issue relates to emerging infrastructure needs. There is a need to develop the capability to assist communities, and others, to anticipate new developments--such things as the distribution and costs to access fiberoptics technology or satellite communications, the increasing employment in the service economy, and the combined effects on a dispersed work force.

Beyond the issues mentioned above, the regional centers serve as mechanisms to facilitate regional activities and address research and extension education agenda wherever those agendas originate. In particular, the role of the RDC's should be:

- To develop a statement of academic, and certainly educational, philosophy on research and extension work with local government. This is needed to help build the philosophy in the administration and much of the faculty in the colleges of agriculture and other administrators in the Land Grant institutions. It is certainly needed with existing advisory groups and many governmental officials.

- To stimulate and support workshops, networks, and conferences for research and extension faculty on issues relating to rural government, and on broader issues of rural communities. The function of brokering ideas, faculty interests and the few funds available is a very important activity for the centers, one that is unique within the Land Grant structure and perhaps unique within public institutions.

- To develop the capability to spread information into the mass media. From the regional base, assist with the dissemination of research and educational information with analyses and implications to media that can greatly expand the portion of the population informed.

PART V: Implications for the Future of Infrastructure Investment

24
The Federal Government's Role in Community Infrastructure in the 1980s and Beyond

Beth Walter Honadle

Despite the evolving relationships among levels of government, there will always be an important role for the Federal government to play in community infrastructure decision-making. The Federal government's responsibilities in this area arise from externalities, inequities caused by interjurisdictional fiscal disparities, and our belief as a Nation in guaranteeing the availability of certain services. The Federal government's role in domestic functions is always changing. As long as Federal deficits remain large, there will be public pressure to cut domestic expenditures. Functions that have been performed by the Federal government directly, or with large infusions of Federal funds, will now be the responsibilities of states and their localities. Despite such inevitable curtailments in direct Federal expenditures on community infrastructure, certain cross-cutting functions related to local facilities are reserved for the Federal government. This brief chapter outlines informational, financial, and institutional roles of the Federal government in the 1980s and beyond.

INFORMATION DEVELOPMENT AND SHARING

The primary role of the Federal government in the area of community infrastructure is to develop and provide information for decision-makers at all levels in the Federal system. Essential activities include (1) monitoring conditions and identifying trends in existing community infrastructure, (2) promoting networks for the sharing of information, (3) conducting basic research and developing new technologies, and (4) serving as a clearinghouse for information generated within and outside the Federal government.

In order to ascertain the magnitude or the existence of a national infrastructure problem, it is first necessary to gather timely, accurate, and consistent data on what facilities exist, where they exist, and the condition of those facilities. Only the Federal government has the resources and scope of responsibility to survey community infrastructure for the Nation as a whole. A recent example of how the Federal government can develop data on community infrastructure is the National Rural Community Facilities Assessment Study (NRCFAS) in which the U.S. Department of Agriculture (USDA) had a private consulting firm conduct a national survey of fire protection, public water supply, transportation, and other community facilities. The data were then analyzed by USDA researchers.

For States and localities to effectively perform expanded roles in public service provision and economic development, it is useful for them to be able to learn from each other. The Federal government is in a good position to foster networks among professionals around the country working in the community facilities field.

The Federal government is a source of technological innovation and basic research. The products of research and development may then be transferred to state and local governments for adoption and tailoring to their own, unique situations. The Federal government is the proper place for research and development because such undertakings are expensive and involve considerable risks. By assuming the considerable front-end costs of innovation, the Federal government enables thousands of localities to adopt tested technologies and to avoid "reinventing the wheel". Among the basic research questions that need to be answered are, (1) What are the relationships between investments in infrastructure and economic development?, and (2) What are the infrastructure needs of the growth sectors today? Knowing the answers to such fundamental questions might help localities avoid costly mistakes.

States and localities look to the Federal government as a clearinghouse for information. It is most convenient and efficient for people who need to find out what is known about a subject, where funding is available, and who is doing what in the field, to be able to go to a one-stop-shop. An example of how the Federal government can play the clearinghouse role is the National Technical Information Service (NTIS) of the U.S. Department of Commerce.

FINANCING INFRASTRUCTURE

The benefits of public services frequently go beyond the boundaries of the service area. For example, an employer in Michigan benefits from the education a job applicant received in a school system in Kentucky. Taxpayers in one community thereby subsidize other communities' needs for trained labor. Poorer jurisdictions cannot afford to provide adequate levels of services to their citizens. Without financial incentives, certain facilities would not be supplied at the level that is desired from a social point of view.

For these reasons the Federal government has a role in the financing of locally provided services. This role may include grants, loans, loan guarantees, and/or tax incentives to provide infrastructure. The reliance on these various funding alternatives is shifting away from categorical grants and toward block grants and loan guarantees. Although the tools may change over time, compensating for externalities and achieving redistributive objectives remain Federal responsibilities.

INSTITUTIONAL ROLES

In a Federal system there is the need to constantly rethink and sort out roles and responsibilities. Studying the consequences of different structures for providing public services is logically a function of the Federal government. An example of a Federal agency that performs this role for policy-makers is the Advisory Commission on Intergovernmental Relations (ACIR). ACIR was created by Congress nearly three decades ago to study and recommend improvements in the American federal system.

Mandates and regulations comprise another significant area of Federal institutional responsibility. Examples include national standards for clean air and pure water and affirmative action in governmental hiring and promotion practices. The right of all Americans to expect a minimum quality of life and equal opportunities to obtain benefits provided by government imply a need for Federal government intervention.

In sum, the Federal government's role is evolving from a direct to an indirect role in supporting rather than providing infrastructure. The primary role that the government can play is developing and sharing basic information for policy-makers. More specific roles are suggested in Chapter 23.

25
Infrastructure Investment: Alternatives and Priorities

Thomas G. Johnson, Brady J. Deaton, and Eduardo Segarra

The objective of this book was to survey the most important issues in the analysis, evaluation, and implementation of infrastructure investments. Among the issues identified are those related to: the limitations of current theoretical formulations of infrastructure investment analysis; the adequacy and reliability of data sources and methodologies used in evaluating infrastructure investments; the effectiveness of land-grant research and extension programs in assisting local governments in infrastructure investment planning and the political and financial issues behind infrastructure investment decision-making. Rather than providing an exhaustive review of all those issues, this book has attempted to determine the current state of our knowledge and understanding of the infrastructure decision-making process so that researchers, as well as decision-makers, are aware of the theoretical limitations, and the financial and institutional constraints when analyzing infrastructure investments.

This book is intended to mark the beginning of a more comprehensive inquiry into rural infrastructure issues. The fiscal and economic health of the nation may very well depend on our committment to this task. The preceding chapters document where we are but also indicate where we aren't. They ask, and lay the foundations for answering the questions, Where would we like to be?, and How do we get there? Partial answers to these questions are sprinkled through the chapters of this volume, but there is a need to organize and prioritize them. That is, answers and/or prescriptive solutions have been identified which address the most pressing issues in infrastructure investment decision-making, but there is a need to be more systematic. The objective of this chapter is to chart a course toward this goal.

NEED FOR CAPACITY BUILDING

The overall, most urgent need is for the creation of local government decision-making capacity. This need comes from the changing roles of the various levels of government and the emerging institutional arrangements among them. Whether Pulver's optimism (Chapter 20) about the future role of the federal government is borne out or not, the task facing local governments is enormous and growing. The infrastructure programs of the past served as "great equalizers" among local governments assuring the least sophisticated local governments relatively easy, equitable access to infrastructure. In the future, the distribution of local government fortunes will more closely reflect the distribution of their decision-making capacity. The completion of the interstate highway program, the increasing role of block grant financing, the emergence of information infrastructure, the internationalization of the economy, and other changes will require much more effective planning, grantsmanship and decision-making by local government officials. The job is so large that only an effective program of capacity building can hope to be sufficient. All institutions involved in outreach must work together to reduce the gap between the most and the least capable local governments.

NEED FOR UNDERSTANDING THEORETICAL FOUNDATIONS

Next, we must continue to enhance and strengthen the theoretical foundations on which infrastructure investment analysis rests. For example, we must consider incorporating stochastic and dynamic elements into applied analyses of infrastructure investment and in extensions of related theories. These theoretical formulations should address the broader implications of investments in infrastructure such as effects on income distribution, social values (Chapter 6), and technological change. The analyses of the income distribution issue would ultimately depend on where the investments were made, who would benefit from them, and who or how they were financed. Such improvements in the theoretical formulations of infrastructure investment analysis would necessarily lead to needed improvements in our methodologies in order to accommodate such factors into the analysis.

NEED FOR IMPROVED METHODS AND DATA

Several chapters in Parts II and III of this book enumerate strengths and weaknesses of both methodologies and data currently available for infrastructure investment analysis. It would seem, therefore, that our methodological alternatives and abilities are being doubly constrained by our somewhat naive theoretical basis, and our inconsistent and incomplete data (Chapter 10). Thus, improvements in our measurement and data collection procedures must be given a high priority. The data issue, however, is not isolated from other issues. That is, the institutional setting in which these activities are carried out directly affects the outcomes. In particular, land-grant research and extension programs should focus on the ability of local governments to collect reliable, complete, and consistent data. Furthermore, research and extension must communicate their respective needs and those of the clientele in order to improve both specification of methodologies and data needs.

Local infrastructure decision-making may be viewed as a triangular arrangement of three major elements. These include: an understanding of underlying relationships (theoretical foundations); our ability to measure the parameters of these relationships and the current conditions (data); and lastly, our ability to predict the future and evaluate our alternatives (methodologies and models).

Involved in this triadic relationship are a number of other important issues. One of these is the validation of our decision-making models. While it would seem that this relates to only one of the three elements, experience (Keeling, 1986) indicates that validation of projects reflect on theory, data and our models. Among our higher priorities is the need for measures of reliability of, and established confidence interval around, our projections of community impacts. These should incorporate determination of the sources of error, and whether they are theory, data, or model related. This will provide a basis for prioritizing our research efforts.

NEED FOR INSTITUTION BUILDING

Finally, because of the changing scope and economic implications of infrastructure investment decision-making, new relationships between federal, state, and local governments must be identified, analyzed, and, at times, suggested as innovations which can be monitored and evaluated. Although the distribution of responsibilities changes and, from the perspective of the ultimate client, the "faces" change from time to time, the overall role played by government in society does not change dramatically. That is, federal, state, and local governments' roles as suppliers of information, regulators, and decision-making entities prevail through time. Therefore, relationships among these and between them and land-grant research and extension programs must improve and be strengthened over time, even as they change. A high priority must be given then to institution building between land-grant institutions and governmental entities to establish improved communication ties.

NEED FOR UNDERSTANDING THE MACRO ECONOMY

Local communities differ significantly in their ability to interpret and respond to shifts in the economy. Combinations of forces such as the national business cycle, international capital flows, reduced federal presence in local government affairs, deregulated banking, and national monetary and fiscal policies present an almost unfathomable web of economic interrelationships to local citizens and their elected local officials. Yet, the task of responding effectively lies with the local governments.

The extension services associated with the nation's Land Grant Universities can play a vital educational role in this area. Our universities possess the range of professional expertise in economics, finance, political science and sociology and the educational delivery system to address the needs of local governments. Educational programs growing out of research-based knowledge must be developed in a more concerted fashion to equip local leaders and local government staff with the needed conceptual and applied tools. A broader understanding of global affairs and international interdependence must be an integral part of these programs.

Community infrastructure represents a very significant component of national capital formation. Accordingly, the contribution of these investments to both public and private sector productivity must be understood. Conceptually, this will require that more research attention be given to identifying the output of public services. The public good nature of most local public services probably leads to significant underinvestment. This is due in part to the influence of free riders who impede the ability of local governements to generate adequate revenue and, in turn, undertake necessary spending desired by the local public.

Our priorities then are to build capacity among local decision-makers, forge improved relationships and lines of communication between the practitioners, theoreticians, and change agents, and critically assess the decision-making information that we produce. Improvements in the theory, data, and methodologies will grow from this assessment. Simultaneously, a renewed committment by Extension is needed to provide educational programs on the global interrelatedness of the local economy. These priorities, while very simplistic, represent a vast undertaking. It is an undertaking upon which the future of our communities depends.

References

Abt Associates. 1980. *National Rural Community Facilities Assessment Study*. Cambridge, Massachusetts: Abt Associates.

Advisory Commission on Intergovernmental Relations. 1970. *Size Can Make a Difference: A Closer Look*. ACIR Bulletin No. 70-8, p. 2. Washington, D.C.: ACIR.

Advisory Commission on Intergovernmental Relations. 1981. *The States and Distressed Communities: The 1980 Annual Report*. Information Report No. M-125. Washington, D.C.: ACIR.

Advisory Commission on Intergovernmental Relations. 1982. *State and Local Roles in the Federal System*. Report A-88. Washington, D.C.: ACIR.

Advisory Commission on Intergovernmental Relations. 1984a. *Financing Public Physical Infrastructure*. Report A-96. Washington, D.C.: GPO.

Advisory Commission on Intergovernmental Relations. 1984b. *Strengthening the Federal Revenue System: Implications for State and Local Taxing and Borrowing*. Report A-97. Washington, D.C.: ACIR.

Advisory Commission on Intergovernmental Relations. 1985. *The States and Distressed Communities: The Final Report*. Report A-101. Washington, D.C.: ACIR.

American Planning Association. 1980. *Local Capital Improvements and Development Management: Analysis and Case Studies*. Washington: GPO (June).

American Public Works Association. 1981. *Revenue Shortfall: The Public Works Challenge of the 1980s.* Chicago, Ill.: American Public Works Association.

Anderson, James E. 1979. *Public Policy-Making,* 2nd edition. New York: Holt, Rinehart and Winston.

Anonymous. 1985. "CSG Protests Inaccurate Treasury Figures." *State Government News* 28(1): 24.

Associated General Contractors. 1983. *America's Infrastructure: A Plan to Rebuild.* Washington, D.C.: Associated General Contractors.

Banovetz, James M. (editor) 1984. *Small Cities and Counties: A Guide to Managing Services.* Washington, D.C.: International City Management Association.

Barkley, Paul W. "Public Goods in Rural Areas: Problems, Policies and Population." Unpublished manuscript. Washington State University, Pullman, Washington.

Batie, Sandra S. 1978. "Discussion: Location Determinants of Manufacturing Industry in Rural Areas." *Southern Journal of Agricultural Economics* 10: 33-36.

Battelle Columbus Laboratories. 1973. *Final Report of the Arizona Environmental and Economic Trade-Off Model.* Phoenix: Arizona Office of Planning and Development.

Beale, Calvin L. 1981. *Rural and Small Town Population Change.* Economics and Statistics Service, USDA, Report ESS-5 (February).

Beale, Calvin L. 1982. "The Population Turnaround and Small Town America." In *Rural Policy Problems: Changing Dimensions,* ed. William P. Browne and Don F. Hadwiger. Lexington, Mass.: Lexington Books.

Beck, Roger and Frank Goode. 1981. "The Availability of Labor in Rural Areas." in *New Approaches to Economic Development in Rural Areas.* Ithaca: Northeast Center for Rural Development Publication 30.

Bigler, C., R. Reeve, and R. Weaver. 1972. *Report on the Development of the Utah Process: A Procedure for Planning Coordination Through Forecasting and Evaluating Alternative State Futures.* Salt Lake City: Utah State Planning Coordinator.

Bluestone, Barry and Bennet Harrison. 1982. *The Deindustrialization of America*. New York: Basic Books.

Boadway, Robin W. 1979. *Public Sector Economics*. Cambridge, Mass.: Winthrop Publishers.

Boadway, Robin W. and David E. Wildasin. 1984. *Public Sector Economics*. Boston: Little, Brown and Company.

Bohm, R.A. and J.H. Lord. 1972. "Regional Economic Simulation Modeling--The TVA Experience." Paper presented at the Annual Meeting of the Northeast Regional Science Association, April 14-15, at University Park, Penn.

Bonnen, James T. 1975. "Improving Information on Agriculture and Rural Life." *American Journal of Agricultural Economics*. 57: 753-63.

Bontrager, Sharon, Gerald A. Doeksen, Shari R. Gilbert, and Masoud Morshedi. 1984. *Users Guide to a Computer Program to Analyze Costs and Returns for Rural Fire Protection*. Computer Software Series CSS-3. Stillwater: Oklahoma State University, Agricultural Experiment Station.

Bowles, Samuel and Herbert Gintis. 1984. *The Mosaic of Domination and The Future of Democracy*. Draft. Amherst, Mass.

Braschler, Curtis. 1984. "Discussion: Agricultural Economists in Rural Development: Responsibilities, Opportunities, Risks, and Payoffs." *Southern Journal of Agricultural Economics* 16(1): 49-51.

Brown, Anthony. 1980. "Technical Assistance to Rural Communities: Stopgap or Capacity Building?" *Public Administration Review* 40 (January/February): 18-33.

Browne, William P. and Don F. Hadwiger, eds. 1981. *Rural Policy Problems: Changing Dimensions*. Lexington, Mass.: Lexington Books.

Bryce, Herrington J. 1979. *Planning Smaller Cities*. Lexington, Mass.: Lexington Books.

Buchanan, James M. 1965. "An Economic Theory of Clubs." *Economics* 32: 1-14.

Buck, A., Daryl J. Hobbs, and D. Meyer. 1984. *Feasibility of High Tech Companies Incubation in Rural University Settings*. SBIR Report. Rolla, Missouri: INCUTECH.

268   References

Bullock, Charles S. and Charles M. Lamb. 1984. *Implementation of Civil Rights Policy.* Monterey, California: Brooks/Cole Publishing Company.

Burchell, R.W. and D. Listokin. 1978. *The Fiscal Impact Handbook.* Brunswick, N.J.: Rutgers Center for Urban Policy Research.

Business Week. 1981. "State and Local Government in Trouble." 26 October 1981, pp. 135-181.

Castle, Emery N., H. Becker Manning, and Frederick J. Smith. 1972. *Farm Business Management.* The MacMillian Company.

Chase, Robert A. and F. Larry Leistritz. 1983. *Profile of North Dakota's Petroleum Work Force, 1981-82.* Ag. Econ. Rpt. No. 174. Fargo: North Dakota Agr. Exp. Sta.

Chicoine, David L. and Norman Walzer. 1984. *Financing Rural Roads and Bridges in the Midwest.* Washington, D.C.: Office of Transportation and Agricultural Marketing Services, USDA.

Choate, Pat. 1980. *As Time Goes By: The Costs and Consequences of Delay.* Columbus, Ohio: The Academy for Contemporary Problems.

Choate, Pat and Susan Walter. 1981. *America in Ruins: Beyond the Public Works Pork Barrel.* Washington, D.C.: The Council of State Planning Agencies.

Christopherson, Gary A. 1983. "Shoring Up Urban America's Health Care Infrastructures: Strategies for Local Governments." *Municipal Management* 1(2): 33-39.

Cigler, Beverly A. 1984. "Small City and Rural Governance: The Changing Environment." *Public Administration Review* 44 (November/December): 540-545.

Cigler, Beverly A. 1985a. "Fiscal Stress: Searching for Causes and Solutions." *Urban Affairs Quarterly* 30(3) (March): 409-415.

Cigler, Beverly A. 1985b. "Infrastructure Decision Making: A Political Scientist's View." Post-conference paper prepared for the National Symposium on Local Infrastructure Investment Decisions, U.S. Department of Agriculture and Department of Agricultural Economics, Virginia Tech, Arlington, Virginia, April 17-19, 1985.

Cigler, Beverly A. 1986a. "Capacity-Building Policy for Local Energy Management." In *Perspectives on Management Capacity-Building:*

Challenge for the Eighties, ed. Beth Walter Honadle and Arnold M. Howitt. Albany: SUNY Press.

Cigler, Beverly A. 1986b. "Small Cities' Policy Responses to the New Federalism." In *Administrating the New Federalism,* ed. Lewis Bender and James A. Stever, pp. 160-181. Boulder, Colo.: Westview Press.

Cigler, Beverly A. 1987. "Rural Infrastructure: Research Needs." *The Rural Sociologist.* 7(7) (January).

Clark, G. and J.W. Wright. 1964. "Scheduling of Vehicles from a Central Depot to a Number of Delivery Points." *Operations Research* 12(4): 568-581.

Clayton, Kenneth C. and David Whittington. 1977. *The Economics of Community Growth: An Impact Model.* Food and Res. Econ. Dept. Staff Paper 40. Gainesville: University of Florida.

Cobb, Roger W. and Charles D. Elder. 1983. *Participants in American Politics: The Dynamics of Agenda-Building.* 2nd ed. Baltimore: The Johns Hopkins University Press.

Colman, William G. 1983. *A Quiet Revolution in Local Government Finance.* Washington, D.C.: Panel on Intergovernmental Systems of the National Academy of Public Administration.

Committee on Agriculture, Nutrition, and Forestry, United States Senate. 1977. *National Conference on Nonmetropolitan Community Services Research,* pp. 27-28. Washington, D.C.: GPO.

Congressional Budget Office. 1983. *Public Works Infrastructure: Policy Considerations for the 1980s.* Washington, D.C.: GPO.

Congressional Budget Office. 1985a. *Efficient Investments in Wastewater Treatment Plants.* Washington, D.C.: GPO (June).

Congressional Budget Office. 1985b. *The Federal Budget for Public Works Infrastructure.* Washington, D.C.: GPO (July).

Congressional Budget Office. 1986. *Federal Policies for Infrastructure Management.* Washington, D.C.: GPO (June).

CONSAD. 1980. *A Study of Public Works Investment in the United States.* Washington, D.C.: U.S. Department of Commerce.

Conway, H. McKinley. 1980. *Marketing Industrial Buildings and Sites.* Atlanta: Conway Publications.

Cooksey, Betsey A. 1979. "Public vs. Private Development of Industrial Parks in Rural Areas of the Eastern United States". *The American Industrial Development Council Journal* 15: 81-99.

Coon, R. C., F. Larry Leistritz, and T. A. Hertsgaard. 1986. *Composition of North Dakota's Economic Base: A Regional Analysis.* Ag. Econ. Rpt. No. 209. Fargo: North Dakota Agr. Exp. Sta.

Copeland, T.E. and J.F. Weston. 1983. *Financial Theory and Corporate Policy.* Reading, Mass.: Addison-Wesly.

Council on Environmental Quality. 1978. "National Environmental Policy Act." *Federal Register* 43 (June 9): 112.

Cummings, R.A. and W.D. Schulze. 1978. "Optimal Investment Strategies for Boomtowns: A Theoretical Analysis." *American Economic Review* 68(3): 374-385.

Danzinger, James N. and Peter Smith Ring. 1982. "Fiscal Limitations: A Selective Review of Recent Research." *Public Administration Review* 42 (January/February): 47-56.

Darling, David L. 1979. *An Industrial Impact Model for Indiana Communities.* Ag. Exp. Sta. Bull. No. 229. W. Lafayette, Ind.: Purdue University.

Dawkins, Peter M. 1984. "Rebuilding America. How Do We Pay the Bill?" *Economic Development Commentary* 8(3): 3-6. National Council for Urban Economic Development.

Debertin, David L., Angelos Pagoulatos and Eldon D. Smith. 1980. "Estimating Linear Probability Functions: A Comparison of Approaches." *Southern Journal of Agricultural Economics.* 11: 65-9.

Denver Research Institute. 1979. *Socioeconomic Impact of Western Energy Resource Development.* Washington, D.C.: Council on Environmental Quality.

Devoy, Robert and Harold Wise. 1979. *The Capital Budget.* Washington, D.C. Council of State Planning Agencies.

Digler, Robert J. 1985. *The Deductibility of State and Local Taxes: Implication of Proposed Policy Changes.* Washington, D.C.: National League of Cities.

Dillman, Don A. and Daryl J. Hobbs, eds. 1982. *Rural Society in the U.S.: Issues for the 1980s.* Boulder, Colo.: Westview Press.

Doeksen, Gerald A., Leonard G. Anderson, Jr., and Vanessa Lenard. 1981c. *A Community Development Guide to Emergency Medical Services: A System Approach to Planning, Funding and Administration.* Agricultural Experiment Station Bulletin, Oklahoma State University.

Doeksen, Gerald A., J. Kuehn, and Joseph F. Schmidt. 1974. "Consequences of Decline and Community Economic Adjustment to It." In *Communities Left Behind: Alternatives for Development*, ed. L.R. Whiting, pp. 28-42. North Central Regional Center for Rural Development. Ames: Iowa State University Press.

Doeksen, Gerald A., Harold Mace, and Marlyr Nelson, 1981. *Planning a Rural Fire Truck.* Oklahoma State University Extension Fact No. 841, Cooperative Extension Service, Oklahoma State University, Stillwater.

Doeksen, Gerald A., James R. Nelson, and M.G. Kletke. 1981. *User's Guide to Computer Program to Analyze Costs and Returns for a Rural Clinic.* Ag. Exp. Sta. Res. Rpt. No. P-810. Stillwater: Oklahoma State University.

Dossani, Nazir and Wilbur Steger. 1980. "Trends in U.S. Public Works Investment: Report on a New Study." *National Tax Journal* 33(2): 97-110.

Erwin, Richard. 1977. *Guide for Local Area Population Projections.* U.S. Bureau of the Census. Washington, D.C.: GPO.

Eyestone, Robert. 1978. *From Social Issues to Social Policy.* New York: John Wiley.

Fisher, Phillip J., Ronald W. Forbes, and John E. Petersen. 1980. "Risk and Return in the Choice of Revenue Bond Financing." *Governmental Finance* 9(3): 9-13.

Florestano, Patricia S. 1981. "Revenue-Raising Limitations on Local Government: A Focus on Alternative Responses." *Public Administration Review* 41 (Special Issue, January): 122-131.

Florestano, Patricia S. and Stephen B. Gordon. 1980. "Public vs. Private: Small Government Contracting with the Private Sector." *Public Administration Review* 40 (January/February): 29-34.

Forbes, Ronald W. and John E. Petersen. 1983. "State Credit Assistance to Local Governments." In *Creative Capital Financing for State and Local Governments*, ed. John E. Petersen and Wesley C. Hough, pp. 225-235. Chicago: Municipal Finance Officers Association.

Ford, Andrew. 1976. *User's Guide to BOOM 1 Model.* LA-6396-MS. Los Alamos, N.M.: Los Alamos Scientific Laboratory.

Forrester, Jay W. 1969. *Urban Dynamics.* Cambridge, Mass.: M.I.T. Press.

Fort, John. 1985. "Use of the Ability to Pay Evaluation in the Grant Review and Award Process." Report to S.C. Office of the Governor.

Foster, Richard. 1982. "Infrastructure: Picking Up the Pieces." *State Legislatures* 8 (10): 14-15.

Fox, William F. 1981. "Can There Be Size Economies in Providing Government Services?" *Rural Development Perspectives*, 4. Washington, D.C.: ERS, USDA.

Francis, Joe D., Bruce L. Brower, Wendy F. Graham, Oscar W. Larson III, Julian L. McCaull, and Helene Moran Vigorita. 1982. *National Statistical Assessment of Rural Water Conditions*, Executive Summary, Department of Rural Sociology, Cornell University, prepared for the U.S. Environmental Protection Agency.

Friedland, William H. 1982. "The End of Rural Society and the Future of Rural Sociology." *Rural Sociology* 47(4): 589-608.

Friedman, Lee S. 1984. *Microeconomic Policy Analysis.* New York: McGraw-Hill.

Gebre-Selassie Haile-Mariam. 1983. "Economic Analysis of Current and Future Needs for Emergency Medical Service Systems." Unpublished Ph.D. Dissertation. Stillwater: Oklahoma State University.

Ghez, G.R. and G.S. Becker. 1975. *The Allocation of Time and Goods Over the Life Cycle.* New York: Columbia University Press.

Gilmore, John S. and M. K. Duff. 1975. *Boom Town Growth Management: A Case Study of Rock Springs--Green River, Wyoming.* Boulder, Colo.: Westview Press.

Gilmore, John S., D. M. Hammond, Keith D. Moore, J. Johnson, and D. C. Coddington. 1982. *Socioeconomic Impacts of Power Plants.* Palo Alto, California: Electric Power Research Institutes.

Gitajn, Arthur. 1985. *Creating and Financing Public Enterprises.* Chicago, Ill.: Government Finance Officers Association.

Gold, Steven D. 1982. *How State Governments Can Assist Local Governments to Raise More Revenue.* Legislative Finance Paper No. 25. Denver: National Conference of State Legislatures.

Golonka, Susan. 1985. "Whatever Happened to Federalism?" *Intergovernmental Perspective* 11(1): 8-18.

Goodwin, H.L., Gerald A. Doeksen, and James R. Nelson. 1979. *Economics of Water Delivery Systems in Rural Oklahoma.* Ag. Exp. Sta. Bull. No. B-745. Stillwater: Oklahoma State University.

Goodwin, H.L. and James R. Nelson. 1981. *Analyzing Economic Feasibilities of Rural Solid Waste Management Systems.* Ag. Exp. Sta. Bull. No. B-758. Stillwater: Oklahoma State University.

Government Finance Officers Association. 1984. *Building Prosperity: Financing Public Infrastructure for Economic Development.* Chicago: Government Finance Officers Association.

Government Finance Research Center. 1983. *Building Prosperity: Financing Public Infrastructure for Economic Development.* Washington, D.C.: Government Finance Research Center, Municipal Finance Officers Association.

Green, Roy E. and B. J. Reed. 1981. "Small Cities Need Grants Management Capacity." *Rural Development Perspectives* 4: 28-30.

Haley, John F. 1979. *A Study of State-Imposed Municipal Bond Validation Requirements.* Washington, D.C.: Government Finance Research Center, Municipal Finance Officers Association.

Hallberg, Milton C. and W.R. Kriebel. 1972. *Designing Efficient Pickup and Delivery Route Systems by Computer.* Ag. Exp. Sta. Bull. No. 782. University Park: Pennsylvania State University.

Halstead, John M., Robert A. Chase, Steve H. Murdock, and F. Larry Leistritz. 1984. *Socioeconomic Impact Management: Design and Implementation.* Boulder, Colo.: Westview Press.

Halstead, John M. and F. Larry Leistritz. 1983. *Impacts of Energy Development on Mercer County, North Dakota.* Ag. Econ. Rpt. No. 170. Fargo: North Dakota State University.

Hamilton, H.R., S.E. Goldstone, J.W. Milliman, A.L. Pugh, E.B. Roberts, and A. Zellner. 1969. *Systems Simulation for Regional Analysis: An Application to River-Basin Planning.* Cambridge, Mass.: M.I.T. Press.

Harl, Neil. 1985. "The Changing Rural Economy: Implications for Rural America." Paper presented at the National Rural Education Forum, Kansas City, Missouri.

Heady, Earl O. and Wildred Candler. 1958. *Linear Programming Methods.* Ames, Iowa: The Iowa State University Press.

Henry, Mark. 1980. "On the Value of Economic-Demographic Forecasts to Local Governments." *Annals of Regional Science* 14(1): 12-20.

Henry, Mark, J. C. Hite, B. Dillman, and E. McLean. 1981. "South Carolina Impact Model-User's Guide." Unpublished manuscript. Department of Agricultural Economics, Clemson University, Clemson, South Carolina.

Hertsgaard, T. A., Steve H. Murdock, Norman Toman, Mark Henry, and R. Ludtke. 1978. *REAP Economic-Demographic Model: Technical Description.* Bismarck: North Dakota Regional Environmental Assessment Program.

Hill, Kenneth D. and Gerald A. Doeksen. 1981a. *User's Guide to Computer Program for Analysis of Costs and Returns for Transportation Systems for the Elderly.* Ag. Exp. Sta. Res. Rpt. No. P-808. Stillwater: Oklahoma State University.

Hill, Kenneth D. and Gerald A. Doeksen. 1981b. *User's Guide to the Computer Program to Analyze Costs and Returns for Emergency Medical Service Systems.* Ag. Exp. Sta. Res. Rpt. No. P-809. Stillwater: Oklahoma State University.

Hill, Melvin B. 1978. *State Laws Governing Local Government Structure and Administration.* Athens, GA: Institute of Government, University of Georgia.

Hirsch, Werner Z. 1968. "The Supply of Urban Public Services." In *Issues in Urban Economics*, ed. Harvey S. Perloff and Lowdon Wingo, Jr. Baltimore: John Hopkins University Press.

Hirsch, Werner Z. 1973. *Urban Economic Analysis*. New York: McGraw-Hill Book Co.

Hite, James C., Mark Henry, and B. Dillman. 1983. "Infrastructure Needs and Resources of Selected State and Local Government Programs in South Carolina." Unpublished manuscript. Department of Agricultural Economics, Clemson University, Clemson, South Carolina.

Hobbs, Daryl J. 1985. "Bridging, Linking, Networking the Gap: Uses of Instructional Technology in Rural Schools." Paper presented at the National Rural Education Forum, Kansas City, Missouri.

Hogan, James. Various times, 1984-85. Government Branch, Bureau of the Census, Personal Communication.

Holland, Stuart. 1972. *The State as Entrepreneur*. London: Weidenfeld & Nicholson.

Honadle, Beth Walter. 1981. "A Capacity-Building Framework: A Search for Concept and Purpose." *Public Administration Review* 41 (September/October): 575-580.

Honadle, Beth Walter. 1982. "Managing Capacity-Building: Problems and Approaches." *Journal of the Community Development Society* 13(2): 65-73.

Honadle, Beth Walter. 1983. *Public Administration in Rural and Small Jurisdictions*. New York: Garland Publishers, Inc.

Hough, Wesley C. and John E. Petersen. 1983. *State Constraints on Local Government Capital Financing*. Legislative Finance Paper No. 36. Denver: National Conference of State Legislatures.

Hough, Wesley C., Catherine L. Spain, and Barbara Weiss. 1985. "Impact of the 1984 Tax Act on Governmental Financing Options." In *Public/Private Partnerships: Financing a Common Wealth*, ed. Barbara Weiss, pp. 111-117. Washington, D.C.: Government Finance Research Center, Government Finance Officers Association.

Howitt, Arnold M. 1978. "Improving Public Administration in Small Communities." *Southern Review of Public Administration* 34 (December): 325-331.

Hushak, Leroy J. 1983. "Advantages and Limitations of Using Traditional Methods to Provide Local Public Services in a New Federalism Era." *American Journal of Agricultural Economics* 65(5): 1118-1123.

Hustedde, R., Ron E. Shaffer, and Glen C. Pulver. 1984. *Community Economic Analysis: A How to Manual.* North Central Regional Center for Rural Development.

Huston, Michael. 1979. "The United States Steel Project--A Comprehensive Approach to Socioeconomic Analysis." In *Boom Towns: Managing Growth*, Proceedings of Mini Symposium, SME-AIME Annual Meeting, New Orleans, Louisiana.

Inman, R.P. 1979. "The Fiscal Performance of Local Governments: An Interpretative Review." In *Current Issues in Urban Economics*, ed. Peter Mieskowski and Mahlon Strazheim, pp. 270-319. Baltimore: Johns Hopkins University Press.

International City Management Association. 1981. *Management Policies in Local Government Finance.* Washington, D.C.: International City Management Association.

International City Management Association. 1984. *Rethinking Local Services: Examining Alternative Delivery Approaches.* Washington, D.C.: International City Management Association.

Iowa State University. 1984. *Financial Trend Monitoring Data Manual.* CRD 193. Ames, Iowa: Cooperative Extension Service.

Irwin, Richard. 1977. *Guide for Local Area Population Projections.* U.S. Bureau of Census. Washington, D.C.: GPO.

Jequier, Nicolas. 1984. "Appropriate Technology for Rural Government." Local Leadership and Rural Development: Implications for Research and Extension. Organization for Economic Cooperation and Development.

Johnson, Thomas G. 1977. "The Theoretical Basis of Benefit-Cost Analysis." Unpublished manuscript. Department of Agricultural Economics, Virginia Polytechnic Institute and State University, Blacksburg, Virginia.

Joint Economic Committee, U.S. Congress. 1984a. *Infrastructure: A National Challenge.* Hearing before the Subcommittee on Economic

Goals and Intergovernmental Policy. Washington, D.C.: GPO (February 19).

Joint Economic Committee, U.S. Congress. 1984b. *Our Nation's Infrastructure.* Hearing before the Joint Economic Committee. Washington, D.C.: GPO (August 9, 31 and September 7, 1983).

Joint Economic Committee, U.S. Congress. 1984c. *Hard Choices: A Summary Report of the National Infrastructure Study.* Washington, D.C.: GPO (April).

Jones, Charles O. (editor) 1977. *An Introduction to the Study of Public Policy,* 2nd edition. North Scituate, Massachusetts: Duxbury Press.

Jump, Bernard, Jr. 1982. "Meeting State and Local Financing Needs in the 1980s: Can the Municipal Debt Market Do Its Share?" *Journal of Public Budgeting and Finance* (Winter): 58-72.

Kamensky, John M. 1984. "Budgeting for State and Local Infrastructure: Developing a Strategy." *Journal of Public Budgeting and Finance* (Autumn): 3-17.

Kaye, Ira. 1982. Chapter 15: "Transportation". In *Rural Society in the USA: Issues for the 1980s,* ed. D. A. Dillman and D. J. Hobbs. Boulder, Colo.: Westview Press.

Kelch, David. 1977. "Industrial Location in the Nonmetropolitan Communities of Kentucky and Tennessee." Ph.D. Dissertation, University of Kentucky.

Keller, A. and J. Luptak. 1983. *North Dakota Energy Development Impact Office, 1981-83 Biennium Legislative Report.* Bismarck, North Dakota: North Dakota Energy Impact Office.

Kendrick, J.W. 1976. *The Formation and Stocks of Total Capital.* New York: Columbia University Press.

Kirlin, John J. and Anne M. Kirlin. 1985. "How Developers and Jurisdictions Approach Bargaining." In *Public/Private Partnerships: Financing a Common Wealth,* ed. B. Weiss, pp. 36-45. Washington, D.C.: Government Finance Research Center, Government Finance Officers Association.

Krutilla, John V. 1964. "Welfare Aspects of Benefit-Cost Analysis." In *Economics and Public Policy in Water Resource Development,* ed. Stephen

C. Smith and Emery N. Castle, pp. 22-31. Ames: Iowa State University Press.

Kuehn, John A., Curtis Braschler, and J. Scott Chonkwiler. 1979. "Rural Industrialization and Community Action: New Plant Locations Among Missouri's Small Towns." *Journal of the Community Development Society* 10: 95-107.

Ladd, Helen F. 1978. "An Economic Evaluation of State Limitations of Local Taxing and Spending Powers." *National Tax Journal* 31: 1-18.

Lamb, Robert and Stephen P. Rappaport. 1980. *Municipal Bonds: The Comprehensive Review of Tax-Exempt Securities and Public Finance.* New York: McGraw-Hill Book Co.

Leistritz, F. L. and K. C. Maki. 1981. *Socioeconomic Effects of Large-Scale Resource Development Projects in Rural Area: The Case of North McLean County, North Dakota.* Ag. Econ. Rpt. No. 151. Fargo: North Dakota Agricultural Experiment Station.

Leistritz, F. Larry and Steve H. Murdock. 1981. *The Socioeconomic Impact of Resource Development: Methods for Assessment.* Boulder, Colo.: Westview Press.

Leistritz, F. L., Steve H. Murdock, N. E. Toman, and T. A. Hertsgaard. 1979. "A Model for Projecting Localized Economic, Demographic, and Fiscal Impacts of Large-Scale Projects." *Western Journal of Agricultural Economics* 4(2): 1-16.

Lenard, Vanessa, Gerald A. Doeksen, and Robert L. Oehrtman. 1983. *An Economic Analysis of EMS Services in Noble County, Oklahoma, 1984.* Dept. of Ag. Econ. Paper No. 83110. Stillwater: Oklahoma State University.

Lenard, Vanessa, Gerald A. Doeksen, and Robert Oehrtman. 1984. *An Analysis of School Bus Routes for the Beaver Oklahoma School System for the 1984-1985 School Year.* Dept. of Ag. Econ. Paper AE-8483. Stillwater: Oklahoma State University.

Lloyd, Robert C. and Kenneth P. Wilkinson. 1985. Community Factors in Rural Manufacturing Development. *Rural Sociology.* 50(1): 27-37.

Lindbloom, C. 1979. "Still Muddling, Not Yet Through." *Public Administration Review* 39(6): 517-526.

Lintner, J. 1965. "The Valuation of Risk Assets and the Selection of Risky Investments in Stock Portfolios and Capital Budgets." *Review of Economics and Statistics* 47(1): 13-37.

MacManus, Susan A. 1981. "The Impact of Functional Responsibility and State Legal Constraints on the 'Revenue-Debt' Packages of U.S. Central Cities." *International Journal of Public Administration* 3(1): 67-111.

Markle, William D., James deBettencourt and Associates. 1982. *The Infrastructure Problem.* Chicago, Illinois: William D. Markle and Associates.

Marlin, John Tepper (editor). 1984. *Contracting Municipal Services: Guide for Purchasing from the Private Sector.* New York: John Wiley & Sons, Inc. and Council on Municipal Performance.

Martin, Kenneth and Kenneth P. Wilkinson. 1984. "Local Participation in the Federal Grant System: Effects of Community Action." *Rural Sociology* 49(3): 374-388.

McDowell, George R. 1978. "An Analytical Framework for Extension Community Development Programming in Local Government." *American Journal of Agricultural Economics* 60(3): 416-424.

McGranahan, David. 1984. "Local Growth and the Outside Contacts of Influentials." *Rural Sociology* 49(4): 530-540.

McNamara, Kevin T., Warren Kriesel, and Brady Deaton. 1984. "Education as an Investment in Human Capital and Manufacturing Employment Growth." Paper selected for presentation at the Southern Agricultural Economics Association Meetings.

Menchik, Mark D. 1985. "Support for Infrastructure." *Intergovernmental Perspectives* 11(1): 21.

Miller, Michael K., Donald E. Voth, and Diana D. Chapman. 1984. "Estimating the Effects of Community Resource Development Efforts on County Quality of Life." *Rural Sociology* 49(1): 37-66.

Molnar, Joseph J. and John P. Smith. 1982. "Satisfaction with Rural Services: The Policy Preferences of Leaders and Community Residents." *Rural Sociology* 47(3): 496-511.

Moody's Investors Service. 1986a. *Moody's Municipal and Government Manual, 1986.* New York: Moody's Investors Service, Inc.

Moody's Investors Service. 1986b. *Moody's Bond Record.* New York: Moody's Investors Service, Inc.

Morse, George W. and John D. Gerard. 1980. *User's Manual for the Rural Ohio Economic Growth Impact Model.* ESO No. 739. Columbus: Ohio State University.

Mossin, J. 1966. "Equilibrium in a Capital Asset Market." *Econometrica* 34(4): 768-783.

Mountain West Research. 1978. *Bureau of Reclamation Economic Assessment Model (BREAM) Technical Description.* Denver: U.S. Bureau of Reclamation.

Muller, Thomas. 1975. *Fiscal Impacts of Land Development: A Critique of Methods and Review of Issues.* URI 98000. Washington, D.C.: The Urban Institute.

Muller, Thomas and Michael Fix. 1979. *The Impact of Selected Federal Actions on Municipal Outlays.* Report of the Joint Economic Committee, U.S. Congress. Washington, D.C.: GPO.

Murdock, Steve H. and F. Larry Leistritz. 1979. *Energy Development in the Western United States.* New York: Praeger Publishers.

Murdock, Steve H. and F. Larry Leistritz. 1980. "Selecting Socioeconomic Assessment Models: A Discussion of Criteria and Selected Models." *Journal of Environmental Management* 10: 241-252.

Murdock, Steve H., F. Larry Leistritz, Rita R. Hamm, Sean-Shong Hwang, and Banoo Parpai. 1984. "An Assessment of the Accuracy of a Regional Economic-Demographic Projection Model," *Demography* 21(3): 383-404.

Murdock, Steve H., F. Larry Leistritz, Lonnie L. Jones, D. Andrews, B. Wilson, D. Fannin, and J. de Montel. 1979. *The Texas Assessment Modeling System: Technical Description.* Technical Rpt. No. 79-3. College Station: Texas Ag. Exp. Sta.

Murdock, Steve H., R.L. Skrabanek, Sean-Shong Hwang, and Rita R. Hamm. 1981. *City and Small Town Population Growth in Texas in the 1970s.* College Station, TX: Texas A & M. University, Dept. of Rural Soc.

Murray, J.A. and B.A. Weber. 1982. "The Impacts of Rapid Growth on the Provision and Financing of Local Public Services." In *Coping with Rapid Growth in Rural Communities*, ed. B. Weber and R. Howell. Boulder, Colo.: Westview Press.

Nath, S.K. 1957. *A Reappraisal of Welfare Economics.* New York: Oxford University Press.

National Association of Towns and Townships. 1985. *Voluntarism and the Measurement of Fiscal Capacity.* Washington, D.C.: National Association of Towns and Townships.

National League of Cities and U.S. Conference of Mayors. 1983. *Capital Budgeting and Infrastructure in American Cities: An Initial Assessment.* Washington, D.C.: National League of Cities.

Nelson, James R. and Gerald A. Doeksen. 1982. *Analyzing the Economic Feasibilities of Rental Apartment Projects in Rural Oklahoma.* Ext. Fact Sheet No. 848. Stillwater: Oklahoma State University.

Nelson, James R. and Gerald A. Doeksen. 1984. "Agricultural Economists in Rural Development: Responsibilities, Opportunities, Risks, and Payoffs." *Southern Journal of Agricultural Economics* 16(1): 41-47.

Nelson, James R. and S.R. Gilbert. 1983. *User's Guide to a Computer Program to Analyze Economic Feasibilities for Rural Mobile Home Park Developments.* Ag. Exp. Sta. Res. Rpt. No. P-841. Stillwater: Oklahoma State University.

Nelson, James R., Ed Henderson, and H. L. Goodwin. 1980. *Economic Analysis of Proposed Improvements for Ottawa County Rural Water District 2.* Dept. of Ag. Econ. Paper No. 80102. Stillwater: Oklahoma State University.

Nelson, James R. and Bud Johnson. 1982. *Analyzing the Economic Feasibilities of Mobile Home Park Developments in Rural Oklahoma,* Ext. Fact Sheet No. 846. Stillwater: Oklahoma State University.

Nelson, James R. and Mohammad T. Mostafavi. 1981. *User's Guide to a Computer Program to Analyze Costs for a Rural Water System.* Ag. Exp. Sta. Res. Rpt. No. P807, Stillwater: Oklahoma State University.

Nelson, James R. and Mohammed T. Mostafavi. 1981. *User's Guide to a Computer Program for Estimating Revenues from Alternative Rural*

Water Rate Structures. Ag. Exp. Sta. Res. Rpt. No. P-830. Stillwater: Oklahoma State University.

Nelson, James R. and Mohammed T. Mostafavi. 1982. *User's Guide to a Computer Program to Analyze Economic Feasibilities of Rural Community Rental Apartment Projects.* Ag. Exp. Sta. Res. Rpt. No. P-832. Stillwater: Oklahoma State University.

Nelson, James R. and Mohammad T. Mostafavi. 1983. *User's Guide to a Computer Program to Analyze Economic Feasibilities of Rural Community Rental Apartment Projects.* Ag. Exp. Sta. Res. Rpt. No. P-841. Stillwater: Oklahoma State University.

Nelson, Marlys K. and Gerald A. Doeksen. 1982. *Fire Protection Services Feasibility Guide for Local Decision-makers in the Rural Ozarks.* Ag. Exp. Sta. Bull. No. B-764, Sillwater: Oklahoma State University.

Nelson, Marlys K. and Michael Fessehaye. 1981. *Central Wastewater Collection and Feasibility Guide for Local Decision-makers in the Rural Ozarks.* AIB-445, Economics Statistics Service. Washington, D.C.: USDA.

Nelson, Marlys K. and Michael Fessehaye. 1982. *User's Guide to a Computer Program to Analyze Costs for a Rural Community's Central Sewer System and Treatment Facility.* Ag. Exp. Sta. Res. Rpt. No. P-827, Stillwater: Oklahoma State University.

Newland, Chester A. 1981. "Local Government Capacity Building." *Urban Affairs Papers* 3: iv-v.

Newsweek. "The Decaying of America." *Newsweek* (August 2, 1982): 12-18.

Odell, Rice. 1982. "Can We Afford to Maintain Our Urban Infrastructure?" *Urban Land* 41(1): 5-9.

Oehrtman, Robert L. and Gerald Doeksen. 1981. "An Adaptation of a Computerized Transportation Location Model to Problems of Rural Development." Mimeograph. Department of Agricultural Economics, Oklahoma State University, Stillwater, Oklahoma.

Olsen, John B. and Douglas C. Eadie. 1982. *The Game Plan: Governance With Foresight.* Washington, D.C.: The Council of State Planning Agencies.

Olsen, R.J., G.W. Westly, H.W. Herzog, Jr., C.R. Kerley, D.J. Bjornstad, D.P. Veyt, L.G. Bray, S.T. Grady, and R.A. Nakosteen. 1977. *MULTIREGION: A Simulation--Forecasting Model of BEA Economic Area Population and Employment.* ORNL/RUS-25. Oak Ridge, Tennessee: Oak Ridge National Laboratory.

Ostrom, Vincent. 1969. "Operational Federalism: Organization for the Provision of Public Services in the American Federal System." *Public Choice* 6: 1-17.

Otto, Daniel M. 1984. *Iowa Economic Growth Model: Assessing Economic Change in Rural Iowa.* Ames: Iowa State University, Cooperative Extension Service.

Petersen, John E. 1977. "Simplification and Standardization of State and Local Government Fiscal Indicators." *National Tax Journal* 30(3): 299-311.

Petersen, John E., Lisa A. Cole, and Maria L. Petrillo. 1977. *Watching and Counting: A Survey of State Assistance to and Supervision of Local Debt and Financial Administration.* Chicago: Municipal Finance Officers Association and the National Conference of State Legislatures.

Petersen, John E. and Wesley C. Hough. 1983. *Creative Capital Financing for State and Local Governments.* Chicago: Municipal Finance Officers Association.

Peterson, George E., Nancy Humphrey, Mary John Miller, and Peter Wilson. 1983. *The Future of America's Capital Plant.* Washington, D.C.: The Urban Institute.

Peterson, George E. and Mary John Miller. 1981. *Financing Infrastructure Renewal.* Washington, D.C.: Urban Consortium.

Peterson, George E. and Mary John Miller. 1982. *Financing Urban Infrastructure: Policy Options.* Washington, D.C.: The Urban Institute.

Pfister, R. 1976. "On Improving Export Base Studies." *Regional Science Perspectives* 6: 104-116.

Pindyck, Robert S. and Daniel L. Rubinfeld. 1981. *Econometric Models and Economic Forecasts.* New York: McGraw-Hill Book Co.

Porter, Douglas R. and Richard B. Peiser. 1984. *Financing Infrastructure to Support Community Growth.* Washington, D.C.: Urban Land Institute.

Premus, Robert. 1982. *Location of High Technology Firms and Regional Economic Development.* Joint Economic Committee, Congress of the United States. Washington, D.C.: GPO.

Quinn, Kevin and Myron Olstein. 1985. "Privatization: Public/Private Partnerships Provide Essential Services." In *Public/Private Partnerships: Financing a Common Wealth,* ed. Barbara Weiss, pp. 66-82. Washington, D.C.: Government Finance Research Center, Government Finance Officers Association.

Randall, Alan. 1981. *Resource Economics.* Columbus: Grid Publishing.

Reeder, Richard J. 1984. *Nonmetropolitan Fiscal Indicators: A Review of the Literature.* Washington, D.C.: ERS, USDA.

Reeder, Richard J. 1985. *Rural Governments: Raising Revenues and Feeling the Pressure.* Rural Development Res. Rpt. No. 51. Washington, D.C.: ERS, USDA.

Reeder, Richard J. 1986. "Fiscal Decentralization: Impacts on Rural Governments." Unpublished paper presented at the National Conference of the American Society for Public Administration, Anaheim, California.

Reid, J. Norman. 1982. "Distinguishing Among Rural Communities: The Differences Really Matter." *Municipal Management: A Journal* 5(2): 83-89.

Reid, J. Norman, Thomas F. Stinson, Patrick J. Sullivan, Leon B. Perkinson, MonaCheri P. Clarke, and Eleanor Whitehead. 1984. *Availability of Selected Public Facilities in Rural Areas.* ERS, USDA. Washington, D.C.: GPO.

Reid, J. Norman and Patrick J. Sullivan. 1984. "Rural Infrastructure: How Much? How Good?." *Rural Development Perspectives* 1(1): 9-14. ERS, USDA.

Reid, J. Norman and Eleanor Whitehead. 1982. *Federal Funds in 1980: Geographic Distribution and Recent Trends.* ERS Staff Report No. AGES820927. Washington, D.C.: ERS, USDA.

Richardson, Harry W. 1973. *The Economics of Urban Size,* Lexington Mass.: Lexington Books.

Rogers, David L., Brian F. Pendleton, and Willis J. Goudy. 1981. "Classifying Community Services: A Comparison of Intuitive and

Empirical Techniques." *Journal of the Community Development Society* 12: 49-62.

Rosenberg, Philip and Sally Rood. 1985. "The Realities of Our Infrastructure Problem." *Municipal Management* 7(3): 84-88.

Ross, P.J., B.L. Green, and R.A. Hoppe. 1984. "Classifying Major Socioeconomic Patterns Among U.S. Non-metropolitan Counties." Paper presented at Annual Meeting, Rural Sociological Society, College Station, Texas A&M University, August.

San Diego Comprehensive Planning Organization. 1972. *Technical User's Manual for the Interactive Population/Employment Forecasting Model.* San Diego: San Diego Comprehensive Planning Organization.

Savas, E.S. 1982. *Privatizing the Public Sector. How to Shrink Government.* Chatham, N.J.: Chatham House.

Schmenner, Roger W. 1982. *Making Business Location Decisions.* Englewood Cliffs, N.J.: Prentice Hall Press.

Schmidt, Joseph F., Robert L. Oehrtman and Gerald A. Doeksen. 1978. "Planning Ambulance Service for a Rural Emergency Medical Service District." *Southern Journal of Agricultural Economics* 10(1): 126-133.

Shabman, Leonard. 1983. "Nonmarket Valuation and Public Policy: Historical Lessons and New Directions." In *Nonmarket Valuation: Current Status, Future Directions.* Southern Natural Resource Economics Committee.

Shaffer, Ron E. 1972. *The Net Economic Impact of New Industry on Rural Communities in Eastern Oklahoma.* Ph.D. dissertation. Stillwater: Oklahoma State University.

Shaffer, Ron E. and Luther Tweeten. 1972. "Measuring the Impact of New Industry on Rural Communities in Oklahoma." In *Research Application in Rural Economic Development and Planning* Ag. Exp. Sta. Res. Rpt. P-665. Stillwater: Oklahoma State University.

Shaffer, Ron E. and Luther Tweeten. 1974. "Measuring Net Economic Changes from Rural Industrial Development: Oklahoma." *Land Economics* 50(3): 261-270.

Sharpe, William F. 1964. "Capital Asset Prices: A Theory of Market Equilibrium Under Conditions of Risk." *Journal of Finance* 19(3): 425-442.

Shryock, H.S. and T.S. Seigel. 1973. *The Methods and Materials of Demography*. Washington, D.C.: GPO.

Skrabanek, R.L. and Steve H. Murdock. 1981. *Texas County Population Changes in the 1970s*, Department of Rural Sociology, 81-5. College Station: Texas A&M University.

Smith, David M. 1981. *Industrial Location*. New York: John Wiley and Sons, 1981.

Smith, Eldon D., Brady J. Deaton and David R. Kelch. 1978. "Location Determinants of Manufacturing Industry in Rural Areas." *Southern Journal of Agricultural Economics* 10: 23-32.

Sofranko, Andrew and Frederick C. Fliegel. 1984. "Dissatisfaction with Satisfaction." *Rural Sociology* 49(3): 353-373.

Sokolow, Alvin D. 1981. "Local Governments: Capacity and Will." In Amos Hawley and Sara Miles (editors) *Nonmetropolitan America in Transition*. Chapel Hill: University of North Carolina press, 704-735.

Sokolow, Alvin D. and Beth Walter Honadle. 1984. "How Rural Local Governments Budget." *Public Administration Review* 44: 373-383.

Sokolow, Alvin D. and Keith Snavely. 1983. "Small City Autonomy in the Federal System: A Study of Local Constraints and Opportunity in California." *Publius* 13: 73-88.

Stafford, Howard A. 1979. *Principles of Industrial Facility Location*. Atlanta: Conway Publications.

Stanfield, Rochelle L. 1982. "The Users May Have to Foot the Bill to Patch Crumbling Public Facilities." *National Journal* 14(48): 17-20.

State Community Development Block Grant Clearinghouse. 1985. "Public Facilities Receive the Most Funds." In *State CDBG Update* 7(3). Washington, D.C.: Council of State Community Affairs Agencies.

Stenehjem, Erik J. 1978. *Summary Description of SEAM: The Social and Economic Assessment Model*. Argonne, Ill.: Argonne National Laboratory.

Stevens, Barbara J., ed. 1984. *Delivering Municipal Services Efficiently: A Comparison of Municipal and Private Service Delivery*. Washington, D.C.: U.S. Department of Housing and Urban Development.

Stinson, Thomas F. 1981a. "Fiscal Status of Local Governments." In *Nonmetropolitan America in Transition*, ed. Amos Hawley and Sara Miles, pp. 704-735. Chapel Hill: University of North Carolina Press.

Stinson, Thomas F. 1981b. "Overcoming Impacts of Growth on Local Government Finance." *Rural Development Perspectives* 4: 12-19. Washington, D.C.: ERS, USDA.

Sulaiman, Jamalludin, and Leroy J. Hushak. 1980. "The Impacts of Industrial Sites on Industrial Employment Growth: A Case Study of Appalachian Ohio." *The American Industrial Development Council Journal* 15: 7-22.

Sullivan, Patrick J. 1983a. *Examining the Rural Municipal Bond Market*, Rural Development Res. Rpt. No. 34. Washington, D.C.: ERS, USDA.

Sullivan, Patrick J. 1983b. *The Cost of Metro and Nonmetro Government Borrowing*, Rural Development Res. Rep. No. 35. Washington, D.C.: ERS, USDA.

Sullivan, Patrick J. 1983c. "Municipal Bond Ratings: How Worthwhile Are They for Small Governments." *State and Local Government Review* 15(3): 106-111.

Sullivan, Patrick J., Judith N. Collins, and J. Norman Reid. 1981. "Local Government: Trends and Prospects." *Rural Development Perspectives* 4: 4-11. Washington, D.C.: ERS, USDA.

Texas Advisory Commission on Intergovernmental Relations. 1984. "Local Government Fiscal Capacity Measures: A Profile of State Studies." Unpublished manuscript. Department of Agricultural Economics, Texas A and M University, College Station, Texas.

Thompson, Dale. 1983. *Infrastructure Sources: A Key to Current Literature for Municipal Officials and Public Managers*. Policy Working Paper No. 11. Washington, D.C.: National League of Cities.

Tiebout, Charles M. 1956. "A Pure Theory of Local Expenditures." *Journal of Political Economy* 64: 416-424.

Tuchfarber, Alfred J. 1983. "Housing: An Infrastructure Issue? A Demographic Profile." *Urban Resources* 1(2): 29-32.

Tweeten, Luther. 1984. *High Technology in Rural Settings*. University of Tennessee, Office for Research in High Technology Education.

Urban Land Institute, 1983. "Financing Local Infrastructure in a Time of Fiscal Constraint." *Urban Land* (August): 16-21.

U. S. Bureau of the Census. 1980. *Annual Housing Survey*, Volume E. Washington, D.C.: U.S. Bureau of the Census.

U.S. Bureau of the Census. 1983. *Governmental Finances in 1981-82*. Series GF82, No. 5. Washington, D.C.: GPO.

U.S. Bureau of the Census. 1984a. *Governmental Finances in 1983-84*, Series GF84, No. 5. Washington, D.C.: GPO.

U.S. Bureau of the Census. 1984b. *State Government Finances in 1984*, Series GF84, No. 3. Washington, D.C.: GPO.

U.S. Bureau of the Census. 1984c. *Census of Governments, 1982: State Payments to Local Governments* 6(3). Washington, D.C.: U.S. Bureau of the Census.

U.S. Bureau of the Census. 1985a. *Local Government in Metropolitan Areas: 1982 Census of Governments 5*. Washington, D.C.: GPO.

U.S. Bureau of the Census. 1985b. *Census of Governments, 1982: Finance Statistics*. Washington, D.C.: U.S. Bureau of the Census.

U.S. Department of Agriculture Office of Rural Development Policy. 1983. *Better Country: A Strategy for Rural Development in the 1980s*, pp. 15-19. Washington, D.C.: USDA.

U.S. Department of Agriculture. 1984a. *Chartbook of Nonmetro-Metro Trends*. Rural Development Research Report, No. 43. Washington, D.C.: ERS, USDA.

U.S. Department of Agriculture. 1984b. *1984 Handbook of Agricultural Charts*. Agricultural Handbook No. 637. Washington, D.C.: USDA.

U.S. Department of Commerce. 1980. *A Study of Public Works Investment in the United States*. Washington, D.C.: GPO.

U.S. Department of Housing and Urban Development. 1982. *Maintaining the Existing Infrastructure: Overview of Current Issues and Practices in Local Government Planning*. Washington, D.C.: U.S. Department of Housing and Urban Development, Office of Policy Development and Research.

U.S. General Accounting Office. 1980. *EPA Should Help Small Communities Cope with Federal Pollution Control Requirements.* Washington, D.C.: GAO.

U.S. General Accounting Office. 1983. *Trends and Changes in the Municipal Bond Market As They Relate to Financing State and Local Public Infrastructure.* PAD-83-46. Washington, D.C.: GAO.

U.S. House of Representatives. 1983a. *Agricultural Communities: The Interrelationship of Agriculture, Business, Industry, and the Rural Economy.* Papers from a Symposium prepared by the Congressional Research Service, Library of Congress, for the Committee on Agriculture. Washington, D.C.: GPO.

U.S. House of Representatives. 1983b. *Issues in National and Local Capital Development.* Hearing before the Task Force on Capital Resources and Development, Committee on the Budget. Washington, D.C.: GPO.

U.S. News and World Report. 1982. "To Rebuild America--$2.5 Trillion Job." 57-61.

U. S. Senate, 1977. *National Conference on Nonmetropolitan Community Services Research.* Papers presented at a U.S. Department of Agriculture-sponsored national conference held at Ohio State University, January 11-13, 1977. Prepared for the Committee on Agriculture, Nutrition, and Forestry (July 12).

U.S. Senate. 1979. *Rural Development: An Overview.* Prepared by the Congressional Research Service, Library of Congress, for the Committee on Agriculture, Nutrition, and Forestry (August 20).

Van Horn, Carl and Donald Van Meter. 1976. "The Implementation of Intergovernmental Policy." In Charles Jones and Robert Thomas (editors) *Public Policy Making in the Federal System.* Volume III. Beverly Hills, California: Sage Publications.

Van Meter, Donald and Carl Van Horn. 1975. "The Policy Implementation Process: A Conceptual Framework." *Administration and Society* 6 (February): 445-488.

Vaughan, Roger J. 1979. *State Taxation and Economic Development.* Washington, D.C.: Council of State Planning Agencies.

Vaughan, Roger J. 1983. *Rebuilding America, Volume 2: Financing Public Works in the 1980s.* Washington, D.C.: Council of State Planning Agencies.

Vaughan, Roger J. and Robert Pollard. 1984. *Rebuilding America, Volume 1: Planning and Managing Public Works in the 1980s.* Washington, D.C.: Council of State Planning Agencies.

Vehorn, Charles L. 1981. "Public Pricing Growing in Rural America." *Rural Development Perspectives* 4: 37-39. Washington, D.C.: ERS, USDA.

Vranna, W. P. and J. Luptak. 1985. *North Dakota Energy Development Impact Office, 1983-85 Biennium Legislative Report* Bismarck: North Dakota Energy Impact Office.

Wallace, L. T., and V. W. Ruttan. 1961. "The Role of the Community as a Factor in Industrial Location." *Papers and Proceedings of the Regional Science Association* 7: 133-42.

Walter, Susan and Pat Choate. 1984. *Thinking Strategically: A Primer for Public Leaders.* Washington, D.C.: The Council of State Planning Agencies.

Watson, Rick. 1982a. *How States Can Assist Local Governments With Debt Financing for Infrastructure.* Legislative Finance Paper No. 19. Denver: National Conference of State Legislatures.

Watson, Rick. 1982b. *State Aid for Local Capital Facilities.* Legislative Finance Paper No. 20. Denver: National Conference of State Legislatures.

Watson, Rick. 1983. *How States Can Assist Local Governments With Debt Financing for Infrastructure.* Washington, D.C.: National Conference of State Legislatures.

Webb, Shwu-Eng. H., Gerald A. Doeksen, and Robert Carroll. 1980. *A Community Development Guide for a Transportation System for the Elderly.* Dept. of Ag. Econ. Paper No. 8024. Stillwater: Oklahoma State University.

Weber, B. A. and R. E. Howell, eds. 1982. *Coping with Rapid Growth in Rural Communities.* Boulder, Colorado: Westview Press.

Weinberg, Mark. 1984. "Budget Retrenchment in Small Cities: A Comparative Analysis of Wooster and Athens, Ohio." *Public Budgeting and Finance* 4: 46-57.

Weiss, Barbara, ed. 1985. *Public/Private Partnerships: Financing a Common Wealth.* Washington, D.C.: Government Finance Research Center, Government Finance Officers Association.

Wilkinson, Kenneth P. 1985. "Rural Community Development: A Deceptively Controversial Theme in Rural Sociology." *The Rural Sociologist* 5(2): 119-124.

Williams, Duane, Terry Boucher, Gerald Doeksen, June Parks, and Lou Stackler. 1983. *A Guidebook for Rural Physician Services: A Systematic Approach to Planning and Development.* Oklahoma State Exp. Sta. Bull. No. B-765. Stillwater: Oklahoma State University.

Williams, Oliver P. 1967. "Life-Style Values and Political Decentralization in Metropolitan Areas." *Southwestern Social Science Quarterly* 48 (December): 299-310.

Wilson, R. 1982. "Risk Measurement of Public Projects." In *Discounting for Time and Risk in Energy Policy,* ed. R. C. Lind. Baltimore: Johns Hopkins University Press.

Winter, R.C., D.J. Santini, D.W. South, C.M. Hotchkiss, and M.J. Bragen. 1981. *Selection of Economic Impact Assessment Models for Use by Communities in the Tennessee-Tombigbee Corridor: Phase I.* ANL/EES-TM-160. Argonne, Ill.: Argonne National Laboratories.

Wisconsin Department of Development. 1985. *Public Infrastructure in Wisconsin: A Strategic Analysis.* Division of Policy Development, Bureau of Research. Madison: Wisconsin Department of Development.

Woods, Mike D. and Gerald A. Doeksen. 1983. *A Simulation Model for Rural Communities in Oklahoma.* Agricultural Experiment Station Bulletin B-770. Stillwater: Oklahoma State University.

Woods, Mike D. and Lonnie L. Jones. 1982-1983. "Measuring the Impact of New Industry in Small Towns." *Municipal Management Journal* 5(1): 48-56.

Zimmerman, Joseph F. 1981. *Measuring Local Discretionary Authority.* Information Report No. M-131. Washington, D.C.: Advisory Commission on Intergovernmental Relations.